WATERGATE
AMERICA IN CRISIS

By the Author

WASHINGTON VS. MAIN STREET: THE STRUGGLE BETWEEN FEDERAL
   AND LOCAL POWER

WATERGATE: AMERICA IN CRISIS

WATERGATE

AMERICA IN CRISIS

Jules Archer

Illustrated with photographs

THOMAS Y. CROWELL COMPANY   NEW YORK

All photographs from United Press International.

Library of Congress Cataloging in Publication Data
Archer, Jules.
Watergate: America in crisis.
Bibliography: p.
Includes index.
SUMMARY: Analyzes the complex events, issues, and personalities involved in the
first resignation of a president in United States history.
1. Watergate Affair, 1972–   —Juvenile literature.
[1. Watergate Affair, 1972] I. Title.
E860.A72   973.924   75–5567
ISBN 0–690–00616–0

1 2 3 4 5 6 7 8 9 10

Contents

PRESIDENT: . . . So believe me, don't ever lie.

DEAN: The truth always emerges. It always does.

PRESIDENT: Also there is a question of right and wrong too.

DEAN: That's right.

PRESIDENT: Whether it is right and whether it is wrong. Perhaps there are some gray areas, but you are right to get it out now.

—from the Watergate tapes, April 16, 1973

"Don't Shoot— You've Got Us!"

In Washington, D.C., a warm, starry Friday night has been Saturday, June 17, 1972, for just one hour when security guard Frank Wills, twenty-four, trudges on his nocturnal patrol of Watergate, a complex consisting of a hotel, apartment houses, and office buildings. He discovers that the lock on a garage-level door has been taped back to prevent its catching. The door leads to the ground-floor stairwell of the office building.

The taping must have been done, Wills decides, by maintenance men moving equipment in or out of the office building the previous day. Stripping off the tape, so that the door is once more locked, he strolls across the street for a coffee-break in the restaurant of the Howard Johnson Motor Lodge opposite Watergate.

Several minutes later, five well-dressed men move silently out of the Watergate Hotel, crossing the darkened driveway to the garage. All are wearing blue surgical gloves to avoid leaving fingerprints. One approaches the door to the office stairwell. Turning the knob confidently, he is perplexed to find the door locked. There is a whispered conference.

Four of the men retreat to the hotel while the fifth works at jimmying the door. Prying it open, he reports by walkie-talkie that all is ready. The others return. The lock of the forced door is again taped back to keep it from locking behind them. Then the five men stealthily climb the rear stairwell of the office building

*An aerial view of the Watergate complex. Lookout Alfred C. Baldwin III was stationed in
the Howard Johnson Motor Lodge (1), while James W. McCord, Jr., and the Cubans
entered the Democratic National Committee headquarters across the street (2). Behind the
complex is the Kennedy Center for the Performing Arts (3).*

to the sixth floor, headquarters of the Democratic National
Committee (DNC).

Forcing entry, they move swiftly into the office and begin
burglarizing it. Files are broken into; documents removed;
cameras positioned to photograph them. In the office of the
secretary to the chairman of the Democratic National Committee, Lawrence O'Brien, two ceiling panels are removed to
implant bugging devices.

Meanwhile Frank Wills, making his rounds again at about
2:00 A.M., discovers the freshly taped door. He realizes that

*Watchman Frank Wills
discovered the taped door that led
to the apprehension of the
Watergate burglars.*

something is wrong and quickly phones the Washington, D.C., police.

Police radio alerts an unmarked tactical squad car.

Plainclothesmen Sergeant Paul Leeper and officers John Barrett and Carl Shoffler, on patrol in the second precinct, speed to Watergate. Informed by Wills about the twice-taped door, the three officers begin a systematic search of the office building, working their way down from the eighth floor as Wills bottles up the lobby.

Their flashlights are observed from the balcony of Room 723 in the Howard Johnson Motor Lodge across the street by Alfred C. Baldwin III, a former FBI agent.

He hurriedly activates his walkie-talkie. "Base headquarters, base one, to any unit—do you read me?"

"I read you," a voice crackles back. "Go on. What have you got?"

"The lights went on on the entire eighth floor."

"We know about that. That's the two o'clock guard check. Let us know if anything else happens."

Baldwin sees two men in windbreakers and slacks, one with a gun drawn, appear on the sixth-floor balcony.

"Base one, unit one—are our people in suits or are they dressed casually?"

"Our people are dressed in suits. Why?"

"Then we've got problems. There are some people dressed casually, and they've got guns. They're looking around the balcony and everywhere, but they haven't come across our people."

In the darkened office of the DNC, Officer John Barrett suddenly glimpses the shadow of a raised arm moving behind a cloudy glass pane above an office partition. He signals Sergeant Leeper and Officer Shoffler to join him. Moving silently down a corridor, they surround the partition.

"Hold it! Stop! *Come out!*"

"Don't shoot," one burglar pleads. "You've got us!"

To the amazement of the plainclothesmen, not one man but five slowly emerge, their rubber-gloved hands elevated.

"Are you gentlemen metropolitan police?" asks one.

"Yes." Sergeant Leeper orders them up against a wall. "Raise your arms and spread your feet. You're all under arrest on suspicion of burglary." Officer Barrett searches them.

The burglars prove to be carrying a total of $1,300 in new, consecutively numbered $100 bills, although the DNC safe has not been touched. Also found on the team are burglary tools, tear-gas pens, a radio transmitter-receiver, walkie-talkies, bugging devices, two 35-mm. cameras, and forty rolls of unexposed film. The five men are courteous, but they refuse to explain what they are doing in the DNC.

Taken to the Second District station house, they give names which are later discovered to be false, and persist in refusing to answer questions. Although they spurn the right to phone for an

*Carl Shoffler of the Washington police was one of the three officers who arrested the
Watergate burglars. Behind him, as he testifies to the Senate Watergate Committee, is
James McCord.*

attorney, two lawyers mysteriously appear for them later that
morning. Douglas Caddy and Joseph A. Rafferty, Jr., advise
them to remain silent, assuring them that bail and other help is
on the way.

Early that afternoon a warrant is issued to search the two
rooms of the Watergate Hotel which the suspects had occupied
under the names given to the police. Sergeant Leeper, two
officers, and an FBI special agent find six suitcases full of
electronic surveillance equipment and burglary tools, along with
another $3,200 in neat packets of new, consecutively numbered
$100 bills. Also found are address books belonging to two of the
burglars. Listed in both are the name and telephone number of
E. Howard Hunt. In one book the entry is followed by the initials
"W. H."; in the other, by the reference "White House." An
unmailed check for Hunt's country-club dues is also found.

It is now obvious to the police that the burglars found in the

DNC headquarters were engaged in more than just a routine heist job. They are charged not only with attempted burglary, but also with attempting to put wiretaps on the Democrats' telephones.

Arraigned at 4:00 P.M. before Superior Court Judge James A. Belson, the five burglars are compelled to reveal their real names. Four are Cubans. Assistant U.S. Attorney Earl Silbert of the Justice Department wants all five held without bail, but Rafferty argues for their release on a minimum bond because all were unarmed and offered no resistance upon arrest.

The non-Cuban defendant, James W. McCord, Jr., approaches the bench. He whispers to Judge Belson that he is a former employee of the Central Intelligence Agency (CIA), suggesting by this information that it might be embarrassing to the government if the men are held in jail.

The judge sets bail at $50,000 for each of the Cubans, $30,000 for McCord. When bail is arranged, all are ordered to report daily to court to ensure their remaining in the city.

Leader of the Cubans is owl-faced Bernard L. Barker, fifty-five. An American citizen, born and raised in Cuba, he was once a member of dictator Fulgencio Batista's secret police. He later served as paymaster for the CIA in the Bay of Pigs organization that in 1961 unsuccessfully attempted to invade Cuba and overthrow Fidel Castro. He is now a Miami real-estate developer.

Eugenio Martinez, forty-nine, is also a former CIA operative and veteran of the Bay of Pigs invasion. Recently involved in smuggling refugees out of Cuba, he works in Barker's real-estate firm.

Virgilio R. Gonzales, forty-five, Cuban-born, is also a former CIA operative who participated in the Bay of Pigs invasion. He is active in right-wing, anti-Castro groups in Miami where he works as a locksmith.

Frank Sturgis (also known as Frank Fiorini), thirty-seven, is an ex-Marine soldier of fortune and ex-CIA operative who ran guns to Cuba. He heads a political group called Cubans for Nixon.

James W. McCord, Jr., fifty-four, is a former security agent for the CIA. Once described by former CIA director Allen Dulles

Eugenio R. Martinez (left) and Bernard L. Barker (right), leader of the Cubans.

as "my top man," he is now employed as "security coordinator" for the Committee to Re-elect the President (CRP), which is headed by the recently resigned Attorney General of the Nixon Administration, John N. Mitchell. McCord's background includes service as a colonel of a secret military unit charged with surveillance of antiwar militants.

The first news of the Watergate break-in that reaches the headquarters of the Committee to Re-elect the President does not disclose the identity of the burglars. Office manager Robert Odle, twenty-eight, scoffs at the lack of security precautions at the Democratic National Committee. "That could never happen here," he boasts, "because I have this guy working for me, Jim McCord—and he has this place tight!"

On June 18 John Mitchell promptly denies any authorization or knowledge of the burglars' actions. "There is no place in our campaign or in the electoral process for this type of activity," Mitchell states. "We will not permit or condone it." But on the same day the *Washington Post* reports that McCord, security coordinator of CRP, was one of the burglars. It becomes known next day that he had been on the committee's payroll for the past six months, and was still working for the organization right up to his arrest.

Two young reporters, Carl Bernstein and Bob Woodward, are assigned to the story by the *Washington Post*. Through a police tip, Woodward learns of the connection of E. Howard Hunt to the case in the discovered address books of two of the burglars. Who is E. Howard Hunt, he wonders, and what is his role at the White House?

Phoning the White House on June 19, Woodward asks to speak to Hunt. The call is transferred to the office of Charles W. Colson, special counsel to the President.

Colson's secretary says Hunt is not there now, but can be reached at Robert R. Mullen and Company, a Washington public-relations firm with close ties to the White House. She tells Woodward that Hunt is employed there as a writer.

Unconvinced, Woodward phones the White House again to ask a personnel office clerk whether Hunt is on the government payroll. The clerk checks and reports that Hunt is a paid consultant working for Colson. Woodward then phones Hunt at Mullen and Company. Identifying himself, he asks bluntly, "Why were your name and phone number in the address books of two of the men arrested at the Watergate?"

"Good God!" Hunt gasps. Then he quickly adds that he has no comment and slams down the phone. Woodward investigates and learns that the razor-faced Hunt, fifty-four, is an author of spy novels, also known to have been a CIA operative—in fact, Barker's boss during the Bay of Pigs invasion. Woodward is unable to reach Colson to question him. Hunt, briefly interrogated by the FBI, vanishes soon afterward and cannot be located.

FBI agents join the Washington police in tracking down leads in the case. U.S. Treasury records trace the $100 bills found on the burglars to the Republic National Bank of Miami and the account of Barker's real-estate firm.

On June 20 a *Washington Post* story links Hunt as a White House consultant to the Watergate burglary.

Ronald L. Ziegler, thirty-three, President Nixon's press secretary, refers disdainfully to the Watergate break-in as "a third-rate burglary attempt" not worth White House comment.

But as *The Nation* later observes, "If it were only a burglary, it would surely be the most unusual burglary in the world, for one of the participants had $114,000 to finance a job that promised to pay off not one penny in loot."

On June 20 Democratic Party chairman Lawrence O'Brien files a $1,000,000 damage suit against those arrested and CRP. "This incident raises the ugliest questions about the integrity of the political process that I have encountered in a quarter of a century," he declares. "There is certainly a clear line to the Committee to Re-elect the President—and there is developing a clear line to the White House."

But except for the dogged reporters of the *Washington Post*, most of the press pays little attention to the Watergate break-in.

On June 30 a former New York City policeman named Anthony T. Ulasewicz, hired as an undercover political investigator for the White House, enters a Washington hotel to meet an earnest-looking, uneasy man using the code name of Novak. Novak tells Ulasewicz he is to act as courier to the Watergate defendants, using the code name "Mr. Rivers." Large sums of cash will be entrusted to him to deliver secretly to the defendants' lawyers.

Novak assures Ulasewicz that there is nothing illegal about the mission, but warns that henceforth they are to communicate only through prearranged calls made in selected phone booths. Ulasewicz even takes to wearing a bus driver's changemaker, so that he always has enough coins handy for his calls to Novak.

For the first of a series of payoffs made during the summer of 1972 Ulasewicz is given $75,000 in cash. Hiding it in his hotel laundry bag, he refers to it in talks with Novak as "my laundry." In phone conversations with the Watergate defendants' lawyers, he cryptically refers to the "cost of a script, a play, and the salaries of the players."

Ulasewicz finds that delivering the money surreptitiously is no easy task. Some lawyers are dissatisfied with the amounts offered out of the brown paper bag in which he carries the money, or they refuse to accept direct payments of cash.

In making deliveries he sometimes arranges to leave packages of cash in airport lockers, taping the key inside a nearby

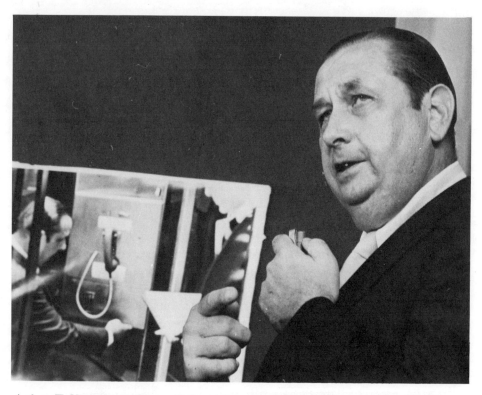

Anthony T. Ulasewicz explains to the Senate Watergate Committee how he arranged delivery of cash payoffs.

phone booth to be found by someone from a designated law firm. Other times the money is hidden in a phone booth or on a window ledge. Ulasewicz watches from a vantage point to make sure the money does not fall into the wrong hands.

In Miami Watergate defendant Barker tells business associates he isn't worried about the trouble he is in because "they" are paying for his lawyer. He does not say who "they" are.

As bagman, Ulasewicz is besieged by increasingly stiffer demands from some of the Watergate defendants. They threaten to talk unless more cash is swiftly forthcoming. Ulasewicz's police background makes him aware that he may be laying himself open to criminal prosecution for obstruction of justice.

"Everything here is not exactly kosher," he warns Novak. Payments made in July and August 1972 have been camouflaged as "helping to pay for the defendants' court costs and living expenses." But by September they undeniably fall into the category of bribery to keep the burglars silent about the identities of those higher-ups who ordered the break-in. Novak nervously agrees with Ulasewicz that they should refuse to make further payments to the defendants and their lawyers.

Novak has good reason for alarm. His real name is Herbert W. Kalmbach, and he is associate finance chairman of CRP under former Secretary of Commerce Maurice H. Stans. He is also President Nixon's personal attorney.

The job of making the payoffs is taken over by wealthy oilman Frederick C. LaRue, a former White House aide once described as John Mitchell's right-hand man. LaRue, now special assistant to Mitchell at CRP, secretly pays out another $230,000 between September 1972 and March 1973, donning gloves to prevent leaving fingerprints on the bills.

Meanwhile the two persistent reporters of the *Washington Post*, Bernstein and Woodward, keep on the trail of the sputtering fuse that leads from Watergate to the White House. It becomes increasingly clear to them that what seemed at first like a simple burglary is, in fact, part of an astounding conspiracy, in which Nixon himself is implicated, to steal a presidential election.

2

In the Beginning

Early clues to understanding the bizarre mystery of Watergate can be found in the life and career of Richard M. Nixon. As a twelve-year-old, he listens to his father rage at the family breakfast table in Whittier, California, against crooked Harding Administration lawyer-politicians on trial for bribery in 1925 in the Teapot Dome oil scandal. Deciding to enter the field of law, he assures his parents, "I will be an old-fashioned kind of lawyer—a lawyer who can't be bought."

This flame of early idealism is soon extinguished, however, by a compulsive drive to succeed at everything he attempts.

At college young Nixon develops an aggressive, competitive spirit. He later recalls with admiration, "Chief Newman, my [football] coach, an American Indian, produced some very fine teams at that small little college at Whittier. . . . There were no excuses for failure. He didn't feel sorry for you when you got knocked down. He had a different definition of being a good loser. He said: 'You know what a good loser is? It's somebody who hates to lose.'"

Nixon attends Duke University Law School and begins practicing law in 1937. He joins the Navy in 1942, where he rises to the rank of lieutenant commander in an air transport supply command.

After World War II he enters Republican politics, determined to be a winner at all costs. Running for Congress in California against Democratic Representative Jerry Voorhis, he selects as his campaign manager lawyer Murray Chotiner, who has made a reputation for himself in Republican politics by winning campaigns through unscrupulous attacks. Chotiner teaches Nixon how to hurl charges that will keep his opponent off balance and on the defensive.

Voorhis is defeated by false accusations that he voted the "Moscow line" in Congress. As cold-war hysteria grows in the United States, Nixon capitalizes on the fear of communism. He wins headlines by joining Senator Joseph McCarthy's attack on the Truman Administration as "riddled with Communists."

In 1949 he brings about the downfall of former New Deal official Alger Hiss for allegedly passing U.S. documents to the Russians. What finally destroyed Hiss, Nixon later writes in his book *Six Crises*, was less what Hiss had done than his attempts to cover it up by lying about it.

Chotiner manages Nixon's 1950 race for a Senate seat against Democratic Congresswoman Helen Gahagan Douglas. Priding himself as a shrewd, masterful campaigner, Nixon tries to supervise every detail himself. Chotiner protests, "Dick, you can either be the candidate or the manager. You can't be both." But Nixon persists in involving himself deeply in campaign strategy and tactics. He uses the same kind of sabotage on Helen Douglas that he used on Jerry Voorhis, labeling her "the Pink Lady."

"During five years in Congress," he charges, "Helen Douglas voted 353 times exactly as has Vito Marcantonio, the notorious Communist party-line congressman from New York."

Outraged, Mrs. Douglas replies, "Although Mr. Nixon is a Republican, he voted 112 times the same way Marcantonio did. I voted 85 per cent of the time with a majority of either the House or my party. I am not a Communist."

Just before Election Day Nixon and Chotiner distribute over half a million bright pink leaflets repeating the Communist slurs against Helen Douglas. She is defeated, and Nixon goes to the Senate. But now a nickname follows him through the years— "Tricky Dicky." Seeking to shed it, he later apologizes for his smear of Mrs. Douglas. "I'm sorry about that episode," he says, adding by way of extenuation, "I was a very young man." But his political ethics improve little over the years.

While hurling Communist accusations at political rivals, he complains constantly that they are smearing him. Eminent journalist Walter Lippmann is to describe him as a "ruthless partisan . . . who divides and embitters people."

In 1952 the Republican party nominates the thirty-nine-year-old senator as its candidate for Vice-President. Disaster threatens, however, when the *New York Post* reveals that under the name of his finance manager, Dana Smith, Nixon controls a secret slush fund set up by seventy-six wealthy California backers.

Smith tries to explain: "Here we had a fine salesman who didn't have enough money to do the kind of selling job we wanted, so we got together and took care of some of those things." He adds frankly, "Dick did just what we wanted him to do."

Later Mrs. Douglas recalls, "He was acceptable to the oil people. He was always against regulating oil drilling. . . . He had all the money he needed because he favored vested interests of every sort."

Presidential candidate Eisenhower's aides urge that Nixon be dropped from the ticket. Nixon accuses Communists of trying to smear him, pleading innocence of any wrongdoing. Eisenhower decides that Nixon must go on television and convince the American people that he is as "clean as a hound's tooth." If he fails, Nixon knows, he will be dropped and his political career finished.

In his famous "Checkers" speech, self-pity and indignation quiver in his voice as he denies using a penny of the slush fund for personal use or giving special consideration to any of his wealthy backers. He points out that his wife, Pat, has no mink coat, only "a respectable Republican cloth coat." In a shrewd appeal to the emotions of millions of dog lovers, he acknowledges accepting only one gift, a cocker spaniel.

"Our little girl—Tricia, the six-year-old—named it Checkers. And you know, the kids love that dog, and I just want to say this right now, that regardless of what they say about it, we're going to keep it." He finishes on a defiant note: "Let me say this:

I don't believe that I ought to quit, because I am not a quitter. . . . I am going to campaign up and down America until we drive the crooks and Communists and those that defend them out of Washington. And remember, folks, Eisenhower is a great man, believe me. He is a great man."

Variety, the show-business weekly, derides the Nixon telecast as a soap opera—"a slick production" aimed at plucking the heartstrings of the unsophisticated. But it works. A flood of favorable telegrams convinces Eisenhower that dropping Nixon from the ticket will hurt the Republicans more than it will help. So he embraces Nixon publicly and tells him, "You're my boy." Nixon's career is saved, but he is secretly bitter at Eisenhower for not having placed personal loyalty to Nixon above insistence upon political honesty.

Nixon also resents the fact that members of the press exposed his secret fund. Convinced that political reporters are his enemy, he is at the same time impressed with the power of television. Manipulation of the facts with an appearance of earnestness before an audience of millions has not only saved him from possible prosecution but also made him Vice-President.

He takes the "low road" in the campaign, insisting that Democratic presidential candidate Adlai E. Stevenson is the Russians' choice. Stevenson replies, "Welcome to Nixonland—a land of slander and smear, of sly innuendo, of the poison pen, the anonymous phone call and hustling, pushing, shoving—the land of smash and grab—anything to win."

But the Eisenhower-Nixon ticket wins two terms.

In 1960 Nixon eagerly seeks the top spot on the Republican ticket. A reporter asks Eisenhower what major Administration decisions Nixon has participated in. "If you give me a week," the President replies, "I might think of one."

Vexed by his nickname of Tricky Dicky, which still pursues him, Nixon tries to develop a new and more dignified image in the 1960 presidential race against Democratic candidate John F. Kennedy. "I do not want to say anything or do anything during the campaign that I will not be able to live with as President," he declares. "I draw the line on anything that has to do with the personal life of the candidate."

Engaging Kennedy in a series of television debates, he

suffers by contrast, projecting an awkward, stiff, synthetic image, while Kennedy impresses viewers as handsome, earnest, and dynamic. "Nixon doesn't know who he is," Kennedy observes privately, "and so each time he makes a speech he has to decide which Nixon he is." Kennedy wins in a tight race.

Frustrated, Nixon determines to return in the future to the no-holds-barred campaign tactics that have always won for him in the past. To gain a foothold for another presidential try, he decides in 1962 to run against California's popular Democratic governor, Edmund G. ("Pat") Brown. Asked if he doesn't find it embarrassing to run for governor after having sought the Presidency, Nixon replies, "It takes an awful lot to embarrass me."

To package his new campaign, Nixon selects an advertising agency executive in charge of the Los Angeles office of J. Walter Thompson. H. R. ("Bob") Haldeman, thirty-six, a thin, unsmiling man with a crew cut, prides himself upon his expertise in selling any product from Black Flag insecticide to political candidates. He recruits campaign aides from among bright, young conservative alumni of the University of Southern California, many of whom work for him.

Ronald Ziegler, a rotund, surly young public-relations man, becomes Nixon's press aide. Another aide, Dwight Chapin, enlists Donald Segretti to whip up support for Nixon among California's youthful voters. Other aides include John Ehrlichman, Haldeman's friend, a lawyer from Seattle; Herbert Kalmbach, Nixon's fund-raiser; and newspaperman Herbert G. Klein.

To sabotage Governor Brown's campaign, two weeks before Election Day the Nixon team conducts a fraudulent poll of voters on behalf of the "Committee for the Preservation of the Democratic Party in California." Almost a million registered Democrats receive mailings branding Brown a left-wing radical; a faked photograph shows him with his arm around Communist longshoreman leader Harry Bridges. Donations solicited to "bring the Democratic party back to the middle of the road" are forwarded to Haldeman for Republican use.

Governor Brown sues, naming Nixon, Haldeman, Ziegler, Chapin, Kalmbach, Segretti, and Klein as perpetrators of the scurrilous and fraudulent mailing. After the election, which

Nixon loses, Judge Byron Arnold of the San Francisco Superior Court finds that the phony "Democratic poll" had been prepared under Haldeman's supervision, then "reviewed, amended and finally approved by Mr. Nixon personally." Found guilty of authorizing unfair campaign practices, Nixon and Haldeman are ordered to pay a fine and court costs.

Shaken by two successive election defeats, Nixon blames the press for presenting him in an unfavorable light. The day after the election he tells reporters bitterly, "Now that all the members of the press are so delighted that I have lost, I'd like to make a statement. . . . For sixteen years . . . you've had a lot of fun [attacking] me. . . . You won't have Nixon to kick around any more because, gentlemen, this is my last press conference."

Seemingly finished as a political candidate, Nixon goes to New York City to practice law. He joins a Wall Street law firm, Mudge, Rose, Guthrie and Alexander, in which pipe-smoking John Mitchell is a senior partner. Nixon is impressed with Mitchell's tough, ultraconservative outlook, and the two become close friends. As the 1960's explode in urban race riots and demonstrations against the Vietnam War, Nixon and Mitchell see eye to eye on the desirability of a crackdown on all social disturbances.

Throughout the Kennedy and Johnson Administrations, Nixon steadily builds political support in the Republican party by doing favors for officials and party chairmen. In 1968 he once more wins nomination to the Presidency, opposing Vice-President Hubert Humphrey, the Democratic nominee. Nixon's hopes of victory are pegged on the serious split between the pro- and anti-Vietnamese war wings of the Democratic party.

Mitchell becomes his campaign manager, raising a slogan of "law and order" aimed at winning over "middle Americans" who are irked by riots and demonstrations. Haldeman and other veterans of the ill-fated California campaign join Nixon's second try for the White House. To sell a "new Nixon" to the public, they engage Madison Avenue public-relations experts.

"There certainly is a new Nixon," Nixon himself states at a carefully staged group interview on television. "I realize, too, that as a man gets older he learns something." Asked how he plans to cope with dissent, he replies, "To me law and order must

After his defeat in the 1962 race for governor of California, Nixon tells reporters,
". . . you won't have Nixon to kick around any more because, gentlemen, this is my
last press conference."

be combined with justice. Now, that's what I want for America."

Behind the scenes, campaign adviser Kevin Phillips discusses whether the support of movie star John Wayne might help or hurt the image of the "new Nixon." Phillips declares, "Wayne might sound bad to people in New York, but he sounds great to the schmucks we're trying to reach through John Wayne—the people down there along the Yahoo belt."

Nixon vows he will listen to "the voice of the great majority of Americans, the forgotten Americans, the nondemonstrators." He calls them "the great Silent Majority."

Telling audiences that he has a plan to end the Vietnam War within six months, he touches his breast pocket to suggest it is there. Privately his only solution is to strengthen the South Vietnam regime militarily—a plan that has already led to disaster for the Johnson Administration. Nixon aide Richard Whalen urges him to tell the American people that the Johnson Administration has lied to them about the war, but Nixon refuses because he supports the war.

The Nixon campaign spends heavily on television commercials. One designed to whip up patriotic fury against the Democrats shows GI's under fire in a shelled trench, followed by a laughing shot of Hubert Humphrey. Other low blows are struck.

"In 40 years of reporting, no public figure repelled me as Nixon the candidate did in 1968," writes correspondent John Osborne in the *New Republic* after the election. "With his simplistic distortions, his shoddy appeal to the Wallace vote in the South and nationally, the packaged crowds and the synthetic situations that the candidate's advance men contrived for him, Mr. Nixon seemed to me to go far beyond the bounds of deception allowed to politicians. . . . It was incredible to me . . . that this man could be the President of the United States."

That thought apparently occurs to millions of Americans in the last days of the campaign, because the polls show a great surge of support to Humphrey. Nixon holds his breath as he squeaks through to a narrow victory, holding on to a lead of a bare seven tenths of 1 percent. He and his men realize that if the campaign had lasted just one or two weeks longer, the Democrats might have swept past them to victory.

Almost as soon as the jubilation dies down at Nixon headquarters, the new President and his aides begin planning how to hold the White House for four more years. Worried by Nixon's hairline majority, they decide that aggressive actions must constantly be taken to throw and keep the Democrats off balance. According to aide Richard Whalen, they regard governing "as little more than an extension of campaigning."

The aides closest to the President have never sought nor held public office, and are restrained by none of the usual caution of professional politicians. Many are public-relations,

The new President with his running mate, Spiro T. Agnew.

advertising, and marketing men engrossed in manipulating public opinion. Intoxicated by unaccustomed power, they gather around the President in the White House as his "palace guard." Herbert L. Porter later recalls, "There definitely did exist a 'we-they' attitude, 'we' being anyone inside the gate, 'they' being all others, particularly the press, and of course the opposition party. On my first or second day in the White House, Dwight Chapin said to me, 'One thing you should realize early on, we are practically an island here.' That was the way the world was viewed."

Forgotten is Nixon's campaign promise, "It's time we once again had an open Administration—open to the ideas from the people and open in its communication with the people—an Administration of open doors, open eyes, and open minds."

As Nixon himself notes in his book *Six Crises*, "Voters quickly forget what a man says."

"Watch What We Do, Not What We Say"

3

It quickly becomes impossible for any but a tight group of aides to get the President's ear after his inauguration in 1969. Access to the Oval Office, either in person or by written memo or report, is rigidly controlled by White House chief of staff Haldeman. Nixon remains largely secluded, not only from the public and the press, but also from Cabinet members and congressional leaders.

His appearances are frequently marked by pomp and ceremony that lead some critics to refer to him derisively as "King Richard." He tenders elaborate receptions of state at which his entrance is heralded by fanfares from the White House band blaring "Hail to the Chief." He designs uniforms for the White House police modeled after the Belgian royal guards until the media ridicules them out of existence.

Protests continue to rack the country—against continuation of the Vietnam War, against racial discrimination, against "the Establishment." Nixon worries that these forces, which swept Lyndon Johnson out of office after only one elected term, may do the same to him. Although only a handful of radical militants resort to violence, he labels all dissenters "young criminals posturing as romantic revolutionaries . . . a severe internal security threat." He criticizes the FBI's surveillance of them as inadequate.

He names John Mitchell, his campaign manager, to be

Attorney General. Mitchell shares Nixon's view that student demonstrators are subversive, imperiling the nation. "These campus riot leaders," he insists, "make it easy for foreign governments to make dupes of us."

At Mitchell's confirmation hearing, Senator Sam J. Ervin, Jr., of North Carolina demands to know whether, as head of the Department of Justice, Mitchell will continue to serve as political adviser to the President. He replies that he will not.

Senator John L. McClellan of Arkansas asks whether he proposes to use wiretaps against criminal suspects. "Carefully and effectively," Mitchell responds, "to protect the privacy and rights of individuals." But he later advises reporters candidly, "Watch what we do, not what we say."

The Nixon Administration more than triples the budget of the Justice Department. Mitchell increases the number of bugging operations by 600 percent and infiltrates the ranks of antiwar, left-wing, and black militant organizations with informers and agents provocateurs. A "Special Service Group" is also set up within the Internal Revenue Service (IRS) to crack down on "extremist organizations."

John Ehrlichman, now Nixon's chief adviser for domestic affairs, is placed in charge of conducting secret surveillance on the President's avowed and suspected opponents. In March 1969 he hires former New York City policeman John Caulfield, who has had experience spying on leftist organizations. On Caulfield's recommendation, Ehrlichman also hires Caulfield's friend, retired policeman Tony Ulasewicz. Caulfield is put on the White House payroll, but Ulasewicz is paid $22,000 a year by Herbert Kalmbach, Nixon's private lawyer, out of leftover campaign funds. For two years Caulfield and Ulasewicz spy on the drinking, sexual habits, domestic problems, and social activities of those whom Nixon considers his political foes.

"It's fair to say that you dealt in dirt, isn't it?" demands Senator Lowell P. Weicker, Jr., later.

"Allegations of it, yes," Ulasewicz admits.

This is one part of the secret strategy of the Nixon Administration to discredit the Democrats' strongest presidential candidates and leading figures. A second operation seeks to link them to radical movements at home and abroad.

The three most influential men in the Nixon White House: H. R. Haldeman, chief of staff; John N. Mitchell, attorney general; John D. Ehrlichman, assistant to the President for domestic affairs.

These sabotage operations are carried out under the direction of White House aides like Charles Colson, Dwight Chapin, Gordon Strachan, and Egil Krogh, Jr.

The two White House assistants closest to the President, Haldeman and Ehrlichman, isolate themselves from the dangerous decisions they hand down by a policy of "deniability." If anything goes wrong, they can deny involvement, blaming their aides.

Egil Krogh, Ehrlichman's chief assistant, privately boasts, "Anyone who opposes us, we'll destroy. As a matter of fact, anyone who doesn't support us, we'll destroy." The latter threat is aimed at Republicans who disapprove of Richard Nixon.

The President is deeply suspicious of Democratic bureaucrats left over from the Johnson Administration. He is convinced that they are leaking embarrassing secrets about his inner-council deliberations to the press to damage his public image and credibility, hurting his chances for re-election.

Nixon rejects the view of the press that one of its tasks is to serve as a vigilant watchdog to keep the American people fully informed of the government's operations. He believes that a President has the right to keep secret whatever information he decides should not be made public. This view is supported by his foreign-policy adviser, Henry Kissinger, who operates a National Security Council (NSC) in the White House basement. The NSC, in effect, usurps the decision-making powers of the State Department, whose career officers are distrusted as sources of news leaks.

Nixon and Kissinger are both enraged, less than four months after the President's inauguration in 1969, when *The New York Times* carries a front-page story revealing that American B-52 bombers have been violating Cambodia's neutrality by bombing suspected North Vietnamese and Vietcong bases in that country. The news is no secret to the Cambodians on whom the bombs are falling, but until now it has been concealed from the American public.

President Nixon insists that news leaks in the government must be traced and stopped. Attorney General Mitchell gives the FBI a signed order to tap the phones of thirteen government officials and four newsmen. Some suspects are members of Kissinger's own staff, named by him as having access to the leaked Cambodia secrets.

Ironically, the source of the exposé is later revealed to be no "security leak" at all. *The New York Times* simply picked it up from a *London Times* story filed by a British reporter in Cambodia who witnessed the bombings.

Although the wiretaps and other forms of surveillance reveal no leaks, they do provide Nixon with political information. FBI Director J. Edgar Hoover tips off the President that ex-Secretary of Defense Clark Clifford is preparing an article attacking Nixon's Vietnam policy. White House aides at once begin planning a political counterattack. "This is the kind of early warning we need more of," Ehrlichman notes in satisfaction. Haldeman adds, "Let's get going."

A wiretap on Kissinger aide Anthony Lake is continued even after he leaves in 1971 to become chief foreign-policy adviser to Senator Edmund Muskie, then Nixon's leading Democratic rival for the Presidency. After Morton L. Halperin leaves the National Security Council, his phone calls are monitored for almost two years. The FBI sends the White House wiretap reports on how certain senators are expected to vote, on the activities of Nixon critics, on Muskie's campaign plans, and on the social habits and political views of White House employees.

While keeping these illegal wiretaps secret, Attorney General Mitchell insists that the President has the right to wiretap any domestic group "which seeks to attack and subvert the Government by unlawful means." Mitchell is worried by information that leaders of the antiwar movement have plans to cripple Nixon's bid for re-election in 1972. The President himself has a morbid fear of demonstrators. When Nixon travels anywhere to make a speech, Haldeman warns advance men they must make certain that demonstrators remain "unseen and unheard" by the President, authorizing "any means—legal or illegal" to achieve that purpose.

All evidences of social unrest and protest are regarded by Nixon and his aides as "threats to national security." Once a Maryland schoolteacher raises an antiwar banner within sight of the White House. When Nixon expresses his annoyance to Dwight Chapin, his appointments secretary seeks some thugs to remove the demonstrator. But White House counsel John Dean gets the park police to persuade the teacher to move his banner out of sight of the President.

Nixon is equally incensed by reporters for the media, whom he feels are prejudiced against his policy of continuing the Vietnam War until North Vietnam submits to his terms. As a candidate he promised to bring peace within six months, but now he insists the American intervention must continue until there is "peace with honor." The *Washington Post* observes, "What President Nixon means by peace is what other people mean by victory." Nixon fears that Southern and Midwestern supporters of the Vietnam War will block his re-election if he accepts a political solution to the war that will give the Communist Vietcong participation in the government of South Vietnam.

On the other hand he knows that he will be defeated if American troops are still fighting and dying in Indochina by Election Day. So he devises a plan of "Vietnamization"—a slow withdrawal of U.S. ground forces over a four-year period, replacing them with American-trained and -equipped South Vietnamese troops, while intensifying U.S. bombing raids. During his first four years in office, another fifteen thousand American boys die in battle and a hundred thousand more are wounded, to prop up the corrupt dictatorship of Nguyen Van Thieu, whom Nixon praises as "one of the four or five greatest leaders in the world."

When he makes a speech, carried on television, defending this policy, network commentators discuss and criticize it afterward. Furious, Nixon has Vice-President Agnew make stinging speeches against this "effete corps of impudent snobs." Agnew accuses them of "instant analysis," with anti-Nixon bias evident in "the expressions on their faces, the tone . . . the sarcasm." Agnew also charges *The New York Times* and the *Washington Post* with left-wing leanings.

On Nixon's orders, White House aides mount an orchestrated attack on those members of the media that refuse to accept his assertions at face value. In October 1969 Jeb Stuart Magruder, in charge of public relations, suggests to Haldeman that the three television networks, *Time*, and *Newsweek* can be frightened into "changing their views" by threatening a tax investigation or antitrust suit.

Haldeman instructs Magruder to mobilize Nixon's "Silent Majority" to "pound the magazines and the networks," protesting criticism of the President as unpatriotic. Nixon speechwriter Pat Buchanan appears on the CBS network to agitate viewers into demanding that "every legal and constitutional means" be taken "to break the power of the networks."

On April 30, 1970, Nixon goes on television to announce that he has sent troops to invade Cambodia to clean out enemy sanctuaries there. He declares that for five years the United States has not done so "because we did not wish to violate the territory of a neutral nation" as North Vietnam has done. He conceals the fact that for the previous fourteen months 3,875 secret air strikes have been authorized against Cambodia.

Nixon even sends Secretary of State William Rogers to testify before the Senate, "Cambodia is one country where we can say with complete assurance that our hands are clean and our heart is pure." Months later an outraged Senate Armed

Services Committee holds hearings to find out why they were not told the truth about illegal bombings that Congress has never authorized against a country with which the United States is at peace. Secretary of Defense James Schlesinger admits that false statistics about the bombings have been supplied to the Senate by the Pentagon, and that 102 American servicemen listed as killed in South Vietnam actually died in Cambodia and Laos.

The President's revelation on April 30 that he has widened the war by invading Cambodia with ground forces infuriates the antiwar movement. Over a half million people march in a Washington protest. The police make mass arrests of 13,400 demonstrators, detaining them in outdoor stockades. Department of Justice lawyers defend the arrests as essential to "national security," but a court later declares the arrests illegal.

Campuses all over America also erupt in demonstrations, some accompanied by bombings and other violence. Deeply upset, Nixon says bitterly, "You see these bums, you know, blowing up the campuses today are the luckiest people in the world, going to the greatest universities, and here they are . . . storming around about this issue."

Protest demonstrations at Kent State and Jackson State lead to the calling of police and national guardsmen to the campus. Six students are killed; many others wounded. Over 440 colleges shut down in a national strike of protest, and the National Student Association demands Nixon's impeachment.

Nixon is shaken by the killings and the uproar, but he insists that the domestic disorders are being financed by hostile foreign nations and demands that the CIA obtain proof of his belief. After investigating, the CIA submits two reports finding that the radical movements are getting no financial aid from abroad. They are "homegrown, indigenous responses to perceived grievances and problems that had been growing for years." Nixon is angered.

"The White House," James McCord later testifies, "had for some time been trying to get political control over the CIA assessments and estimates, in order to make them conform to 'White House policy.' . . . This also smacked of the situation which Hitler's intelligence chiefs found themselves in . . . when they were put in the position of having to tell him what they thought he wanted to hear about foreign military capabilities and intentions, instead of what they really believed."

Rejecting the CIA reports, Nixon takes action on a pre-election plan he has described in his book *Six Crises*: "To set up a new and independent organization carrying out covert para-military operations." His determination to do this is reinforced by his dissatisfaction with the FBI also, because Director J. Edgar Hoover, worried about his own reputation if the FBI is caught violating civil liberties, wants the political wiretaps stopped.

The President appoints Tom Charles Huston, ex-chairman of Young Americans for Freedom, who has worked in army intelligence, to draw up plans for a Nixon-controlled operation against domestic dissenters and critics. Huston first suggests using the Internal Revenue Service as an instrument to punish those who oppose the President. "What we cannot do in a courtroom via criminal prosecution," Huston tells Haldeman, "IRS could do by administrative action."

A special service group is set up in the IRS to monitor over a thousand tax-exempt political groups, including the Students for a Democratic Society (SDS) and the Black Panthers. The IRS is told that the White House wants Democratic party chairman Lawrence O'Brien sent to "the penitentiary" on tax-fraud charges. IRS Commissioner Randolph Thrower resigns, protesting against use of the agency as a "personal police force."

The White House arranges its own contacts within the IRS. They provide Haldeman with tax data to be used politically against those considered unfriendly to the President.

Huston develops a wide-ranging plan that sets up an independent intelligence agency to maintain permanent, intensive surveillance of antiwar activists, minority leaders, and others whom Nixon considers a threat to "national security." He advocates collecting information by illegally bugging phones in homes and offices; intercepting and opening mail; planting spies and agents provocateurs on campus; tax harassment; and other violations of the Bill of Rights.

This top-secret new intelligence superagency is to be run from the White House. It will also coordinate intelligence from the FBI, CIA, and military counterintelligence agencies. Explaining the planned use of "surreptitious entry," the Huston plan states: "Use of this technique is clearly illegal; it amounts to burglary. It is also highly risky and could result in great embarrassment if exposed. However, it is also the most fruitful tool and can produce the type of intelligence which cannot be obtained in any other fashion."

After "careful study," the President approves the Huston plan on July 23, 1970. FBI Director Hoover, however, refuses to cooperate. Tom Huston reports scornfully that Hoover fears that "if we do these things, the 'jackals of the press' and the ACLU [American Civil Liberties Union] will find out."

Hoover tells Mitchell bluntly that he will participate in the Huston plan only if Nixon gives him specific authority in writing to violate the law. Huston warns Haldeman, "We don't want the President linked to this thing with his signature on paper" because if the plan leaks, "all hell would break loose." Nixon rejects Hoover's demand.

When Hoover warns that the Administration is playing with dynamite, Mitchell advises the President to lay the Huston plan aside for a while. Hoover tells newsman Andrew Tully, "I was forced to put the kibosh on one crazy intelligence scheme against subversives." But the Huston plan is not dead.

Nixon later insists that he formally cancelled it five days after authorizing it. But Huston testifies under oath that the President didn't, and Nixon never produced any written evidence that he did so. On the contrary, six months after the Huston plan was laid aside, it is distributed as a handbook within a new secret intelligence unit of the Department of Justice—the Internal Security Division. The ISD, under Assistant Attorney General Robert C. Mardian, analyzes intelligence and directs undercover operations.

Mardian is an ultraconservative who seeks to wiretap suspected "domestic subversives" and fire government employees considered "disloyal" to the Nixon Administration. Working closely with Mardian is G. Gordon Liddy, whose name is soon to surface in connection with Watergate and other government-authorized break-ins.

The Huston plan is the fountainhead of all the illicit breaking-and-entering operations authorized by the Nixon Administration in the name of collecting intelligence for "national security" purposes. Lawyers for defendants in the trials the government is prosecuting complain that their homes and offices are being broken into and papers important to their clients' defense stolen.

When existence of the Huston plan is exposed later to the Senate Watergate Committee, Chairman Sam Ervin observes that it shows evidence of "a Gestapo mentality." It calls for a scheme for spying so widespread, Senator Ervin says, that it would be "a great shock to the American people" if they knew. Part of this scheme is exposed in December 1974, when *The New York Times* reveals that all through the first Nixon Administration the CIA violated its charter by spying on thousands of American citizens who oppose the Vietnam War.

As the midterm elections of 1970 approach, Nixon is anxious for a Republican sweep at the polls to create a bandwagon boom for his own re-election in 1972. He orders his aides to intimidate the media into giving more favorable coverage to his Administration by accusing them of biased reporting.

This attack is led by his special counsel, ex-Marine superpatriot Charles "Chuck" Colson, who writes Haldeman, "It is time for us to generate a PR [public relations] campaign against the Democrats and CBS." Haldeman replies, "Absolutely." Colson mobilizes over thirty political "attack groups" across the country.

During September the Nixon Administration lodges twenty-one complaints about biased television news coverage. Meeting with heads of the three networks, Colson seeks to bully them into submission, threatening that the Federal Communications Commission may refuse license renewals to their member stations. CBS vice-chairman Frank Stanton is warned that failure to "play ball" will result in Administration action "to bring you to your knees on Wall Street and Madison Avenue."

The networks hastily reassure Colson that any "imbalance" in presenting the news will be corrected at once.

"The harder I pressed them," Colson jubilantly reports in a memo to Haldeman on September 25, 1970, "the more accommodating, cordial and almost apologetic they became. . . . They are damned nervous and scared, and we should continue to take a very tough line." The Justice Department files antitrust suits

Charles W. Colson, special counsel to President Nixon.

against all three networks to keep the pressure on. When reporters accuse the White House of attempting to muzzle the media, Nixon aides ridicule the accusation as "paranoiac."

Historian Henry Steele Commager observes, "Never before in our history . . . has government so audaciously violated the spirit of the Constitutional guarantee of freedom of the press."

Nixon worries about another threat to his re-election hopes: ex-Governor George Wallace of Alabama, who is seeking to regain his power base by running in the 1970 Democratic primary for governor. Wallace has been gaining political strength since his 1968 run for the Presidency as a third-party candidate. If he tries again in 1972, he may siphon off enough votes from "Middle America" to cause Nixon to lose.

Haldeman's aide Lawrence M. Higby secretly funnels $400,000 of leftover campaign funds into Alabama in an attempt to defeat Wallace in the state primary. After Wallace wins, he learns that the IRS has plans to prosecute his brother for unreported income. Wallace then announces that he will not be a third-party candidate against Nixon in 1972 but will run in the Democratic primaries. This will split the Democratic vote, while preserving the votes of Middle America for Nixon. The IRS does not prosecute Wallace's brother.

To help Republican candidates in the 1970 election, Nixon sends Vice-President Agnew around the country to make vitriolic attacks against student dissenters, Democrats, and the press. Republicans complain that Agnew's diatribes are so heavy-handed that they may backfire. He disclaims personal responsibility. "Any schoolchild," he points out, "would know that the Vice-President is just an extension of the President."

The Republicans gain two seats in the Senate but lose a dozen in the House, plus eleven governorships and key state legislatures. They poll badly in many of the largest states crucial to presidential elections. The omens are grim for Nixon's hopes of re-election. "In 1970," columnists Robert Novak and Rowland Evans note, "the Presidency of Richard Nixon hit bottom." Press secretary Herbert Klein is asked about rumors that Nixon may decide not to run again. "You just don't know the man," Klein replies. "Richard Nixon simply loves being President of the United States."

But Nixon is increasingly haunted by fears that the vexatious Vietnam War may make him a one-term President. He quickly organizes a new "game plan" for his next two years in office.

At a meeting with his senior aides at his home in Key Biscayne, Florida, it is decided that he must develop a lofty new image as "the President." All traces of Nixon the tricky politician must be erased, while the "low road" of tough partisan brawling is assigned to others in the Administration. Nixon tells newsmen at a televised press conference, "Now I am going to wear my hat as President of the United States."

Ron Ziegler, replacing Herbert Klein as press secretary, introduces a policy of giving newsmen as little information as possible. Using evasive language, he answers questions with nonanswers, giving rise to a sarcastic new term among newsmen —"Ziegling." Asked in February 1971 whether the Administration is secretly planning to invade Laos, Ziegler replies elliptically, "The President is aware of what is going on in Southeast Asia. That is not to say anything is going on in Southeast Asia."

Reporters learn that the FBI is secretly investigating CBS correspondent Daniel Schorr, apparently to "get something on him." The White House hastily issues a statement to the effect that Schorr is merely being checked out routinely for a possible presidential appointment. Haldeman later admits that this is a lie. Another newsman who is anathema to Nixon is Dan Rather of CBS. Early in 1971 Ehrlichman tries unsuccessfully to pressure CBS News president Richard Salant into transferring Rather from Washington.

Rather later describes other White House techniques used against conscientious reporters: "They now have a journalistic goon squad operating inside. The idea is to crowd you, to harass you when they can with phone calls complaining about pieces. . . . We ought to understand what is going on. They have a $400-million-a-year public relations operation. A very large part of the money is spent for partisan/political/ideological propaganda. . . . Now if they did this with Republican Party funds, that would be one thing. But these people are by and large on the public payroll."

A Supreme Court decision in February 1971 compels Nixon to end the wiretaps on government officials and newsmen. But by now an "Inter-agency Evaluation Committee"—essentially the secret police unit blueprinted by the Huston plan—is operating in the White House.

A computer expert is summoned to develop an intelligence bank of dossiers on political friends and enemies, for use in putting Administration pressure on them to support whatever measures the President wants. The expert's firm is so shocked by this plan for computerized political blackmail that it refuses to cooperate.

Nixon becomes extremely worried that same month when the Harris public-opinion poll shows that the leading contender for the Democratic presidential nomination, Edmund Muskie, holds a 43–40 lead over him.

By May 1971 the poll shows Muskie forging ahead with a dismaying 47–39 lead over the President. There is panic at the White House. It is decided to sabotage the campaigns of Muskie and Edward Kennedy, the two leading Democratic contenders. Nixon wants to run against either George McGovern or George Wallace, considering them easiest to beat.

Mitchell, although still Attorney General, takes charge of major campaign decisions. To offset gloom in the Republican camp over Democratic gains in the polls, he assures the press doggedly, "This country is going so far right that you are not even going to recognize it."

In view of what is soon to happen, two significant statements are made about how much the President knows of his aides' campaign activities. Nixon says in an early 1971 interview, "When I am the candidate, I run the campaign"; Magruder later acknowledges, "The President, Bob Haldeman, and John Mitchell . . . were in constant consultation with each other over major activities."

These statements contradict the President's later defense in the Watergate scandal that he was too busy with the nation's affairs to have much to do with decisions of the re-election campaign, which he insists were made by others.

The Ellsberg Affair

4

Nixon's persistence in refusing to end the Vietnam War by a political settlement comes under sharp attack from Daniel J. Ellsberg, forty-one, a Defense Department analyst who had taken part in a 1965 intelligence operation in South Vietnam under Major General Edward Lansdale. A former supporter of the war, Ellsberg had become completely disillusioned by the American intervention.

Returning home, he was assigned by the Pentagon to work on a 47-volume analytic study called *A History of the Decision-Making Process on Vietnam Policy*. It candidly detailed the lies told by the Johnson Administration and the Pentagon to deceive the American people and the Congress into supporting the corrupt Saigon regime.

"They could hang people for what's in there," McNamara confides to a friend after reading the report. According to David Halberstam, in his book *The Best and the Brightest*, McNamara's chief aide, John McNaughton, admits to Ellsberg, "If what you say in that briefing is true, we're fighting on the wrong side." The Pentagon quickly classifies it top secret.

But Ellsberg is determined to get the truth to the public. Without authorization he releases copies of the classified documents that are soon known as the Pentagon Papers to *The New York Times*, which begins publishing them on June 13, 1971. Shocked, Nixon calls a meeting of his aides, which Colson later describes as "a kind of panic session." The news leak indicates a "disloyal" higher-up in the Nixon Administration. What embarrassing Nixon political secrets may be leaked to the press next?

By destroying the legitimacy of the American presence in Vietnam, the leaked report also hurts Nixon's chances of re-election for having further continued the war for two and a half years. Moreover, it threatens his plans for a foreign-policy triumph in the election year of 1972—dramatic trips to Peking and Moscow to end the cold war with pacts of "détente." He and Kissinger worry that the Chinese and Russians will now feel they cannot be trusted to keep secret talks secret.

They order Attorney General Mitchell to go to court to stop *The Times* and also the *Washington Post* from publishing further installments of the Pentagon Papers. But the Supreme Court upholds the people's right to know the truth.

Nixon angrily tells Haldeman and Colson, "I don't give a damn how it is done, do whatever has to be done to stop these leaks and prevent further unauthorized disclosures. I don't want to be told why it can't be done. . . . I don't want excuses. I want results. I want it done, whatever the costs."

Illegal wiretaps are placed on the phones of two *Times* reporters and ten White House aides. But the truth emerges only when Ellsberg publicly reveals that it was he who released the Pentagon Papers. Nixon recalls having once met him with Lansdale, during a visit to Saigon during the Johnson Administration, when they explained they were trying to compel the Saigon regime to hold an honest election.

"Oh, sure, honest," Nixon had grinned. "Yes, honest, that's right—so long as you win!"

On June 28 a Los Angeles grand jury indicts Ellsberg in California for theft and violation under the Espionage Act, later adding conspiracy and other charges. Ellsberg's friend Anthony Russo is also indicted with him for conspiring to steal and release the papers.

The prosecutors are pressing charges at the Administration's insistence. Prosecuting Ellsberg is part of Nixon's political strategy for re-election. "The President," Colson later reveals, "on numerous occasions urged me to disseminate damaging information about Daniel Ellsberg . . . and others with whom

Ellsberg had been in contact." Nixon wants direct evidence found to link Ellsberg with antiwar Democrats in the camps of Muskie and Kennedy.

"This case won't be tried in the court," Colson tells Ehrlichman, "it will be tried in the newspapers. So it's going to take some resourceful engineering." He indicates to Haldeman that Ellsberg will make a "natural villain" for the Nixon campaign "to the extent he could be painted evil."

But Mardian, who heads the Internal Security Division, is tipped off by his friend, FBI assistant director William Sullivan, that the Ellsberg trial could boomerang. The FBI has records of the seventeen illegal wiretaps Nixon authorized after *The Times* story on the Cambodia bombings. They include fifteen conversations involving Ellsberg.

This illegally gathered information could throw the case out of court, and also cause an uproar in the press. Sullivan believes that J. Edgar Hoover is preserving it to blackmail Nixon with, in case the President tries to fire him.

"This is so hot I can't even talk to you about it," Mardian later tells White House counsel John Dean. When the President is told about the wiretap logs, he at once orders Ehrlichman to obtain them from Sullivan. Turned over to the White House without Hoover's knowledge, they are locked away in Ehrlichman's safe. In pretrial hearings the government, responding to a court order, vows that there has been no electronic surveillance of Ellsberg's conversations.

To implement the scheme to discredit Ellsberg and the Democrats, Nixon sets up a secret investigative unit nicknamed the Plumbers, under the supervision of Ehrlichman. The unit is headed by Egil Krogh, Jr., thirty-one, an aggressive White House lawyer, and David Young, thirty-two, a lawyer from Kissinger's National Security Council staff.

"I told Mr. Krogh that as a matter of first priority, the unit should find out all it could about Mr. Ellsberg's associates and his motives . . . ," the President later recalls. "Not then knowing what additional national secrets Mr. Ellsberg might disclose, I did impress upon Mr. Krogh the vital importance to the national security of his assignment."

This explanation is not supported by notes taken by

*Egil Krogh, Jr., head of the
secret investigative unit called
"the Plumbers."*

Ehrlichman during a July 1 discussion with Nixon. He writes, "Espionage—not involved in Ellsberg case." He further notes, "Leak stuff out—this is the way we win."

On the same day Colson phones an old friend, retired CIA career spy E. Howard Hunt, who is bitter at the Kennedy clan. Hunt is convinced that the CIA's Bay of Pigs invasion of Castro's Cuba collapsed because President John F. Kennedy, supported by his brother Robert, refused to save it with air power.

Colson asks Hunt to help the Nixon campaign link Ellsberg to Senator Edward Kennedy, a dove on Vietnam. "Ellsberg could be turned into a martyr of the New Left," Colson explains, "[or] this thing could be turned into a major public case against Ellsberg and co-conspirators."

Colson also wants Hunt to cripple Kennedy's candidacy among Roman Catholics by proving that his brother John, as President, ordered the overthrow and murder of South Vietnam's

Howard Hunt, hired by Colson as a "consultant."

president Ngo Dinh Diem. "I believe," Hunt later recalls, "it was desired by Mr. Colson . . . to demonstrate that a Catholic U.S. Administration had, in fact, conspired in the assassination of a Catholic chief of state in another country."

Colson gets an OK from Haldeman to hire Hunt as a $100-a-day "consultant" with an office in the White House. At the same time Hunt retains his public-relations job with Robert R. Mullen and Company as a cover.

In a July speech to the Virginia Bar Association, Attorney General Mitchell defends the right of the government to wiretap domestic "subversives" as "necessary to protect the national security." Shocked, Representative Emanuel Celler, chairman of the House Judiciary Committee, calls this a "police state" view. Former Attorney General Ramsey Clark declares, "That's an utterly lawless philosophy. The President is bound to obey the Constitution like all other Americans."

Asked about Mitchell's views at a press conference, Nixon implies that the government eavesdrops on private conversations without court orders in only a few special cases. "We will wiretap," he says, "only when a wiretap is necessary."

When he is asked about his reluctance to end the war in Vietnam, he replies, "I would remind all concerned that the way we got into Vietnam in the first place was through overthrowing Diem, and the complicity in the murder of Diem."

He orders the Plumbers to search through files of classified cables in the State Department for some that will prove President Kennedy ordered Diem's overthrow and murder. Hunt is given the job, but can find a few cables indicating only that the Kennedy Administration knew Diem's generals were planning a coup and were not opposed to it.

"Do you think you could 'improve' on them?" Colson asks Hunt. Hunt replies that he'd need technical aid to do so.

"Well, we won't be able to give you any technical help. This is too hot. See what you can do on your own."

Hunt manages to forge two cables linking the late President and the Democrats directly to Diem's assassination. Colson leaks them to *Life* reporter William Lambert, suggesting an article called "How Kennedy Killed Diem." But Lambert is suspicious of Colson. Unable to authenticate the cables, he decides not to write the story. Hunt deposits the forged cables in his office safe to leak elsewhere later in the campaign if Edward Kennedy becomes the Democratic candidate.

The Plumbers set up shop in Room 16 in the basement of the Executive Office Building, adjoining the White House, with Hunt as the key operative under Krogh and Young. When it is learned that Ellsberg has been a patient of Dr. Lewis J. Fielding, a Beverly Hills, California, psychiatrist, Hunt is assigned to uncover Ellsberg's psychiatric record. "We should go down the line to nail the guy cold," Colson tells Hunt.

Hunt later explains, "Our government trains people like myself to do these things and do them successfully. It becomes a way of life for a person like me." His life style is in the gaudy image of a James Bond—French food, wine, elegant china and crystal, glamorous women, daring missions in disguise under aliases. He describes the Plumbers unit as uniquely "above the FBI and the CIA," since it works directly for the White House.

A second secret agent, recommended by Krogh and hired by Ehrlichman, joins Hunt in the Plumbers. Bushy-moustached G. Gordon Liddy, a gun-loving ex-FBI agent, has been an assistant district attorney in Dutchess County, New York. Demonstrating a flair for the flamboyant, he once electrified a jury during a trial by suddenly firing a pistol loaded with blanks.

Local Republican officials, who consider Liddy a dangerously unstable "wild man" with high political ambitions, get rid of him by recommending him to Gerald Ford, then House minority leader, for a Treasury job in Washington. But the Treasury Department, too, soon grows eager to lose him—"We couldn't control him," one official later recalls—and Liddy finds a new government berth with the Plumbers.

To help Hunt assemble damaging information on Ellsberg's personal problems, Mitchell arranges to have two FBI men question Dr. Fielding on July 20, 1971. The psychiatrist refuses to reveal confidences between doctor and patient. The FBI agents are equally unsuccessful in trying to interrogate Ellsberg's associates.

Meanwhile Assistant Attorney General Mardian turns over

*G. Gordon Liddy, hired by
Ehrlichman as one of the
Plumbers.*

to Hunt and Liddy copies of the fifteen Ellsberg phone conversations in the secret FBI wiretap records. The Plumbers study them for derogatory material and leads.

Another news leak embarrasses and angers the President on July 23 when *New York Times* reporter William Beecher breaks a story revealing details of the American negotiating position in the SALT (Strategic Arms Limitation) talks with the Soviet Union. Although this occurs long after the illegal wiretap program he has ordered for political reasons, Nixon later seeks to justify the wiretaps by repeatedly referring to the SALT-talks leak as the chief reason.

He now suggests to Ehrlichman and Krogh that they give lie-detector tests to thousands of government employees. "I don't know how accurate they are," he says, "but I know they'll scare the hell out of people." He adds, "This *does* affect the national security. . . . This isn't like the Pentagon Papers." Yet he later persistently justifies his cover-up of the Plumbers' illegal acts involving Ellsberg on grounds of "protecting national security."

On July 28 Hunt writes Colson, "I am proposing a skeletal

operations plan aimed at building a file on Ellsberg that will contain all available overt, covert and derogatory information. This basic tool is essential in determining how to destroy his public image and credibility."

He suggests to Krogh and Young that an undercover operation be organized to gain access to Ellsberg's case record in Dr. Fielding's office files. When they send Ehrlichman a memo requesting permission, it returns with written approval "if done with your assurance that it is not traceable."

But an even more direct order comes from the President. "Do whatever [is] necessary," he tells Krogh, "to dig up more on Ellsberg." John Dean later testifies, "I asked him [Krogh] if he had received his authorization to proceed with the burglary from Ehrlichman. Krogh responded that no . . . he had received his orders right out of the Oval Office. I was so surprised to hear this that I said, 'You must be kidding.' And he repeated [it] again."

Ehrlichman phones CIA Deputy Director Robert Cushman. Identifying Hunt as a White House consultant on security matters, he asks the CIA to cooperate with Hunt on a "highly sensitive mission." Cushman arranges to furnish Hunt and Liddy with physical disguises, false identification papers, an experimental camera in a tobacco pouch, and a disguised tape recorder. In August, with the approval of the President, Hunt and Liddy fly to Los Angeles to case the operation. They return with photos of Dr. Fielding's office building and outer office which are developed for them by the CIA.

Meanwhile Young, Mardian, and Pentagon counsel J. Fred Buzhardt meet with Congressmen Edward Hébert and Leslie Arends to plan hearings of the House Armed Services Committee on the Pentagon Papers leak. Proposed witnesses to be called for interrogation include prominent Democrats like ex-Secretary of Defense Clark Clifford and his assistant Paul Warnke, both of whom are now active in Senator Muskie's primary campaign for the presidential nomination.

The purpose of the investigation, Young explains in a memo to Ehrlichman, would be to "develop a very negative picture around the whole Pentagon study affair . . . and then to identify Ellsberg's associates and supporters on the New Left with this negative image. . . . Do we want to prosecute or do we want to bring such material out through the congressional investigation?"

Young adds, "I am sending you a separate Hunt-to-Colson memorandum which attempts to select the politically damaging material involving the Democratic hierarchy. . . . If the present Hunt/Liddy project No. 1 is successful it will be absolutely essential to have an overall game plan developed for its use in conjunction with the congressional investigation."

Ehrlichman writes Colson, "On the assumption that the proposed undertaking by Hunt and Liddy would be carried out and would be successful, I would appreciate receiving from you by next Wednesday a game plan as to how and when you believe the materials should be used."

The Plumbers develop a plan for breaking into Dr. Fielding's office. Krogh and Young assure Ehrlichman that "Hunt/Liddy project No. 1" will be nontraceable to the White House. Hunt now demands that the CIA provide him with a secretary, a "safe house" in Los Angeles to operate from, and a credit card he can use under an alias. But Cushman has second thoughts about getting the CIA deeper involved in what is obviously domestic espionage. He orders the CIA to extend no further cooperation to Hunt.

The FBI, too, proves balky. An FBI report contradicts Nixon's insistence that Ellsberg had Democratic collaborators. "The FBI is disposed to think," Young writes in a memo, "that Ellsberg is the sole prime mover." Nor will the FBI support a White House claim that Ellsberg turned over a more complete version of the Pentagon Papers to the Russian Embassy.

Nixon is now convinced more than ever that he can rely upon only his own intelligence unit—the Plumbers.

At Ehrlichman's request, Colson borrows $5,000 in untraceable cash to finance the Hunt-Liddy operation. He gets it from a friend, public-relations man Joseph Baroody, who is later repaid out of a dairy-industry campaign contribution.

Krogh gives the money to Hunt and Liddy, warning them not to break into Dr. Fielding's office themselves, because of their White House ties. Hunt goes to Miami to assemble a burglary team from Cubans he directed in the CIA Bay of Pigs invasion. He asks Bernard L. Barker, "Would you be willing to help me in a matter of national security which is above both the CIA and the FBI?"

Barker, impressed that Hunt is working directly for the White House, promptly agrees. Hoping that Hunt in turn will use his influence to aid Barker's exile organization to launch a new attempt to overthrow Castro, Barker recruits Eugenio Martinez and Felipe de Diego to help him.

The break-in is planned for the Labor Day weekend.

Late at night in California on September 3, 1971, Hunt is staked out to keep an eye on Dr. Fielding's home to make sure he remains there. Liddy stands guard outside the office building, maintaining contact by walkie-talkie with the three Cubans as they break in through a window on the ground floor.

Jimmying Dr. Fielding's office door, the Cubans pry open a locked file cabinet and locate a folder on Ellsberg. De Diego holds up all the records in it, one by one, as Martinez photographs them. Hunt is chagrined, however, when the records produce nothing in any way derogatory to Ellsberg.

"It was a clean operation," he reports to Krogh. "There were no fingerprints left behind. But it failed to produce." When Hunt tries to show Martinez's photos to Colson, Colson covers his eyes and snaps, "I don't want to know what you have been doing!" As a lawyer Colson knows that if he has specific knowledge of the break-in and fails to report it to the police, he is guilty of a felony.

Hunt knows that the CIA must have secret files on Ellsberg because of the international aspects of the Pentagon Papers leak. He gets David Young to appeal for a "psychological profile" of Ellsberg prepared from its data. CIA Director Richard Helms reluctantly complies. But the CIA report delivered to the Plumbers is also disappointing.

"There is no suggestion that the subject thought anything treasonous in his act," it discloses. "Rather he seemed to be responding to what he deemed a higher order of patriotism. His exclusion of the three volumes of the Papers concerned with the secret negotiations would support this."

Krogh and Young gloomily report to Ehrlichman that the Nixon Administration is likely to fail in its prosecution of Ellsberg because he gave classified information only to the press, not to a foreign power. Moreover the Defense Department, embarrassed by congressional criticism of its "top secret" classification of the Pentagon Papers to conceal government lies about Vietnam, has declassified them, an admission that national security was not involved.

Hunt persists in the project to smear Ellsberg. Working from the CIA report, the FBI wiretap records, and newspaper clippings, he draws up a 28-page dossier that he hopes will do the job. But Young rejects it as useless, and it ends up shelved in the safe of Hunt's White House office.

"By God," J. Edgar Hoover confides to newsman Andrew Tully, "Nixon's got some former CIA men working for him that I'd kick out of my office. Some day that bunch will serve him up a fine mess!"

Dirty Tricks

5

When things look bleakest for Nixon's re-election chances, in the spring and summer of 1971, he and his aides determine to hold the White House if they have to steal the election. They resort to intimidation of the media, political sabotage, and dirty tricks. The Democratic party and its candidates are to be blamed for every violent demonstration in the country and smeared by rumors that their campaign funds include "Communist money."

In charge of all slippery chores is Charles Colson, described by White House aide Kenneth Clawson as a "tough doer, the kind of fellow who does the necessary dirty work." Once, plotting to burglarize the Brookings Institute for some documents, Colson proposes to set fire to the building as a cover. A horrified Caulfield rushes out of Colson's office to warn White House counsel John Dean that Colson is crazy and had better be stopped. Dean flies out to San Clemente to see Ehrlichman, who phones Colson to halt the operation.

"I might have said it . . . ," Colson acknowledges later. "It is characteristic of me. . . . But I certainly never meant it." Although few officials have the President's ear, Colson sees or talks to him on the telephone almost every day.

Colson's campaign to intimidate the television networks is intensified in the fall of 1971. He charges "consistent bias" against Nixon in network newscasts, pressuring television executives to order that the President be presented in only a favorable light.

"Attacks on the press by officers of the government have become so widespread and all-pervasive," notes the American Civil Liberties Union, "that they constitute a massive federal-level attempt to subvert the letter and spirit of the First Amendment."

Nixon sets up the Office of Telecommunications headed by Clay Whitehead, who insists that all local television stations be responsible for what is said on any network newscasts and documentaries they carry. Under Whitehead's proposal a local station will lose its broadcasting license if the Federal Communications Commission (FCC) decides that it presents "biased" news programs.

The FCC is headed by Nixon appointee Dean Burch, ultraconservative, former campaign manager for Barry Goldwater. The threat is clear to local television-station owners, who in any event, according to the show business weekly *Variety*, are "about 99% for the Administration and about 99% against any hard Nixon news." They pressure NBC, CBS, and ABC to curb unfavorable news or views of the Nixon Administration on network programs, and the networks begin to find excuses for not presenting "controversial views."

Colson, Haldeman, Ehrlichman, and the President himself contribute names to a list of over two hundred individuals and organizations labeled "political enemies." The list is maintained by White House counsel John Dean, who later reveals that Nixon wants "the use of the Internal Revenue Service to attack our enemies" by tax audits. In a September 1971 memo to Haldeman and Ehrlichman, Dean discusses "how we can use the available federal machinery to screw our political enemies."

The enemies list includes university presidents, businessmen, celebrities, anti-Vietnam War leaders, civil-rights organizations, labor leaders, reporters and newspapers, ten Senators, every black member of the House of Representatives and six other Congressmen. In a memo to Haldeman's aide Lawrence Higby, Dean singles some out as designated by Colson "worthwhile for go status."

Next to the name of Morton Halperin, a former member of

the National Security Council, who became an executive of Common Cause, Dean notes, "A scandal would be most helpful here." CBS correspondent Daniel Schorr is called "a real media enemy." Dean suggests that Doyle, Dane, and Bernbach, a pro-Democratic advertising agency, "should be hit hard starting with Dane." Targeting Muskie fund-raiser Arnold Picker of United Artists, Dean observes, "Success here could be both debilitating and very embarrassing for the Muskie machine."

When Dean later exposes the enemies list in testimony before the Senate Watergate Committee, House minority leader Gerald Ford remarks, "If you have so many enemies that you have to keep a list, you're in trouble." Haldeman tries to explain the list away as simply a compilation of political opponents for the purpose of "not inviting them to White House social functions." Correspondents laugh.

In November 1971 Dean and Caulfield ask Haldeman to compel IRS Commissioner John Walters to make "changes in personnel and policy" that will let the White House use the IRS against the enemies list as it sees fit. When Long Island newspaperman Robert Greene writes an exposé of government funds lent to millionaire Charles G. "Bebe" Rebozo, the President's closest friend, Haldeman reportedly recommends that Greene should "have some tax problems." Similarly Caulfield recommends both an IRS tax audit and an FBI investigation for the producer of a film unfavorable to the President.

Some on the enemies list are kept under surveillance. According to Kalmbach, Haldeman orders him to give up to $50,000 to Ulasewicz to spy on House Speaker Carl Albert and to bug the home phone of columnist Joseph Kraft.

Out of the same fund of campaign cash, Kalmbach pays $1,300 a month and $35,000 in expenses to Donald Segretti, who is brought into the re-election campaign to head a dirty-tricks squad. Segretti's sponsors are Haldeman's aide Gordon Strachan and Nixon's appointments secretary Dwight Chapin. They, Segretti, and Ron Ziegler are USC alumni, who once belonged to the Trojan Knights, a campus political club. The club's tactics included ripping down posters of rival candidates for the student senate, stealing the opposition's leaflets, stuffing ballot boxes, and packing the student court to suppress complaints. When Segretti

Donald H. Segretti, head of the
"dirty tricks" squad.

asks Strachan for a White House position, his friends agree that he's just the man to run a dirty-tricks program to help re-elect the President. Haldeman gives him the job.

Segretti travels around the country, using the alias of Simmons, as he sets up a political espionage-sabotage network. Impressing upon recruits the need for absolute secrecy, he promises them plenty of money and a good position after Nixon's re-election. Army friend Alex Shipley asks him, "How can we be taken care of if no one knows what we're doing?"

"Nixon knows that something's being done," Segretti replies. "It's a typical deal—'don't tell me anything, and I won't know.' " He describes the work—infiltrating Democratic candidates' headquarters to spy and steal documents; forging campaign literature to discredit them; sending out phony press releases; sabotaging Democratic fund-raising dinners; starting brawls at Democratic rallies; spying on candidates' families to dig up dirt that can hurt their campaigns.

Great fun, Segretti promises, with lots of excitement, free travel, and a limitless expense account. He urges Shipley to sign on and recruit five other operatives. Shipley refuses, but Segretti finds more than enough willing recruits.

Chapin instructs Segretti to sow dissension among the leading Democratic candidates during their primary campaigns, turning them against each other so bitterly that they will refuse to unite behind the primary winners in the general election.

As Frank Mankiewicz, campaign director for Senator George McGovern, later testifies in Congress, Segretti's sabotage activities do indeed deeply divide Democratic candidates, badly hurting reunification of the party behind McGovern.

When the polls show Senator Muskie leading Nixon in popularity by nine points, the President and his aides hold an emergency meeting at Key Biscayne. A decision is reached to concentrate on sabotaging the primary campaigns of Muskie and Edward Kennedy, the two leading contenders for the Democratic nomination. Nixon wants McGovern to get the nomination, considering him the weakest candidate and the easiest to defeat.

"We're out to swing the convention to McGovern . . . ," Segretti informs Indiana party worker Charles Svihlik, age twenty-four, "to literally destroy strong candidates like Muskie."

Chapin, Colson, and Hunt feed Segretti ideas for dirty tricks. Muskie finds his primary campaign in New Hampshire going mysteriously haywire. Democratic voters are enraged when they are awakened after midnight by phone calls allegedly from "Harlem Youth for Muskie Volunteers," urging votes for Muskie. The ultraconservative *Manchester Union Leader* prints a spurious letter from a "Paul Morrison" of Florida, quoting Muskie as having slurred New Englanders of French Canadian descent by calling them "Canucks."

The paper runs a front-page editorial headlined "Muskie

One of Segretti's counterfeit posters is displayed by Senate Watergate Committee counsel Samuel Dash.

Insults Franco-Americans," declaring, "We have always known that Senator Muskie was a hypocrite." It also runs a news item representing Muskie's wife as fond of drinking, smoking, and off-color jokes. Outraged, Muskie makes a speech in Manchester in the midst of a snowstorm. Branding the Morrison letter a lie, he becomes so emotional in defending his wife's reputation that his eyes fill with tears and he chokes up.

This public display of "instability" costs him heavily, dropping his share in the New Hampshire primary from 65 to 48 percent. He still wins, but his status as the front runner among the various Democratic candidates is badly hurt.

Segretti's sabotage operations are transferred to the supervision of the Plumbers for the Florida primaries. When Hunt and Liddy fly to Miami to guide Segretti, Hunt suggests organizing an attack on Republican headquarters and blaming it on Democratic supporters. Instead they decide to "screw up" the

Democratic campaign by making each candidate believe the others are trying to sabotage him.

Releases on "Muskie" letterheads are sent to the press, reporting a faked poll to the effect that 51 percent of interviewees consider Edward Kennedy unfit for the Presidency. Hired "Muskie supporters" picket the campaign headquarters of Senator Henry Jackson, while phony Jackson and Humphrey supporters picket Muskie's headquarters. A fraudulent Jackson news release accuses Muskie of having stripped his Senate office of government typewriters for use by his campaign workers in Florida.

A low point is reached when Segretti supplies Florida saboteur Robert Benz with counterfeit "Citizens for Muskie" letters. Mailed three days before the Florida primary, these falsely accuse Jackson and Humphrey of having run afoul of the law because of sexual misconduct. This dirty trick, reported to Chapin and Strachan, immensely amuses them.

Evil-smelling liquids are released at a Muskie fund-raising picnic to break it up. A Wallace rally is flooded with fake Muskie leaflets reading, "If you liked Hitler, you'll just love Wallace." Outraged voters give the Florida primary to Wallace, with Muskie finishing a poor fourth behind Jackson and Humphrey. The Democrat whom the polls have shown able to beat Nixon in 1972 has now been so effectively sabotaged that he is unlikely to gain his party's nomination.

The President and his aides decide that the Republican National Committee (RNC) is too stodgy to fight the kind of bare-knuckles campaign they want, to be sure of winning. In March 1972 they form the Committee for the Re-election of the President (CRP), with headquarters only 150 yards from the White House.

While Segretti continues to pervert the electoral process, CRP uses other tactics to make it seem that the President has more popular support than he actually has, hoping to create a bandwagon effect.

In early May 1972 Nixon, desperate to force North Vietnam to yield to his conditions for peace before Election Day, announces his decision to mine Haiphong Harbor. As protest sweeps the nation, the CRP appeals to officials of veterans organizations. A manufactured telegram campaign lets Ziegler announce that wires received at the White House are running "6 to 1" in support of Nixon's action.

When Washington television station WTTG runs an opinion poll on the mining, CRP forges almost four thousand ballots. A half-page ad appears in *The New York Times* to answer that paper's editorial criticism. It asks, "WHO CAN YOU BELIEVE—THE NEW YORK TIMES OR THE AMERICAN PEOPLE?" The ad is signed by "the November Group," which claims to represent citizen support for the President. It actually represents only the advertising agency placing the ad, which originates with Colson and is paid for by Herbert Porter at CRP.

An antiwar rally with Daniel Ellsberg as the principal speaker is scheduled to take place outside the Capitol on May 4, 1972. Two days before, FBI Director J. Edgar Hoover dies, and the Nixon Administration decides to have his body lie in state inside the Capitol rotunda. At a signal from Colson, the Plumbers prepare to disrupt the antiwar rally.

Barker flies to Washington with nine Cuban vigilantes, including Martinez, Gonzales, Sturgis, and de Diego. Their instructions are to denounce Ellsberg as a traitor, beat him up, then run. But they prematurely attack dissenters at the rally, and two of them are arrested by the police. The pair are released and the rest scattered when a mysterious "man in a gray suit" (Hunt?) assures a police lieutenant that they are "good men" and "anti-Communists."

On May 15 Arthur Bremer, an emotionally disturbed youth, shoots and cripples Governor George Wallace in Maryland, ending his race for the Democratic nomination. According to Howard Hunt, Colson immediately asks him to fly to Milwaukee, break into Bremer's apartment, and try to find evidence that can link Bremer to left-wing causes. Hunt rejects the idea as far too risky.

When McGovern's victories in several primaries make him the front-runner, the sabotage apparatus is retooled to wreck his campaign as the party's choice. Spy Tom Gregory, who worked at Muskie's campaign headquarters, is now ordered by Hunt to volunteer at McGovern's headquarters. He is told to make detailed sketches of the offices of McGovern's campaign managers, obviously as a prelude to bugging them.

In June, as the Democrats prepare to hold their convention in Miami the following month, the Plumbers offer one of the Cubans $700 a week to recruit Florida hippies to throw rocks, break windows, and urinate in public to "give the voters a bad impression of the people supporting McGovern." He declines because he's already working for the FBI and the Miami police.

At CRP, Liddy proposes to hire a woman to disrobe at the Democratic Convention to suggest an immoral image of the party to television viewers. Although this plan is rejected, young men are hired to wear conspicuous McGovern campaign buttons while behaving in a flagrantly homosexual manner in front of television cameras.

Once he is re-elected, Nixon is determined to punish those members of the media who persist in seeking to run down the truth about Watergate and related misdeeds. On September 15, 1972, he gives Dean a number of names for the enemies list. "They are asking for it," he says, "and they are going to get it. We have not used the power in this first four years, as you know. . . . We have not used the [Tax] Bureau and we have not used the Justice Department, but things are going to change now!"

"What an exciting prospect!" Dean enthuses.

In the final months of the campaign the President decides to use the IRS to harass the Democratic campaign. Ehrlichman sends Dean to IRS Commissioner John Walters to demand tax audits of key figures on the enemies list, on 575 McGovern supporters, and on DNC chairman Lawrence O'Brien.

Walters balks, warning Ehrlichman that the resultant scandal could make Watergate look like "a Sunday School picnic." He also reveals that O'Brien has already been audited several times, and his tax reports found in good order.

"I'm tired of your goddam foot-dragging tactics," Ehrlichman snarls. He later admits, "I wanted them to turn up something and send him [O'Brien] to jail before the election."

Nixon observes darkly that Walters' boss, Treasury Secretary George Shultz, had better "lay down the law" to Walters. The President assures Dean that after his re-election he will replace all reluctant bureaucrats with new bureau chiefs who will be "responsive to the White House."

Dirty tricks are played on Republicans who refuse to go along with Administration policy, like Representative Paul McCloskey of California, who opposes Nixon's prolongation of the Vietnam War. McCloskey's campaign for re-election is dealt a low blow when Colson tries to smear him as a supporter of homosexuals by arranging and publicizing a fraudulent contribution to the McCloskey campaign on behalf of the Gay Liberation Front.

Nixon does not hesitate to help the re-election of about one hundred conservative Democrats who support him. According to Strachan, the President sees to it that they receive only token Republican opposition in their bids to return to Congress. They, in turn, join the opposition to the exposure of a Republican President's guilt in the Watergate cover-up.

Outraged when Nixon's sabotage of one hundred local Republican campaigns is disclosed, Senator Lowell Weicker later demands, "Did we have any sort of an election contest . . . was there a contest in 1972 for the House or for the Senate?"

On September 28, 1972, Alex Shipley, whom Segretti tried unsuccessfully to recruit for the dirty-tricks campaign, tells what he knows to *Washington Post* reporter Carl Bernstein. A Justice Department contact admits to Bernstein, "Yes, political sabotage is associated with Segretti. . . . There is some very powerful information, especially if it comes out before November 7th [Election Day]."

"I was shocked when I learned about it," another Justice Department official confides. "I couldn't believe it. These are public servants? God. It's nauseating. You're talking about men who run the Government!" He adds that not only John Mitchell is involved. "It was strategy—basic strategy that goes all the way to the top. Higher than him, even."

Despite the Watergate arrests, dirty tricks persist right up to Election Day. When McGovern schedules a speech to explain his plan to end the Vietnam War, someone falsely claiming to be his television adviser phones CBS officials to cancel it. To deprive McGovern of news coverage in campaign trips around the country, calls are made to local reporters falsely announcing that he will be six hours late in arriving. Hired goons disrupt McGovern rallies, starting fights and creating a disorderly image for the Democratic campaign.

In October the *Washington Post* characterizes the Nixon Administration's "Department of Dirty Tricks" as "rancid."

When a grand jury convenes to probe facts uncovered about the Watergate break-in, Segretti admits to John Dean that he's frightened. Subpoenaed as a witness, how can he avoid implicating Chapin, Strachan, and Kalmbach without committing perjury? Dean tells him not to worry because the Department of Justice has everything "under control."

Dean later testifies that he informed Assistant Attorney General Henry E. Petersen, who is in charge of the Department of Justice's inquiry into Watergate, that Segretti was recruited by Chapin and Strachan and paid by President Nixon's private lawyer, Herbert Kalmbach, but that his campaign activities were in no way involved with Watergate. "I said that these facts, if revealed, would be obviously quite embarrassing, and could cause political problems during the waning weeks of the election. Mr. Petersen said that he understood the problem."

Petersen consults with acting FBI director L. Patrick Gray, appointed to the job by Nixon after J. Edgar Hoover's death. Both Petersen and Gray know that there are links between Hunt and Segretti, because of several recorded long-distance phone calls between them initiated by Hunt. But Gray tells Petersen, "On the basis of information available . . . we need not go into the area of the Segretti sabotage operations."

Segretti disappears until after the election.

6

Too Much Money

When Nixon first entered the White House in 1969 his campaign finance chairman, Maurice Stans, turned over $1,700,000 in unspent funds to Herbert Kalmbach, his assistant fund-raiser. Haldeman orders the President's lawyer to keep the money in cash in various safe-deposit boxes. It represents unreported contributions from corporations, which are forbidden by law to contribute to federal political campaigns.

The law is flouted by both parties in a number of ways. Most corporate contributions are made in the names of company officers and employees. Some are disguised as payments to advertising agencies, which act as political fronts. Others are paid as "retainer fees" to law firms in which candidates have an interest.

Some corporations withdraw large sums from a foreign subsidiary, then "launder" the money through one or more foreign banks to make it untraceable before it is finally turned over to the candidate. Sometimes cash or checks are given to a dummy committee, with a name like "United Friends of Good Government," which then channels the money to the candidate's campaign. Finally, sometimes cash changes hands under the table.

Corporations violate the campaign law for two basic reasons: first, as heavy contributors they expect a successful can-

didate to help them obtain profitable federal contracts, press for laws that favor their interests, and get them out of difficulties with government agencies; second, in many cases they are practically blackmailed into making a large contribution on the implied threat of otherwise having difficulties in these areas.

Corporate contributions have become such an open scandal that in January 1972 Congress feels compelled to pass a new Fair Campaign Practices Act. When it takes effect on April 7, it will compel all contributors of over $100 to be publicly listed by name, address, and business affiliation. Nixon dares not be put in the position of vetoing the bill. But Stans, resigning as Secretary of Commerce to head CRP's Finance Committee, gets him to stall signing it until the last minute, to give Republican fund-raisers extra time to pick up unreported contributions.

In the months before the April seventh deadline, Stans sends half a dozen men around the country collecting huge sums in cash and checks. Big corporations have been told, rather than asked, how much they are to contribute. Demands are made on defense contractors to contribute 1 percent of their profits from government contracts.

"I was solicited by Mr. Herbert W. Kalmbach," George A. Spater, board chairman of American Airlines, testifies later, "who said that we were among those from whom $150,000 was expected. I knew Mr. Kalmbach to be . . . the President's personal counsel." American Airlines, which needs government approval for a planned merger with Western Airlines, obliges.

McDonald's board chairman contributes over $200,000. The Nixon Administration's price commission grants it a price hike. Soon after the Combined Insurance Company of Chicago is allowed to increase premium rates, its board chairman makes a $1,000,000 donation through dummy committees.

By April 7 CRP has raised $22,000,000. In the last few days alone, $2,000,000 pours into the lap of Hugh Sloan, CRP's treasurer, and is kept unrecorded in Stans's safe for a month. It is then divided among Stans, Haldeman, and Kalmbach for funding CRP's spies, saboteurs, and undercover operations. Herbert Porter, CRP's scheduling chief, later admits that the money kept in the secret fund was earmarked for campaign dirty tricks. On April 6 Gordon Strachan picks up $350,000 from

Sloan for a secret slush fund, controlled by Haldeman, which is later returned to CRP and used as hush money for the Watergate defendants.

Some campaign contributions become involved in the Watergate affair. One consists of four Mexican checks forwarded by Daguerre Manuel Ogarrio, a lawyer who has laundered through Mexican banks a campaign contribution from Robert H. Allen, president of Gulf Resources and Chemical Corporation of Houston, Texas. The second is a cashier's check from Kenneth Dahlberg, chairman of CRP's Minnesota branch, representing $25,000 in cash given him by soybean millionaire Dwayne Andreas.

G. Gordon Liddy, as counsel for CRP's Finance Committee, recommends in April 1972 that these undeclared contributions, totaling $114,000, be laundered further and converted into cash. Given the checks by Sloan, Liddy flies to Miami, where Bernard Barker deposits them in his company account in a Miami bank. The money is afterward withdrawn in three cash payments and returned to Liddy, who brings the cash back to Sloan minus $2,500 he deducts for operational expenses.

Becoming aware of CRP attempts to conceal these and other campaign links to Watergate, on July 23, 1972, Democratic National Committee chairman Lawrence O'Brien charges CRP with "the most outrageous conspiracy of suppression that I have witnessed in a generation of political activity . . . an example of the frantic Republican effort to conceal, lock up, or otherwise submerge a growing scandal that reaches into the White House itself."

In response to O'Brien's $8,000,000 damage suit against CRP on behalf of the Democrats for the Watergate break-in, CRP files a $2,500,000 countersuit, charging O'Brien with using the federal courts as "an instrument for creating political headlines."

On August 1, 1972, the *Washington Post* reveals that cash found in the possession of the Watergate burglars when they were arrested has been traced to the Ogarrio and Dahlberg checks deposited in the Miami bank account of Bernard L. Barker. When the checks are identified as unreported contributions given to Stans for the Nixon re-election campaign, the General

Accounting Office (GAO), the investigative bureau of Congress, is prodded into planning an audit of Nixon's campaign finances.

Stans indignantly accuses the GAO of reaching "false and unwarranted conclusions." If there have been any violations of the new election law, he insists, they are only minor and technical. Nixon is informed that the planned GAO audit was asked for by Carl Albert, Democratic Speaker of the House.

"Maybe we better put a little heat on him," Haldeman suggests on September 15. The President replies, "I think so, too." The references are to data the White House spy system has gathered on Albert's personal problems. Haldeman says, "What we really ought to do is call the Speaker and say, 'I regret to see you ordering the GAO down here because of what it's going to cause us to do to you.'"

Nixon agrees. He is also concerned about another possible probe by Representative Wright Patman, Democratic chairman of the House Banking and Currency Committee, who wants to investigate discrepancies of almost $1,000,000 in CRP's books. Nixon orders his aides to have House minority leader Gerald Ford apply pressure to stop the probe. "After all," he points out, "if we ever win in the House, Jerry will be the Speaker. . . . Jerry has really got to be led on this."

For whatever reason, the GAO indefinitely postpones its audit of Nixon's campaign finances. And the Justice Department persuades the members of Patman's committee to vote against a House investigation, on grounds that public hearings could jeopardize the rights of defendants in the pending Watergate trial.

Patman is frustrated in his determination to summon more than forty principals in the Watergate affair, to explore possible violations of the campaign laws. He declares angrily, "I predict that the facts will come out, and when they do I am convinced they will reveal why the White House is so anxious to kill the committee's investigation. The public will fully understand why this pressure was mounted."

He tries to get Mitchell, Stans, Dean, and others to testify before him voluntarily, but they decline. Charging a "massive cover-up" to sabotage "free, open elections," Patman warns that Nixon "has pulled down an iron curtain of secrecy."

The final tally of campaign funds shows that the Republicans have collected a record $58,000,000—"the largest amount of money ever spent in a political campaign," Stans acknowledges—while the Democrats have only $14,000,000. With over four times as much money, Nixon and his men have over four times the power to influence American voters.

The Watergate affair also leads to the exposure of other financial scandals. In March 1971, after the dairy industry has done nothing to redeem an earlier pledge to raise $2,000,000 for the President's re-election, Agriculture Secretary Clifford Hardin rejects dairymen's request for an increase in federal milk subsidies. Treasury Secretary John Connally urges the President to reverse this decision, mentioning the dairymen's pledge.

"If you can get more help for 'em," he tells Nixon, "[they] will be more loyal to you." Nixon replies that since Congress is likely to vote the increase anyway, "I think the best thing to do is just relax and enjoy it." Connally agrees, reminding the President, "You're in this thing for everything you can get out of it." Connally is later indicted on charges of taking a $10,000 bribe from the dairy industry to use his influence in getting increased milk subsidies.

Nixon tells Ehrlichman, "All right, make the best deal you can." Murray Chotiner, the President's one-time campaign manager, is dispatched to tell dairy-industry leaders "that Mr. Ehrlichman expected the dairy industry to reaffirm its $2 million 'commitment' in light of a forthcoming increase in milk price supports."

The following night, after the dairymen have made a first $25,000 contribution at a Republican dinner, the President meets with fourteen of them and tells them, "You are a group that are politically very conscious. And you're willing to do something about it. . . . I appreciate that. And I don't have to spell it out. . . . Others keep me posted as to what you do."

On March 25, 1972, Kalmbach verifies to Nixon that the dairymen have reaffirmed their pledge of $2,000,000. On the same day Secretary Hardin reverses himself and announces a 5 percent increase in milk subsidies, worth an estimated $500,000,000 in extra profits to the dairy industry.

A second financial scandal involves International Telephone and Telegraph (ITT), the nation's largest and most powerful conglomerate, with huge business holdings all over the world. Its president is Harold Geneen, a man whose decisions can tumble governments. It is later revealed that ITT and the Nixon Administration, which gave the CIA $8,000,000 for the purpose, undermined the left-wing Allende government in Chile and brought about its downfall.

During Nixon's first term in office, ITT seeks to swallow a number of companies through mergers that are fought by Richard McLaren, chief of the Justice Department's antitrust division. Geneen pressures the White House to call off McLaren's suits. Word is passed through Ed Reinecke, Lieutenant Governor of California, that ITT is prepared to donate half the cost of holding the Republican Convention in San Diego, where Nixon wants it to be held.

Reinecke tells Attorney General Mitchell, who subsequently has a discussion with ITT's lobbyist in Washington, Mrs. Dita Beard. Soon Ehrlichman phones Richard Kleindienst, Mitchell's deputy, and orders him to stop McLaren's appeal to the Supreme Court against the ITT mergers. Kleindienst replies that he can't. On April 19, 1971, he receives a phone call from the President, who angrily repeats the order.

"The ITT thing—stay the hell out of it!" Nixon roars. "Is that clear? That's an order!" When Ehrlichman tells the President that the problem is McLaren's "very strong sense of mission," Nixon snaps, "Get him out—in one hour!"

But he reverses himself two days later, after Mitchell warns that he's playing with "political dynamite," risking an investigation by Senator Philip Hart's Antitrust and Monopoly Subcommittee which can get Nixon "chewed to pieces."

On June 25 Dita Beard writes a confidential company memo: "Other than . . . John Mitchell, Ed Reinecke, Bob Haldeman and Nixon . . . no one has known from whom the 400 thousand commitment had come. . . . I am convinced our noble commitment has gone a long way toward our negotiations on the mergers eventually coming out as Hal [Geneen] wants them. Certainly the President has told Mitchell to see that things are worked out fairly. . . . If it gets too much publicity, you can

Richard G. Kleindienst, deputy attorney general.

believe our negotiations with Justice will wind up shut down. Mitchell is definitely helping us but cannot let it be known."

She concludes, "Please destroy this, huh?"

Nine days after ITT arranges to make its contribution, the Justice Department announces its withdrawal of the Supreme Court antitrust suit against the company, along with a settlement on terms favorable to ITT.

Columnist Jack Anderson manages to get hold of the Dita Beard memo, which has not been destroyed, and publishes it in February 1972. Anderson accuses Mitchell, who is about to resign as Attorney General to head CRP, of having engineered the deal with ITT for a political bribe.

Kleindienst has already been confirmed as Mitchell's successor, but the Dita Beard memo leads the Senate Judiciary Committee to reopen its hearings. Kleindienst swears under oath that he has known nothing of ITT's political offer. He is asked whether the White House ever used any pressure to compel him to drop the ITT antitrust suit.

"I was not interfered with by anyone at the White House,"

he asserts. "I was not importuned; I was not pressured; I was not directed." The President subsequently praises Kleindienst's "honesty . . . integrity . . . [and] devotion to the law."

Mitchell also testifies under oath: "The President has never talked to me about any antitrust suit that was in the [Justice] Department. . . . Specifically, with respect to ITT, no, I have never talked to the President about it."

Reinecke likewise denies involvement. All three are later indicted for perjury. Dita Beard's testimony is also sought, but she has suddenly disappeared. It turns out that she has been whisked off to a Denver hospital by G. Gordon Liddy, and is "too ill" to testify. E. Howard Hunt, disguised in a red wig and dark glasses, is dispatched by Colson to talk to her on behalf of "high levels of the Administration." Dita Beard then issues a statement insisting that her ITT memo is a forgery. But an FBI investigation reveals that it is genuine.

Another memo surfaces at the hearings, this one from

Jack Anderson, with a copy of the Dita Beard memorandum, before the Senate Judiciary Committee.

Dita Beard, lobbyist for ITT.

Colson to Haldeman expressing fear that still secret documents about ITT might be exposed, especially one that can "lay this case on the President's doorstep."

The Senate Judiciary Committee hesitantly votes to let the Senate's confirmation of Kleindienst's nomination stand, but senators Edward Kennedy, John Tunney, Birch Bayh, and Quentin Burdick dissent vehemently. Kleindienst, they charge, "played a determinative role in the events leading to the settlement of the ITT cases, and . . . attempted to withhold . . . the full facts."

Kennedy adds, "The doors of the White House are open

wide to every chairman of the board, but they're bolted tight against the average citizen. They said it was just coincidence when ITT gave $400,000 for the GOP convention this year, at the very time when a major antitrust case was pending and settled favorably. I don't call that coincidence. I call that corruption."

A third financial scandal erupts over wealthy financier Robert Vesco, who is in trouble with the Securities and Exchange Commission (SEC) because they suspect him of looting $224,000,000 from a mutual fund he controls, International Overseas Services. In the summer of 1971 he made a secret $200,000 contribution in $100 bills to CRP under the impression that Mitchell and Stans would help get him off the SEC hook. His cash is accepted, but to Vesco's chagrin the SEC refuses to call off its investigation.

According to Harry Sears, head of CRP in New Jersey and one of the Vesco company's directors, Stans explains, "That SEC situation has gotten just too hot to handle." Vesco groans, "My God, and I gave all that money!" He demands that Sears put pressure on Stans. Stans replies, Sears alleges, "Harry, as far as the Vesco contribution is concerned, there's no record of it."

Just after Nixon's re-election Stans discusses the matter during a goose hunt in Texas with J. Bradford Cook, Jr., the SEC counsel. Stans asks whether the SEC intends to inquire into Vesco's contribution to CRP. Cook replies that he hasn't yet decided. He also mentions that he would very much like to become the new chairman of the SEC. Stans says he'll "put in a good word" at the White House.

Cook gets the job. He deletes all references to Vesco's secret $200,000 cash gift to CRP from the SEC's investigative report on IOS. But the *Washington Star-News* ferrets out the story and publishes it in December 1972. CRP, already having its hands full trying to hold the lid on the Watergate scandal, quickly returns $200,000 to Vesco. Cook is compelled to resign, and the SEC begins criminal proceedings against Vesco, who flees the country.

Protesting their innocence, Mitchell and Stans are indicted on charges of conspiracy, attempted obstruction of justice, and perjury in regard to the Vesco contribution. They are acquitted

Maurice H. Stans and John N. Mitchell, after their acquittal in the Vesco case.

Charles G. "Bebe" Rebozo, Nixon's closest friend.

in 1974 by a jury that fails to find sufficient evidence against them.

As though these financial scandals are not bad enough, another one swirls around the President's closest friend and financial adviser, Charles G. "Bebe" Rebozo. It stems from a $100,000 cash campaign contribution given Rebozo by billionaire Howard Hughes, at a time when Hughes's attorneys are trying to get approval of some mergers in Nevada from the Antitrust Division of the Department of Justice. Rebozo later claims to have kept this cash in a safe-deposit box for three years, then returned it to Hughes.

Columnist Jack Anderson, however, charges that the original cash was used for Nixon's private benefit. Later probes, following Anderson's leads, question the source of $36,000 used to improve the President's home in Key Biscayne, $300,000 in jewelry held by Nixon's private secretary Rose Mary Woods, and $135,000 worth shared by the President's wife and two daughters.

Even more damaging are the revelations emerging out of the Watergate investigations that Nixon's years in the White House have made him a near millionaire; that $17,000,000 in government funds have been spent on his two homes in Key Biscayne and San Clemente; and that he has used tax dodges to pay less income tax than a roadworker or a janitor.

To millions of hard-pressed taxpayers fighting inflation, this is perhaps the worst scandal of all.

(Opposite) The Nixon estates: San Clemente, California (top); Key Biscayne, Florida (bottom).

7

The Gemstone Plot

The summer after Nixon takes office in 1969, a tragic accident occurs when a car driven by Senator Edward Kennedy plunges off a bridge into a tidal pool on Chappaquiddick Island, Mass. He escapes unhurt, but his passenger, secretary Mary Jo Kopechne, is drowned. The incident creates great public attention, and Kennedy's less than satisfactory account of how it happened arouses considerable skepticism.

Nixon and his aides, who view Kennedy as the most serious future obstacle to the President's re-election, lose no time in seeking to exploit the Chappaquiddick incident. Four hours after they learn of it, Caulfield sends Ulasewicz to the scene. Posing as a reporter, Ulasewicz asks embarrassing questions at press gatherings to discredit Kennedy. The phone in Miss Kopechne's family home is wiretapped. Colson sends Hunt to Chappaquiddick to probe for incriminating facts. Haldeman wants Kennedy shadowed twenty-four hours a day, but Caulfield warns that a "tail" might be arrested as a suspected assassin.

When CRP is organized in 1971, the White House wants it staffed with an intelligence-gathering operation to spy out any harmful information about Democratic candidates and gain advance knowledge of their campaign plans in order to disrupt them. Caulfield develops a plan he calls Sandwedge, and offers his services as spymaster, but Mitchell prefers a lawyer with a background in intelligence work.

G. Gordon Liddy is chosen and transferred to CRP as its "general counsel," along with Hunt. The new unit is, in effect, still the Plumbers, but now operating under Mitchell instead of Krogh and Young. A third member is added to their team— former CIA agent James McCord, who is recommended by Caulfield as CRP's "security coordinator" for CRP and also the Republican National Committee.

Until Mitchell resigns as Attorney General on February 15, 1972, to become chairman, the Committee to Re-elect the President functions under his deputy, Jeb Magruder.

While still heading the Justice Department, Mitchell orders Liddy to prepare a broad-gauged intelligence plan to use against the Democrats. Liddy informs Magruder that Mitchell has promised $1,000,000 to carry it out. Magruder suggests that for a plan of that magnitude, Liddy had better prepare a documented presentation, with a budget breakdown. Liddy gets McCord to instruct him in the use, cost, and capabilities of various bugging devices.

On January 27, 1972, there is a meeting of Mitchell, Magruder, Liddy, and White House counsel John Dean in the Attorney General's office during which Liddy gives a half-hour presentation of his plan, called Gemstone.

Using his charts, Liddy describes highlights of Gemstone. Radical antiwar leaders are to be kidnapped and held captive in Mexico until the Republican convention is over, so that they will be unable to organize demonstrations against it. A yacht is to be hired and staffed with call girls to entice members of the Democratic National Committee, both to gain confidential information and to compromise the Democrats whose misbehavior will be recorded by secret cameras and bugging equipment.

Mugging squads are to be hired to rough up anti-Nixon demonstrators. The Democratic National Committee's headquarters in Washington is to be broken into and bugged by placing electronic listening devices in the walls, ceilings, and phones. Other targets are also designated to be broken into for political information. Electronic devices are to be used to eavesdrop on communications between Democratic campaign planes and ground offices.

Liddy's last chart breaks down the cost of each operation of Gemstone. Total budget needed: $1,000,000.

John Dean is appalled by Liddy's proposals. He testifies later, "I said right in front of everybody, very clearly, I said, 'These are not the sort of things . . . that are ever to be discussed in the office of the Attorney General of the United States.' " But Mitchell merely objects to Gemstone as too expensive and indicates trimming is in order; he later claims that he rejected the plan altogether, but no witness bears this out.

"All three of us were appalled," Magruder later testifies. "The scope and size of the project was something that at least in my mind was not envisioned. . . . Mr. Mitchell [told Liddy to] go back to the drawing board and come up with a more realistic plan." Asked if the Attorney General said anything to discourage Liddy's illegal proposals, Magruder replies, "I would say he was encouraged."

Magruder reports the gist of the meeting in a phone call to Strachan at the White House, to keep Haldeman posted on campaign plans developed by CRP. A few days later, Dean, apparently no longer shocked, tells Liddy that prospects for a revised Gemstone plan "look good." But he warns that "some means would have to be found for deniability for Mr. Mitchell." And the money used for the project will have to be untraceable. Liddy gets McCord to agree to join an operation to bug the DNC headquarters when the plan is approved.

At a second meeting in Mitchell's office on the morning of February 4, Liddy presents a less ambitious version of Gemstone with a budget of half a million dollars. Emphasis is now placed on bugging the offices of Lawrence O'Brien at the headquarters of the Democratic National Committee and of leading Democratic candidates. But a final decision is postponed because Mitchell still considers Gemstone too costly.

Magruder later explains why bugging Lawrence O'Brien's office is given such high priority: "At that time we were particularly concerned about the ITT situation. Mr. O'Brien had been a very effective spokesman against our position on the ITT case, and I think there was a general concern that if he was allowed to continue as Democratic national chairman . . . he could be very difficult in the coming campaign."

There are also other reasons. O'Brien is close to Edward Kennedy, the potential candidate Nixon fears most. A wiretap on his phone can provide Nixon and his men with advance knowledge of the campaign plans of Kennedy, or of whoever wins the Democratic nomination, so that they can be promptly sabotaged. Finally there is a desire to "get something" on O'Brien because, as a former consultant to Howard Hughes, it is feared that he may have damaging documents about the mysterious, unreported $200,000 cash contribution which Hughes made to Nixon through Bebe Rebozo.

On February 15, 1972, Mitchell resigns his post as Attorney General, and his deputy, Richard Kleindienst, a right-wing Republican who managed Goldwater's pre-convention campaign in 1964, is named to take Mitchell's place. Before taking over on March 1 as Nixon's campaign manager, Mitchell vacations at the President's home in Key Biscayne.

Nixon, meanwhile, is growing increasingly touchy about the anti-Vietnam War demonstrators. In March he sends a memo to Dean, complaining that "McGovern and the so-called peace groups" are inciting and financing "demonstrations against me, members of my family and others during the campaign." The President insists that he has "hard evidence" for this charge, but Dean later reports, "We never found a scintilla of viable evidence."

On the contrary, at political trials pushed by the Nixon Administration to smear the peace movement, FBI agents admit under cross-examination that they were instructed to infiltrate antiwar groups and encourage acts of violence. A public angered by illegal acts is more likely to re-elect Nixon. Once when Haldeman receives a memo informing him that anti-Nixon violence is expected at a Nixon rally, he returns it with the enthusiastic endorsement, "Great!"

Liddy, meanwhile, prepares a third Gemstone plan, budgeted down to $250,000. This time he gets Hunt to solicit the support of his friend Colson. Colson phones Magruder at CRP and says, "You all either fish or cut bait. This is absurd to have these guys over there and not using them." Colson insists that

Magruder "get on the stick and get the Liddy operation in effect so we can get the material."

Dean describes Liddy's plan to Haldeman—"muggings and buggings and prostitutes and the like," Dean later testifies. Haldeman says cautiously, "I shouldn't have any part of that." Nevertheless he is anxious to launch the operation against Lawrence O'Brien. Through his aide, Gordon Strachan, he brings additional pressure on Magruder to get moving on Gemstone.

Magruder flies to Key Biscayne to present Liddy's third espionage plan to Mitchell and his right-hand man, Frederick LaRue. "No one was particularly overwhelmed with the project," Magruder later testifies, "but I think we felt that the information could be useful. And Mr. Mitchell agreed to approve the project, and I then notified the parties of Mr. Mitchell's approval."

One of the parties is Strachan, who sends Haldeman a March 31 memo that CRP "now has a sophisticated intelligence gathering system including a budget of 300 [$300,000]." Haldeman later "cannot recall" having seen Strachan's memo.

As approved, Gemstone calls for break-ins to plant electronic eavesdropping devices and photograph confidential documents at the headquarters of the Democratic National Committee in the Watergate complex, at Democratic presidential candidates' headquarters, and at the Democratic National Committee's convention headquarters in the Fontainebleau Hotel at Miami.

Mitchell later denies Magruder's version of the Key Biscayne meeting. He insists he once more rejected Liddy's plan with words like, "We don't need this. I am tired of hearing it. Out." But LaRue afterward in his testimony fails to uphold Mitchell, stating that he never heard Mitchell flatly reject Gemstone at Key Biscayne. And Robert Mardian, former head of the Internal Security Division of the Justice Department, testifies that Mitchell acknowledged to him having approved a $250,000 budget for Liddy.

Mitchell does not deny that, first as Attorney General of the United States, then as the President's campaign manager, he

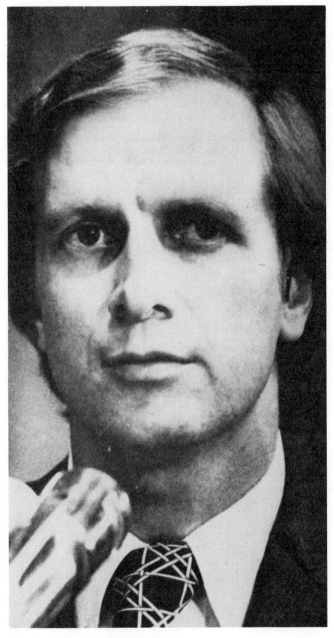

Gordon C. Strachan, aide to Haldeman.

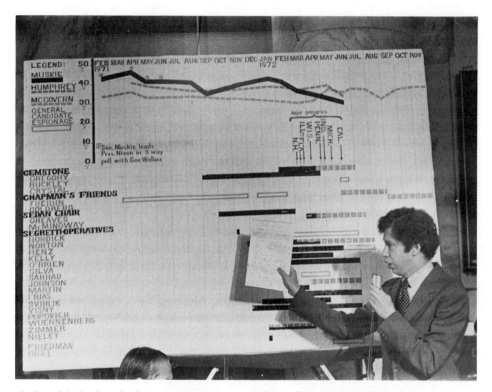

*A chart showing how funds were spent to spy on and disrupt Democratic candidates'
campaigns is displayed at the Senate Watergate Committee hearings.*

listened three times to a long list of proposed criminal acts to be
carried out on behalf of the President's re-election.

"Call Liddy and tell him it's approved," Magruder tells his
assistant, Robert Reisner. "Tell him to get going in the next two
weeks." Reisner relays the order to Liddy.

Friction develops between Magruder and the temperamen-
tal Liddy, who resents Magruder's manner and dislikes taking
orders from someone four years younger. Magruder wants to fire
Liddy, but others urge that Liddy merely be transferred to CRP's
Finance Committee. Here he works as counsel under Maurice
Stans and treasurer Hugh Sloan.

Following the authorization of Gemstone, it is scheduled for
discussion in the Oval Office on April 4, 1972. Strachan later
testifies that he included a memo on it in Haldeman's folder of

matters to be discussed that day with the President and Mitchell.

Hunt begins making frequent trips to Miami, where Barker is recruited for Gemstone with the assurance that it is vital to America's national security. "Get your men in training going up and down stairs," Hunt orders. "They must be in good physical shape."

On April 7 Liddy asks Hugh Sloan for $83,000 as the first payment in the $250,000 budget authorized for him. At Sloan's request, Stans consults Mitchell about it. Mitchell asks Magruder why Liddy needs such a large sum. Magruder explains that it's for "front-end money" to purchase espionage equipment and get Gemstone organized. Mitchell authorizes the payment to Stans, who is told that Magruder will authorize future payments to Liddy.

"What are the payments for?" Sloan asks Stans.

"I don't know what's going on in this campaign," Stans replies, "and I don't think you ought to try to know."

Sloan pays Liddy $83,000 out of a batch of $100 bills that had come from Barker's bank. Some of this money goes to Hunt for Barker and his men. Liddy gives $65,000 to James McCord, who buys $51,000 worth of tape recorders, transmitters, antennas, walkie-talkie units, and other electronic equipment. Liddy tries to buy ten pistols to arm his squad, but without success.

On May 1 McCord recruits former FBI agent Alfred C. Baldwin for a job as a CRP security guard, planning to use him in the Gemstone operation. Hunt orders the Cubans—Barker, Martinez, Sturgis, Pico, de Diego, and Gonzales—to fly to Washington on May 22. The plan is for a double Gemstone mission over the Memorial Day weekend.

One team of Cubans, directed by Hunt, is to break into the headquarters of the Democratic National Committee in Watergate. Magruder instructs Hunt that first priority here will be to place a wiretap on Lawrence O'Brien's phone. At the same time a second team of Cubans plus McCord, directed by Liddy, will force entry into McGovern headquarters.

McCord briefs the conspirators on the use of walkie-talkies to maintain regular communication between the break-in teams and the outside men, to assure the safety and efficiency of the missions. He installs large radio receivers in Room 419 of the

James W. McCord demonstrates bugging devices used at the Democratic National Headquarters.

Howard Johnson Motor Lodge, directly across the street from Watergate. Baldwin is stationed there, to serve first as a lookout for Hunt's break-in team, then as monitor of intercepted conversations once the wiretaps are in place.

The operation is launched close to midnight on May 26—three weeks before the subsequent break-in at Watergate results in the arrests of McCord and four Cubans. This first operation is a dismal, even comic, fiasco. Hunt and Gonzales are unable to pick the lock of a stairwell door leading into the Watergate office building. Worse, they find themselves locked into a corridor and forced to spend the night there.

The Liddy team fares no better. They don't dare risk breaking into McGovern headquarters because of a man standing near the front door. They can't be sure whether he's a guard or just a drunk. The reckless Liddy wants to shoot out the street light and rush the team inside under cover of darkness, but an alarmed McCord talks him out of it.

The conspirators try again the following night. This time they concentrate on Watergate, breaking in by a different route. Hunt manages to tape a door latch that will let the Cubans enter the office building through a garage connecting it to the hotel. He also tapes back the locks of several doors from the stairwell leading to the offices of the DNC on the sixth floor. Then he rejoins Liddy in their room in the Watergate Hotel.

Wearing rubber gloves and using pencil flashlights, Barker and his men break into the DNC through the taped doors. Spotting them from his balcony across the street, Baldwin reports to Hunt over a walkie-talkie. Hunt phones McCord. "My people are in. You can go in now."

Joining the Cubans, McCord wiretaps the phone of Fay Abel, O'Brien's secretary, and puts another bug in the phone of R. Spencer Oliver, executive director of the Association of State Democratic Chairmen. Meanwhile Barker, following Hunt's orders, searches through the files. He is unable to find any documents showing illicit campaign contributions from violent left-wing organizations or from Cuba, or any documents mentioning Kennedy. But he has Martinez photograph security plans for the Democratic convention, plus documents relating to O'Brien and to contributors to the DNC. These films are afterward developed in a Miami photography shop, whose owner subsequently identifies Barker and Sturgis as the men who brought the film in to him.

The Watergate burglars retreat, their mission completed. That night a separate plan to sabotage McGovern headquarters goes awry. Thomas Gregory, working there for the Committee to Re-elect the President under false pretenses, hides in the furnace room until after midnight. He emerges only to find someone in the office working late. Mumbling an incoherent explanation, he hastily leaves. From then on, a night security guard is posted inside McGovern headquarters, and CRP is forced to drop its attempts to wiretap or burglarize them.

Instead a woman reporter traveling aboard McGovern's campaign plane is paid a bribe of $1,000 a week to act as a spy. She is later quoted by the *Washington Star-News* as admitting that her secret assignment is to get "really dirty stuff" on the behavior of those aboard the campaign plane.

McCord and Baldwin begin monitoring the wiretaps placed inside the headquarters of the DNC. The bug in the phone of Fay Abel fails to function, but Oliver's phone calls come through loud and clear. Baldwin writes up transcripts of some two hundred conversations. Examining these logs, McCord selects the most pertinent information and forwards it to Liddy.

Liddy's secretary, Sally Harmony, types the logs on special Gemstone stationery. Each report begins, "Confidential informant says . . . ," so that CRP officials can legally deny having received information from wiretapped phones. Liddy gives eight transcripts, along with documents photographed by Martinez in the DNC, to Magruder, who takes them to Mitchell.

Mitchell is disappointed. He calls Liddy in, according to Magruder, and points out that "this was not satisfactory and it was worthless and not worth the money that he [Liddy] had been paid for it." Crestfallen, Liddy explains that the tap on Fay Abel's phone hadn't worked, and that Oliver's phone is mostly being used by girls working in the DNC for private conversations with boyfriends. Liddy promises to "correct these matters and hopefully get the information . . . required."

Mitchell later denies Magruder's version of this meeting, calling it a "palpable, damnable lie." But Robert Reisner, Magruder's aide, testifies that at about this time he placed a Gemstone file among the papers that Magruder took to Mitchell's office for discussion.

Because the wiretap source of the Gemstone material makes it political dynamite, Magruder does not dare risk sending copies to the White House by messenger. Instead Strachan comes to CRP to examine them. Finding that they "lack substance," he so advises Haldeman, who later "cannot recall" receiving reports on Gemstone. But Magruder testifies, "Everything that we did was staffed to Mr. Strachan so that he could alert other officials at the White House as to our activities."

Mitchell now orders a second break-in at Watergate, according to testimony by both McCord and Dean, this time to wire O'Brien's whole office, so as to pick up actual as well as telephone conversations and also to obtain more documents. The Cubans are summoned back from Miami, and on June 16 Barker flies to Washington with Martinez, Sturgis, and Gonzales.

In the early dark hours of June 17, supervised by Hunt and Liddy from a Watergate Hotel room over walkie-talkies, McCord and the Cubans make their second successful invasion of the DNC, as described in the first chapter. They remove two ceiling tiles in O'Brien's office to plant electronic eavesdropping equipment and begin photographing documents from the files. Suddenly they are caught red-handed by the Washington metropolitan police.

Hunt and Liddy are warned over a walkie-talkie by Baldwin, who is watching from his balcony, and they bolt from the hotel. Hunt rushes across the street to Baldwin's motel room and phones C. Douglas Caddy, a Washington attorney once affiliated with the Mullen Company. Then he orders Baldwin to pack up all the eavesdropping equipment and take it to McCord's home.

"Get it the hell out of here!" he snaps. "Get yourself out of here! We will be in touch. You will get further instructions." Grabbing a briefcase with McCord's electronic devices, he rushes off to his office in the Executive Office Building. Here he puts McCord's briefcase in his safe and takes out $10,000 in cash provided for him by Liddy for use in an emergency. He delivers this money to an attorney on behalf of the five arrested burglars.

The cover-up of Watergate has begun.

8

The Cover-Up Begins

It is now three and a half weeks before the Democratic convention. The President has flown south to spend the weekend on an island in the Bahamas owned by his friend Robert Abplanalp. Mitchell, LaRue, Mardian, and Magruder are in Los Angeles at the Beverly Hills Hotel, planning to attend a "Celebrities for Nixon" party.

They are stunned by a phone call from Liddy to Magruder revealing that McCord and the five Cubans have been arrested. Meeting on the morning of Saturday, June 17, they instantly begin plotting to cut off all leads from the Watergate burglars to CRP and the White House—a cover-up that soon becomes standard operating procedure for everyone involved.

They recognize that the danger involves more than just exposure of the Gemstone plot, although that alone can badly damage the President's chances of re-election. The Cubans also have dangerous knowledge of other criminal break-ins, including the burglary of Dr. Fielding's office. If Hunt and Liddy are caught, Segretti's dirty-tricks campaign may also be exposed, as well as attempts to smear the Kennedys by Hunt, Colson, Caulfield, and Ulasewicz. A wide-ranging investigation could surface Nixon's illegal wiretaps of government officials and newspapermen or bring to light the truth about the ITT, milk fund, and Vesco affairs.

"I do not think there was ever any discussion," Magruder later recalls, "that there would *not* be a cover-up."

He hastily phones his assistants at CRP, Robert Odle and Robert Reisner, ordering them to remove incriminating files from his desk, including Gemstone folders, and to take them home with them. Magruder also phones Haldeman at the President's home in Key Biscayne to warn him about what has happened.

Nixon's four aides in Los Angeles decide that Kleindienst, Mitchell's successor as Attorney General, must order the release of the Watergate burglars, at least of McCord. "After all, *we* were the government," Magruder later explains. "Until very recently John Mitchell had been Attorney General of the United States. It did not seem beyond our capacities to get one man out of the Washington, D.C., jail. . . . It seemed inconceivable that with our political power we could not erase the mistake we had made."

A phone call from Magruder sends Liddy to see Kleindienst, whom he tracks down at the Burning Tree Country Club, near Washington. Explaining that the White House may be implicated in the arrests, Liddy states, "You've got to get my men out of jail." Kleindienst refuses, replying, "You get the hell out of here, kid. Whatever you have to say, just say to somebody else. Don't bother me!" The present Attorney General has no intention of making himself vulnerable to a charge of having interfered with the judicial process for political reasons.

On Saturday morning at CRP Liddy tells Sloan, according to Sloan's later testimony, "My boys got caught last night. I made a mistake by using somebody from here, which I told them I would never do. I'm afraid I'll lose my job."

When McCord's identity is uncovered, Mitchell issues a statement to the press on June 18, indicating that he was merely a private security agent who was employed by CRP and let go months earlier, for acts "wholly inconsistent with the principles upon which we are conducting our campaign." The Watergate burglars, he insists, "were not operating either in our behalf or with our consent."

On the evening of that same Sunday, June 18, White House

counsel John Dean returns from a four-day trip to Manila. Phoning his assistant, Fred Fielding, upon arrival in San Francisco, he learns of the Watergate break-in and arrests. He is urged to fly back to Washington at once because serious problems have arisen. During this Sunday the President, still at Key Biscayne, phones Charles Colson at the White House several times.

When Dean sees Strachan the following morning, Strachan confides that in a phone talk with Key Biscayne, Haldeman has ordered him to shred the "Political Matters" file in Haldeman's office, along with wiretap logs and Gemstone reports.

"The cover-up was in operation when I returned to my office on Monday, the 19th," Dean later testifies, "and it just became the instant way of life at that point in time."

Ehrlichman tells him to analyze White House involvement in the break-in. As the President's counsel, Dean soon becomes coordinating director of all the cover-up activities.

Returning from California on June 21, Magruder tells Sloan that the money found on the burglars is a problem because it can be traced to Liddy and thus to the committee. Magruder is prepared to claim that the funds were given to Liddy for the "legitimate" purpose of infiltrating anti-Vietnam War groups, in order to gather intelligence that might prevent violence at Nixon rallies, but that Liddy had misused the funds on his own initiative.

The only trouble with that story, Magruder explains, is that no one would believe that $200,000—the amount Magruder had authorized Sloan to pay to Liddy—had been allotted for such an operation. Will Sloan back up Magruder's testimony that Liddy had been given only about $75,000?

Sloan refuses to perjure himself.

"You may have to," Magruder tells him.

Another source of dangerous information is bottled up, according to Dean, when Ehrlichman orders Dean to have Liddy get Hunt out of the country. Hearing of it, Colson protests, "You will have the White House party to a fugitive from justice!" Ehrlichman tries to rescind the order, but Liddy informs Dean that Hunt has already fled to parts unknown.

Colson is worried about incriminating evidence locked in

John W. Dean III, White House counsel.

Hunt's office safe. Dean promises to have the safe drilled open and the contents disposed of.

Liddy confesses to Dean that he has "goofed." He blames Magruder: "I was pushed without mercy by Magruder to get in there and get more information. . . . Magruder said, 'The White House is not happy with what we are getting.' " Vowing that he's "a good soldier" and will never talk, Liddy melodramatically volunteers to stand at an appointed street corner to be shot down by assassins hired to seal his lips.

When reporter Bob Woodward of the *Washington Post* writes the story linking Hunt, a White House consultant, with the break-in, Nixon speechwriter Pat Buchanan scoffs to the press that the whole affair amounts to no more than "a few Cubans reading Larry O'Brien's mail." But by this time there is consternation in the White House and at CRP that if the full story of Watergate is allowed to emerge, all the skeletons in the Administration closet—what Mitchell later calls "the White House horrors"—will rattle out and appall the nation.

The first of a series of strategy meetings is held in Mitchell's Watergate apartment on the night of June 19. Dean, Magruder, Mardian, and LaRue discuss with Mitchell ways of containing the scandal. All agree that the White House must be kept out of it at all costs.

As a first step, the files on Gemstone and other politically sensitive matters must be destroyed. When Magruder reveals that he has some of Liddy's intelligence files, there was, according to LaRue, "a response from Mr. Mitchell that it might be good if Mr. Magruder had a fire."

The strategy agreed upon is to limit involvement, if possible, only to those caught red-handed in Watergate. Magruder offers to take the full blame, because he knows that he is bound to be implicated anyway as the official who authorized payments to Liddy. The offer is rejected because it is common knowledge that the power to disburse such large sums rests only with Mitchell and Stans. The scandal of implicating either of them could be ruinous in the November election.

It is decided to keep the investigation in the hands of the FBI, which has a reputation of being above politics. Acting FBI director L. Patrick Gray III is a strong Nixon supporter who is expected to cooperate in limiting the investigation. Nixon's men feel certain that Gray, a former submarine commander, can be depended upon to carry out orders from higher authorities.

After this meeting there is a rush to destroy all incriminating evidence and cut off any trail that may lead from the burglars to higher-ups. Mardian and LaRue direct the housecleaning at CRP, warning the staff to "close ranks" against inquiries.

Liddy carries a foot-thick pile of documents to the paper shredder. His secretary, Sally Harmony, shreds all her notebooks and takes many of his personal files and belongings to her own home. Magruder destroys his copies of spy logs. Kalmbach and Porter get rid of sensitive financial documents in their files. Stans and Sloan destroy reports of campaign contributions received before the disclosure law of April 7.

They also divide up approximately $81,000 in campaign cash from Stans's office safe. Sloan stashes his half at home in a trunk; Stans puts his in a sealed envelope in his desk drawer. Both later turn this money over to Mardian who gives it to LaRue, who pays it to lawyers of the Watergate defendants.

A reporter talking with lawyer Edward Bennett Williams, who represents the Democrats in their civil suit for damages against CRP, is told, "Forget about the burglaries. The story is money. Keep your eye on the money."

Liddy and Hunt are both named to the FBI by Baldwin, who is telling all he knows. Through telephone records, FBI agents learn that Barker made fifteen calls from Miami to Liddy at an unlisted number at CRP, several of them the day before the break-in. When the agents question Liddy, he refuses to answer. Since this is reported in the press, Mitchell has no choice but to order him fired from his position as counsel to CRP's finance committee.

The FBI searches in vain for Hunt. The White House insists that his services were severed three weeks before the break-in. All White House directories are hastily recalled, and reissued with the page listing Hunt's phone number replaced by one on which it is missing. A White House memorandum of record is changed to indicate that Hunt left as a consultant on March 29. But Dorothy Hunt, his wife, reveals to the press that he is still working for the White House.

Hunt and Liddy can no longer be protected, but CRP officials determine to stop the investigation at that level. Herbert Porter, who schedules Nixon rallies for CRP, is asked by Magruder to back up the story of what Liddy was supposed to do

Herbert L. Porter, campaign scheduling director.

with the money paid him by CRP. Flattered by Magruder's report that Mitchell and LaRue consider him "someone we can count on . . . a team player," Porter agrees to commit perjury.

On Dean's orders, Hunt's safe is broken open and the contents removed to Dean's office. Included are a pistol, electronic bugging equipment, Hunt's "psychiatric profile" on Daniel Ellsberg, his forged cables pinning Diem's assassination on President John F. Kennedy, a memo linking Colson to the forged cables and to spying at Chappaquiddick, and Hunt's notebooks filled with other incriminating information.

According to Dean, he consults Ehrlichman, who tells him to shred the documents and "deep six" a briefcase with the pistol and bugging equipment. Dean asks what he means by "deep six." Ehrlichman replies, "When you cross over the bridge on your way home just toss the briefcase into the river." When Dean offers to give it to *him* to "deep six," Ehrlichman replies dryly, "No, thanks."

Dean decides to turn over the contents of Hunt's safe to the FBI, but only after removing the forged cables, Hunt's notebooks, and other documents that can force new lines of investigation.

After the President returns to the White House from Key Biscayne on June 20, he has ten personal meetings or phone consultations with Haldeman, Ehrlichman, Colson, and Mitchell during which, he later alleges, he is told nothing about Watergate or the cover-up. When a tape recording of one Watergate conversation with Haldeman is subsequently subpoenaed, 18½ minutes of it are found to have been erased. No one at the White House can explain how it happened.

That same day Liddy meets with LaRue and Mardian in LaRue's apartment to demand that CRP fulfill a moral commitment to provide bail for himself, Hunt, McCord, and the Cubans, and to "take care of" them and their families financially. To make sure Mitchell's aides understand what is at stake, he reveals other illicit activities even more damning than Watergate that the Plumbers performed for the White House.

When Liddy relates how he spirited away ITT lobbyist Dita Beard to a Denver hospital to prevent her from having to testify before the Senate Judiciary Committee, Mardian asks who told him to do so. Liddy replies that he had had "the express authority of the President of the United States, with the assistance of the Central Intelligence Agency."

LaRue and Mardian, well aware of Liddy's implied threat that the Watergate burglars may spill everything if they are not "taken care of" immediately phone Mitchell.

Mitchell comes to LaRue's apartment after Liddy has left. He subsequently admits to the Senate Watergate Committee that Mardian and LaRue tell him of Liddy's lurid confessions, and he claims that this is the first time he learns about "the White House horror stories." When Mitchell is asked why he did not then inform the President, he replies that if he had, Nixon might have felt compelled to reveal the truth to the nation and that this would have "blown the lid off" the election.

Robert C. Mardian, former assistant attorney general and campaign coordinator.

Dean moves to restrict the probe of Watergate. He hints to Assistant Attorney General Petersen that the White House may not be able to stand a wide-open investigation.

On June 21 John Ehrlichman tells FBI acting director Patrick Gray to deal directly with Dean on Watergate matters. Gray informs Dean that the cash found on the Watergate burglars has been traced to the Ogarrio and Dahlberg checks deposited in Barker's bank account. Could a CIA unit in Mexico be involved in the laundered Mexican checks, Gray wonders, especially since all the burglars are former CIA men?

Gray obligingly requests guidance from the White House on how to handle any CIA aspects of Watergate. Nixon swiftly seizes Gray's theory as a pretext for narrowing the FBI's investigation. He instructs his aides to "ensure that the investigation not expose either an unrelated covert operation of the CIA, or the activities of the White House investigations unit [the Plumbers]."

At an impromptu news conference on June 22 the President is asked if he has had any investigation made to determine possible links between the Watergate break-in and the White House. "Mr. Ziegler and also Mr. Mitchell . . . have stated my position, and have also stated the facts accurately . . . ," Nixon answers. "The White House has had no involvement in this particular incident."

Mitchell's wife, Martha, suddenly phones United Press International reporter Helen Thomas, with whom she is friendly, saying that she is "sick and tired of the whole operation. . . . Politics is a dirty business. . . . They don't want me to talk. . . ." She is abruptly cut off when her assigned security guard rips the phone wires out of the wall.

On the morning of June 23, 1972, just six days after the break-in, Nixon and Haldeman hold a historic conference which indicates that the President is not only fully aware that the cover-up is going on but is also a participant in it. At one point the word "Gemstone" is mentioned.

Haldeman says, "Now, on the investigation; you know the Democratic break-in thing, we're back in the problem area because the FBI is not under control. . . . The way to handle this now is to have [Deputy CIA Director Vernon] Walters call Pat Gray and just say, 'stay to hell out of this—this is ah, business here we don't want you to go any further on it.' "

Nixon expresses surprise that Gray won't cooperate in stopping the FBI from probing the Mexican checks from Ogarrio, which can uncover the laundering of illegal contributions by CRP, and CRP's illicit use of campaign funds.

"Pat does want to," Haldeman explains. "He doesn't know how to, and he doesn't have any basis for doing it." If the CIA certifies that national security is involved, Gray will then have an excuse for curbing the investigation.

Nixon suggests that they get Ogarrio and Dahlberg to say they contributed their checks directly to Barker for his Cuban exile organization. Haldeman warns, "But then we're relying on more and more people all the time. That's the problem. . . ." He suggests that getting the CIA to stop the FBI is the best solution.

Nixon replies, "Right, fine." He reminds Haldeman, "We protected [CIA Director] Helms from one hell of a lot of things. . . . Play it tough. . . . Don't lie to them [the FBI] to the extent of saying no involvement, but just say this is a comedy of errors, without getting into it. . . . Say, 'Look, the whole problem is that this will open up the whole Bay of Pigs thing. . . . Don't go any further with this case—period!' "

The President has now definitely made himself a member of the conspiracy to obstruct justice, covering up the Watergate break-in by deceiving both the FBI and the CIA—a course he persistently pursues for more than two years.

During this conversation Nixon also asks whether Mitchell knew in advance about the break-in. Haldeman: "I think so. I don't think he knew the details, but I think he knew." Nixon asks whether Liddy is responsible: "Is it Liddy? Is that the fellow? He must be a little nuts." Haldeman answers: "He is."

Nixon behind the scenes is far different from the image he projects in public. At one point he talks about spending time phoning key people around the country to get their help in the re-election campaign, while "we're here in Washington, you know, supposedly doing the business of the government."

He discusses appearances his family should make during the campaign. Haldeman cautions, "Be careful not to overuse them and cheapen them." Nixon says, "I couldn't agree more." Haldeman recalls that at a Boston museum someone had refused to shake hands with Nixon's daughter Tricia and suggests that she be scheduled only for carefully controlled television interviews or Republican groups. Nixon agrees: "Middle America type people. . . . The arts, you know, they're Jews, they're left-wing. Stay away." Millions of Jewish Americans, preparing to vote for Nixon's re-election, have no suspicion of this bigoted view.

The tenor of the President's discussion with Haldeman on June 23 clearly indicates only one consideration uppermost in his mind—re-election. The interests of the country are important to him only as they affect his campaign. When Haldeman tries to discuss financial problems caused by the British pound, Nixon says impatiently, "It's too complicated for me to get into." Haldeman then reports that Federal Reserve Board Chairman Arthur Burns is worried about the instability of the Italian lira.

Nixon exclaims, "Well, I don't give a —— about the lira. . . . There ain't a vote in it."

Haldeman points out that Nixon's foreign-policy record is his strongest argument for re-election. "I just think you've got to hit that over and over again," the President instructs him emphatically. "We gotta win!"

To put the CIA cover-up strategy into effect that afternoon, Haldeman and Ehrlichman meet with CIA Director Richard Helms and his deputy, General Vernon Walters. Nixon's aides concentrate on Walters because, in Dean's words, "He was such a good friend of the White House, and the White House had put him in the deputy director position so they could have some influence over the agency."

According to Walters' later testimony, Haldeman declares that the Watergate investigation is "causing trouble and is being exploited by the opposition." It is "leading to a lot of important people and this could get worse." Haldeman asks Helms what connections there are between the CIA and Watergate. None, replies Helms firmly, and says he has so informed Gray.

But Haldeman persists. It is the President's wish, he explains, that Walters call on Gray to suggest that since five suspects have already been arrested, this should be sufficient, and that it would not be advantageous to have the inquiry pushed. The President is particularly concerned about any further probes into the Mexican money, because an FBI investigation might uncover CIA activities there.

Walters subsequently phones Gray, mentioning that he's just talked to "the White House." He warns that if the FBI persists in investigating the Watergate funds, it is likely to expose a CIA operation. Gray replies, according to Walters, "This is a most awkward matter to come up in an election year, and I will see what I can do."

Gray then orders an immediate halt to FBI efforts to interview Ogarrio. Dean also urges him to block any interviews with Dahlberg, the other source of the Watergate funds.

Later that day Haldeman reports that Nixon's plan is going forward and will probably be successful in suppressing a thorough FBI investigation. "No problem," he assures the President.

9

The Payoffs

Meanwhile the FBI investigation into the Watergate break-in proceeds routinely at a lower level with field agents unaware of any White House decision to curb it. When Donald Segretti is to be interviewed on June 25, because phone records have disclosed long-distance calls between him and Hunt, Chapin and Strachan arrange for Dean to see Segretti first and warn him not to reveal his relationship with them or with Herbert Kalmbach. On orders Segretti destroys all his records.

Two FBI agents ask Dean whether Hunt has an office in the White House. Dean claims that he doesn't know, but they locate it, finding a gun and a walkie-talkie unit in Hunt's desk. Hunt's outside employer, Robert R. Mullen and Company, is found to have collected $10,000,000 in Nixon campaign contributions, recorded by donors as "advertising expenses."

L. Patrick Gray lets Dean as White House counsel sit in on FBI interviews with White House aides and others involved in Watergate. In this way Dean keeps tabs on how much the FBI is finding out, so that the White House can stay one step ahead of the investigation, preparing cover-up stories to match and explain away incriminating facts.

At CRP, Treasurer Hugh Sloan continues to resist pressure from Magruder and LaRue to underestimate the funds paid to Liddy. Upset, Sloan complains to Chapin in the White House that there is a "tremendous problem and something has to be done." Chapin suggests that Sloan go off on a long vacation because "the important thing is that the President be protected."

When FBI agents seek to interview him, Sloan seeks advice from Ehrlichman. "Don't tell me any details," Ehrlichman says, cutting him short. "I do not want to know." Sloan then consults Mitchell, who tells him enigmatically, "When the going gets tough, the tough get going." As Sloan ruefully testifies later, "I understood that I was not getting any particularly helpful guidance." He refuses to lie.

The major problem for the White House, however, is keeping Liddy, Hunt, McCord, and the Cubans silent by providing the money Liddy has demanded for them. How can it be paid without entangling CRP or the White House in the mess? Yet if it is not and one of them talks in resentment, the scandal may even deny Nixon renomination at the Republican National Convention, which is less than sixty days off.

Dean informs Walters on June 26 that some of the accused men are "getting scared and 'wobbling.' " Can't the CIA find a secret way to put up funds for them as bail and, if they're convicted, pay them salaries while they're in jail? Walters hastily shoots down this idea, warning that involving the CIA could lead to a "multi-megaton explosion, and is simply not worth the risk to all concerned."

In the interests of national security Patrick Gray continues to yield to pressures to postpone FBI interviews that can surface dangerous facts. Dean gets a delay for Kathleen Chenow, secretary to the Plumbers, so that she can be coached on how to conceal Hunt and Liddy's early missions for the White House. Helms gets a delay for two CIA men who know of the help given to Hunt in the plot to defame Ellsberg. But Gray has trouble stalling interviews with Ogarrio and Dahlberg, which his chief assistants insist are essential. They warn Gray that unless he gets a written statement from Helms that for reasons of national security the interviews must not take place, the FBI could be accused of having taken part in a conspiracy to cover up Watergate.

More storm clouds gather over acting FBI director Gray on June 28 when Dean informs Ehrlichman that he still has two

Left, Vernon A. Walters, deputy CIA director. Right, Richard C. Helms, CIA director.

folders of "sensitive materials" from Hunt's safe. Ehrlichman says
that Gray is now on his way to the White House. Why not turn
them over to him? Dean does so in Ehrlichman's presence. He
warns Gray that the documents "should never see the light of
day," because while they don't pertain to Watergate, they have
national security implications that would be "political dynamite" if they were ever revealed.

Gray later testifies that he construes this as a direct order to
burn the files, relayed from the President through Dean. After
all, "he [Dean] was standing right there in the presence of the
top assistant to the President." So the acting head of the nation's
chief law-enforcement agency destroys vital evidence, involving a
major defendant in the Watergate crime he is presumably
investigating, for political reasons.

A fresh thunderbolt is suddenly hurled at the White House
when Dean receives a cryptic message: "The Writer has a
manuscript to sell." The "Writer" is novelist-spy Hunt's code
name; the "manuscript" obviously refers to the truth about
Watergate and the spy operations that preceded it. The implica-

tion is clear: unless the White House buys his silence, Hunt can sell his revelations to the press for money which he needs for living and legal expenses.

The message is a blackmail threat.

On June 28 Dean meets with Mitchell, LaRue, and Mardian to discuss, in Dean's words, "the need for support money in exchange for the silence of" Hunt, Liddy, McCord, and the Cubans. It is decided that Dean is to ask Ehrlichman for permission to contact Herbert Kalmbach in California, asking the President's lawyer to raise cash and make "covert payments to and for the benefit of persons involved in the Watergate break-in." Dean gets this permission from Ehrlichman.

Kalmbach flies to Washington for what Dean tells him is an "ultra-important assignment." Following orders, he meets Dean in Lafayette Park, across from the White House, and is told to make broad arm gestures, so that they don't appear conspiratorial to anyone who may be observing them. "It was like a Grade B thriller," Kalmbach later testifies.

Dean explains the situation in terms of funneling money for bail, family support, and lawyers' fees to the Watergate Seven, but stresses the need for "absolute secrecy."

Visiting CRP, Kalmbach nervously asks Stans for up to $100,000 for an important and confidential White House assignment. Stans gives him unreported contributions of $75,000 in $100 bills. Next day Kalmbach meets Dean again, and they agree upon Ulasewicz as a courier to deliver the money.

While on June 30 Ron Ziegler again tells the press that there is "no White House involvement in the Watergate incident," the President, Haldeman, and Mitchell hold a crucial meeting. Haldeman insists that Mitchell should resign at once as director of Nixon's campaign. He warns the President, "You run the risk of more stuff . . . surfacing on the Watergate caper type of thing." Nixon expresses the hope that nothing more comes out, but admits, "There is always the risk. . . . I'd cut the loss fast." He suggests that Mitchell's resignation be announced in "human terms," so that anyone connecting it to Watergate will seem churlish or spiteful.

On July 1 Mitchell resigns to "meet the one obligation which must come first: the happiness and welfare of my wife and

Herbert W. Kalmbach, Jr., the President's personal attorney.

daughter." But Martha Mitchell gives UPI reporter Helen Thomas a different reason: "I gave him an ultimatum. . . . I'm not going to stand for all those dirty things that go on."

She reveals that she had been held a political prisoner in California by five security men, who even sedated her with an injection. "Why would anyone do such a thing?" she fumes. "They're afraid of my honesty!" The White House quickly leaks rumors that Martha Mitchell is emotionally disturbed and that her husband has resigned to take care of her.

Lawrence O'Brien charges that Mitchell's resignation has nothing to do "with the alleged distress of his wife, but everything to do with the fact that big operators had been caught red-handed while attempting to spy on the Democratic Party."

Nixon replaces Mitchell at CRP with Clark MacGregor, a liaison man between the White House and Congress. Four days later, the FBI finally interviews Mitchell, who denies having any personal knowledge of the Watergate break-in.

Dean, meanwhile, receives copies of eighty FBI interviews and other investigatory data from the Justice Department. He relays key evidence to Haldeman or Ehrlichman. "I felt certain . . . this information was being given to the President," Dean alleges. Once Gray asks Dean uneasily whether he used an FBI report on Segretti to coach Segretti in giving testimony before the grand jury. Dean says he did not.

Dean's presence at FBI interviews as the eyes and ears of the President has an inhibiting effect on how candidly interviewees dare respond to questions. CRP and White House officials also constantly drop false clues to lead FBI agents off in the wrong direction. Through all this the Administration keeps assuring the public that it is cooperating with the FBI investigation "to the fullest extent."

Mitchell tells the FBI on July 5 that he knows nothing about Watergate except what he reads in the papers. He later explains that since Nixon's re-election was very much at stake, "We weren't volunteering any information."

On July 6 Gray is finally driven by his top aides to demand a formal letter from Helms or Walters asking that the FBI not pursue its investigation of the Mexican funds or of Dahlberg. Otherwise this phase of the Watergate probe can no longer be delayed. Walters replies that the CIA has no reason to make such a request and that he will resign before he permits the agency to be used as a cover-up for Watergate.

Deeply worried, Gray orders that FBI interviews with Ogarrio and Dahlberg take place. His anxiety increases when his aides warn him that an Administration cover-up *is* under way. They agree with Walters that the President ought to be told what his aides are doing. At this point no one in the FBI or the CIA imagines that the President of the United States is himself the chief conspirator.

In a phone talk Gray tells Nixon, "People on your staff are trying to mortally wound you by using the CIA and FBI, and by confusing the question of CIA interest in, or not in, people the FBI wishes to interview."

Expressing no surprise, Nixon merely asks Gray for his recommendation. Gray replies that the case cannot be covered up and will lead higher. He recommends that the President get rid of the people involved, even at the highest levels. Nixon then asks if Walters' opinion is the same, which Gray confirms.

There is a pause as the President realizes that the pretext of stopping dangerous FBI interviews "to protect the CIA" has failed. He merely says, "Pat, you just continue to conduct your aggressive and thorough investigation."

The date is July 6, 1972, and the President has just been warned by the acting FBI director and the deputy director of the CIA that members of his staff are engaged in obstructing justice—which he well knows, since they are doing so under his direction. He nevertheless later insists that he was unaware of any cover-up until long after his re-election.

Keeping his coconspirators as his closest advisers, he subsequently tells the American people in a television address, "There has been an effort to conceal the facts—both from the public— from you—and from me." He also declares solemnly, "I took no part in—or was I aware of" the cover-up.

When FBI agents interview Ogarrio, he tells them about laundering $100,000 in Nixon campaign funds through Mexican banks, after which the money was forwarded to Stans. Dahlberg tells FBI agents about giving Stans a cashier's check for the $25,000 cash contribution he received from Andreas. Stans tells the FBI that he turned the contributions over to Sloan, but cannot explain how or why they ended up in Barker's bank account and then as burglary funds.

Meanwhile the Department of Justice inquiry into Watergate, led by Assistant U.S. Attorney Silbert, continues to prepare evidence for the grand jury that will decide who is to be indicted for trial. The prosecutors and the FBI both report their findings to Assistant Attorney General Henry Petersen, who in turn relays them to his superior, Kleindienst, and to designated White House officials.

Petersen, a staunch admirer of the President, is determined to keep the prosecution strictly confined to the Watergate break-in. Silbert follows his policy.

Although Segretti's FBI interview reveals his involvement in the dirty-tricks campaign, he is only questioned about his connection with Hunt in regard to Watergate. This satisfies Petersen, who has been urged by Dean to be careful about getting into Segretti's non-Watergate activities because such revelations could hurt Nixon in the last weeks of the campaign.

To the vast relief of the White House, Silbert also decides not to pursue information obtained from Ogarrio and Dahlberg by the FBI. Calling it irrelevant to Watergate, Silbert simply refers the data to the Justice Department, where it is ignored. When Gray's top aides insist that he press for a separate full investigation of obvious violations of campaign-funding laws, Petersen recommends against it.

As CRP and White House witnesses are called before the grand jury, cover-up stories are presented in a concerted effort to limit the culpability for the Watergate break-in to Liddy, Hunt, McCord, and the four Cubans. Dean reports to the President how well each witness makes out in keeping the trail from leading higher up. After Strachan, Haldeman's aide, is questioned, Dean reassures Nixon that the prosecution is "soft."

"They didn't ask Strachan any questions about Watergate. They asked him about Segretti. They said, 'What is your connection with Liddy?' Strachan just said, 'Well, I met him over there.' They never really pressed him. Strachan appeared, as a result of some coaching, to be the dumbest paper pusher in the bowels of the White House."

Before Hugh Sloan is called before the grand jury, LaRue makes a final effort to persuade him to perjure himself about the sum of money paid to Liddy, or at least to keep silent, pleading the Fifth Amendment, in order not to contradict the testimony Magruder and Porter plan to give. Sloan refuses to do either. LaRue "suggests" that he resign from CRP, which on the following day, Sloan does.

After his mysterious absence, Hunt suddenly surfaces to testify before the grand jury on July 19. Incriminating information about White House and CRP higher-ups is not revealed under questioning by prosecutor Silbert.

Before Magruder talks to the FBI on July 20 and goes before the grand jury on August 17, he is rehearsed in his story, he alleges, by both Dean and Mitchell. They assure him that if he has to go to prison, he and his family will be taken care of, and there will be a "good opportunity for Executive clemency."

After Magruder's testimony, Dean asks Petersen how he made out. Nobody really believed his story, Petersen reports, but Magruder's quick tongue helped him escape indictment for perjury "by the skin of his teeth."

Magruder later explains why he agreed to commit perjury: "If it had gotten out that people like Mr. Mitchell and others had been involved at that point in time, I honestly thought that Mr. Nixon's re-election would be negated."

Dean reports to the President that he is getting excellent cooperation in restraining the scope of the Justice Department probe from Petersen, who has "realized the problems of a wide-open investigation in an election year." Petersen agrees not to call Colson, Chapin, Krogh, Young, and Stans before the grand jury. In an unusual procedure, they are questioned under oath by the prosecutors at the Department of Justice, not before the grand jurors. Petersen also agrees to Dean's suggestion that no witnesses be asked questions that can establish "embarrassing" links between Segretti and Strachan, Chapin, or especially Kalmbach.

"I told Silbert . . . 'we are not investigating the whole damn realm of politics,'" Petersen later tells the President, "'and I don't want you questioning him about the President's lawyer.'" Nixon comments, "Right."

George McGovern accepts the Democratic presidential nomination. Vice-presidential nominee Thomas F. Eagleton (left) and Chairman Lawrence F. O'Brien (right) flank the podium.

Silbert, criticized later for his unaggressive prosecution of the Watergate case, protests, "I never dreamed, it never occurred to me, that a former Attorney General of the United States would lie to the grand jury!"

Reporters Bob Woodward and Carl Bernstein continue to pursue the Watergate mystery on their own, and the *Post* publishes bits and pieces of the puzzle as they discover them. The evidence they unearth more and more points to criminal guilt high up in the Nixon Administration.

But most of the press ignores Watergate to concentrate on a political sensation that has arisen out of the Democratic National Convention, which had nominated George McGovern for the Presidency, with Senator Thomas Eagleton as his running-mate.

Three weeks earlier, aware that Eagleton will be a likely choice, Ehrlichman calls for an FBI file on him. The file indicates that Eagleton has been hospitalized three times for a nervous breakdown, a fact that Eagleton does not reveal to

McGovern before his selection. As soon as he is nominated, this information is leaked anonymously to the press.

McGovern at first announces that he is standing behind Eagleton "1000 per cent," but then feels compelled to drop him for a new choice, Sargent Shriver. The Democrats are badly hurt by unfavorable news stories and editorial comment. "This obsessive coverage," notes the *Nation*, "is at striking odds with the virtual blackout on the scandal involving the Committee to Re-Elect the President."

The Bernstein-Woodward revelations, nevertheless, make Kalmbach increasingly nervous about his role in channeling large sums of cash secretly to the Watergate Seven. He tells Ehrlichman, "John, I am looking right into your eyes. . . . You know that my family and my reputation mean everything to me. . . . Tell me first that John Dean has the authority to direct me in this assignment, and that it is a proper assignment, and that I am to go forward on it."

According to Kalmbach, Ehrlichman assures him that the payoffs are proper, but that unless he maintains secrecy the Democrats and the press "could have our heads in their laps." Kalmbach then secures another $75,000 for payoffs from the board chairman of Northrop Corporation, who has offered to provide additional campaign funds.

Colson seeks to encourage all on the White House staff not to hesitate to do anything to ensure the President's re-election. In a pep-talk memo he declares, "The statement in last week's UPI story that I was once reported to have said that 'I would walk over my grandmother if necessary' is absolutely accurate." Several Nixon aides later try to excuse their illegal acts by explaining that they were brainwashed into believing that winning a second term for Richard Nixon was so important, it justified any means toward that end.

This concept of loyalty also extends to Nixon's White House aides. Strachan tells Dean that he is ready to commit perjury to avoid involving Haldeman in the Segretti affair. He and Chapin both know that Haldeman approved Segretti's activities and authorized Kalmbach to make payments to him. Chapin lies to the prosecutors that he knows nothing about Segretti's dirty-tricks campaign or payments for it.

Before Segretti himself appears before the grand jury, he is examined in the prosecutor's office. He admits everything, incriminating Chapin, Strachan, and Kalmbach. But according to Young, Segretti is then told "not to worry, that those weren't the questions that would be asked" when he is examined before the grand jury.

On August 22, 1972, Richard Nixon is renominated at the Republican National Convention, which is held in Miami instead of San Diego because of the ITT uproar. He promises to run a "high-minded . . . affirmative" campaign without "gut-fighting." He feels confident of winning because of the split in Democratic ranks over the choice of ultra-liberal George Mc-Govern and the disastrous Eagleton affair—but only if he can keep the lid on the Watergate scandal as tightly as possible until after Election Day.

The half-hearted prosecution of Watergate by the Justice Department angers the Democrats. Lawrence O'Brien insists that a special prosecutor with no links to the White House must be appointed. Kleindienst replies that criminal indictments will be handed down before Election Day—the result of "the most extensive, thorough and comprehensive investigation since the assassination of President Kennedy." "No credible, fair-minded person," he adds, "is going to be able to say that we whitewashed or dragged our feet on it."

But Frank Mankiewicz, McGovern's campaign manager, observes that Kleindienst's investigation of Watergate has been as credible as "sending a fox to find out what goes on in the chicken coop."

10

"Four More Years"

On August 29, six days after his renomination, Nixon declares at a press conference, "Within our own staff, under my direction, counsel to the President, Mr. Dean, has conducted a complete investigation of all leads which might involve present members of the White House staff or anybody in the government. I can state categorically that no one in the White House staff, no one in this Administration, presently employed, was involved in this very bizarre incident."

The term "presently employed" allows the President to exclude any reference to Mitchell, Sloan, Liddy, Hunt, McCord, and Segretti. The statement, nevertheless, is still untrue regarding others who have not yet been compromised, including Nixon himself. He adds, "This kind of activity has no place whatever in our political process. . . . We want the air cleared as soon as possible. . . . What really hurts is if you try to cover it up." He vows that the White House has been cooperating fully with the FBI and Justice Department investigations.

Listening to the news conference on television, John Dean is astonished at the President's statement that on Nixon's orders he has conducted a "complete investigation," which has showed that no one in the Administration was in any way involved in Watergate. "I had had no opportunity whatsoever to discuss this matter with the President," Dean later testifies. "I had no phone conversations, nothing. I was flabbergasted. . . . Here was the

President of the United States reassuring the American people on the basis of a report that didn't exist. . . . I began to think about the fact that I might be being set up in case the whole thing crumbled."

Should the truth come out, in other words, Nixon could say that he had had no idea of it because he had relied on the so-called Dean investigation, which had exonerated everybody in his Administration. The President, of course, knows through his top aides that what Dean has really been doing is interfering with the Watergate investigation to keep the truth bottled up.

When reporters later try to question Ron Ziegler about whether the White House has discovered who ordered the bugging of the Democrats and why, Ziegler evades the questions by merely advising them to read the President's statement.

On August 31 the *Washington Post* reports that both Liddy and Hunt were in the Watergate Hotel during the break-in of the Democratic National Committee. The White House is deeply worried by the persistent revelations of Bernstein and Woodward, suspecting—correctly—that many of their scoops come from news leaks within the Administration. Woodward's chief informer warns him that he is under FBI surveillance.

The informer also confides that a network of over fifty people—"all underhanded and unknowable"—have been involved in gathering secret intelligence in order to wreck the campaigns of Democratic candidates for the White House and that what has been going on is "beyond belief." He also tells Woodward that the White House is desperately trying to continue to contain the scandal.

The impartiality of the FBI investigation comes under further question when Gray tours the country making political speeches in behalf of the Nixon campaign. He even sends a teletype message to twenty-one FBI field offices, asking for special data "in order for John Ehrlichman to give the President maximum support on campaign trips." Gray goes to Cleveland to speak when a White House memo reminds him that Ohio will be "crucially vital to our hopes in November."

Attorney General Kleindienst also goes on the campaign trail, praising Nixon's Administration for its law-enforcement programs. He attacks McGovern as an Ellsberg sympathizer,

Carl Bernstein and Bob Woodward of the Washington Post.

charging that his election to the Presidency would be a "disaster
for the rule of law in America."

The President's re-election strategy is based largely on
campaigning as a great peacemaker. In this election year he has
made historic trips to Peking and Moscow to sign agreements
ending the cold war—"détente," it is called—an ironic accomplishment for a cold warrior who built his political career by
alarming Americans about the Russians and Chinese. Henry
Kissinger is also under orders to wind up American involvement

in the Vietnam War on "honorable terms" before Election Day—four years after Nixon's 1968 promise to end the war in six months.

On September 7 Lawrence O'Brien tells reporters that Watergate lookout Baldwin has admitted to his lawyers that there were actually two break-ins at the Democratic headquarters in Watergate.

Two days later the *Washington Post* announces that the Justice Department has completed its investigation without implicating any officials of either the White House or the Committee to Re-elect the President. No attempt has been made to question Martha Mitchell about "those dirty things that go on" nor to probe into Segretti's illegal dirty-tricks campaign.

The "thorough investigation" promised by Kleindienst has ended within three months, confined to the narrowest possible probe of the Watergate break-in, while ignoring the question of who issued the orders and provided the money for it. In addition, the Justice Department has been providing the White House with daily reports, helping all implicated to invent "scenarios" to explain away incriminating facts.

"They know everything at the Committee," one of Bernstein's sources informs him. "They know that the indictments will be down in a week and that there will only be seven. Once, another person went back to the D.A. because the FBI didn't ask the right questions. That night her boss knew about it."

Kalmbach becomes increasingly worried by news reports of hush money being paid to the Watergate Seven. By the end of the summer he has paid them between $210,000 and $230,000. Despite new orders from Dean and Ehrlichman, he finally refuses to raise any more funds for the burglars. The job is then handed to LaRue.

On September 15, 1972, to the vast relief of Nixon and his men, the federal grand jury indicts only Hunt, Liddy, McCord, and the four Cubans. The seven men are charged with conspiring to obtain illegally information from the DNC, breaking and entering, stealing and photographing documents, planting telephone taps and bugs to pick up office conversation, and monitoring these devices for a three-week period prior to arrest.

The cover-up has worked so far. None of the Watergate

Seven has talked. Top officials will apparently escape exposure and punishment, and the re-election of Richard M. Nixon seems a certainty. Unaware that Watergate is just the tip of an iceberg of high crimes and misdemeanors, fully 668 newspapers support the President while only 38 endorse McGovern.

On the day of the indictments, Haldeman praises Dean to Nixon as a skillful manipulator who has made sure "you don't fall through the holes." Nixon summons Dean to congratulate him: "You had quite a day today, didn't you? You got Watergate under the way, huh? . . . The way you've handled it, it seems to me, has been very skillful . . . putting your fingers in the dikes every time that leaks have sprung here and sprung there."

The President adds, "We are all in it together. This is a war. We take a few shots and it will be over." He reveals a thirst for revenge. "I wouldn't want to be on the other side right now, would you?" He vows to "fix" Edward Bennett Williams, the lawyer pressing the Democrats' civil suit against CRP, after the election "because he's a bad man." Dean replies that he's been keeping the enemies list of those who have proved "less than our friends."

"I want the most comprehensive notes," the President orders, "on all those who have tried to do us in. . . . they are asking for it and they are going to get it. . . ." He is determined to cripple the *Washington Post* by refusing it federal licenses to operate its television and radio stations when it is time for their renewal by the FCC. "The *Post* is going to have damnable, damnable problems out of this one," he vows. He also wants the IRS pressed harder to rake over O'Brien's tax returns.

When tactics are discussed for coping with Watergate until Election Day, Nixon suggests, "You just try to button it up as well as you can and hope for the best. . . ." Haldeman assures him, "It has been kept away from the White House, and of course completely from the President."

On this same day that the Watergate Seven are indicted, George McGovern charges that "at all stages of this investigation it remained a political case under the total direction and control of Mr. Nixon's political operatives, working through Mr. Kleindienst." The next day Henry Petersen indignantly replies, "In no instance has there been any limitation of any kind by anyone on the conduct of the investigation." But FBI agents are under orders not to follow up any leads they uncover without specific approval from the Justice Department.

"No Administration can investigate itself," observes Harvard Law School professor James Vorenberg, "and expect that the public will have confidence in that investigation."

It is for this reason that the Democrats have brought their civil suit against CRP, hoping to force out the whole truth about Watergate before Election Day. But on September 21 Judge Charles R. Richey of the U.S. District Court announces that it is impossible to try the civil suit before the criminal trial is over. According to Dean's later testimony, CRP's lawyer, Kenneth Parkinson, confides in him that "Judge Richey was going to be helpful wherever he can."

On September 29 the *Washington Post* publishes a sensational new disclosure—that a secret slush fund in Stans's safe paid for other espionage activities besides Watergate, and was under the control of Mitchell (even while Attorney General). Mitchell brands the story a reckless fabrication.

In October Dean tells Hugh Sloan he "could be a real hero around here if he took the Fifth [Amendment]" before any investigative bodies, keeping silent about the amount of cash paid to Liddy. But Sloan, thoroughly disillusioned with the Nixon Administration, refuses and even confides some of what he knows to reporter Carl Bernstein.

Vice-President Agnew insinuates that the Democrats were the real culprits behind the Watergate burglars: "Someone set up these people and encouraged them to undertake this caper to embarrass the Republican party!"

Fresh danger threatens when Representative Wright Patman tries to hold hearings on CRP's handling of campaign money, until Dean persuades Patman's committee to vote him down by arming Republican members with a letter from Henry Petersen stating that the hearings could jeopardize a fair trial for the Watergate defendants. "Another sigh of relief was made at the White House," Dean later reports, "that we had leaped one more hurdle in the continuing cover-up."

At a news conference on October 5, a reporter brashly asks

the President why "you people" don't make "a clean breast" of the truth about Watergate. Nixon replies that a "thorough investigation" involving 133 FBI agents and 1,500 interviews has exonerated all "responsible" CRP and White House officials.

Denying that he has interfered with the FBI probe, he insists, "I wanted every lead to be carried out to the end." He adds indignantly, "I have noted that this Administration has been charged with being the most corrupt in history, and I have been charged with being the most deceitful President in history. . . . I am not going to dignify such comments."

On the same day the *Los Angeles Times* reports that for weeks before the Watergate break-in on June 17, Alfred Baldwin had been delivering illegal wiretap transcripts to CRP officials.

Senator Sam Ervin, Jr., chairman of the Senate subcommittee on Constitutional Rights, announces his intention to probe why the Justice Department will not prosecute the Watergate case until after Election Day. When five men are "caught red-handed in a burglary," Ervin points out, any lawyer who can't prepare the case within fifteen minutes "ought to have his law license taken away."

On October 9 Woodward's White House informant discloses that the Nixon Administration had financed four separate operations, involving fifty agents like Segretti, to sabotage the Democrats' campaign. He quotes Mitchell as saying, "If this all comes out, it could ruin the Administration—I mean, *ruin* it!" Next day, primed with new facts, Woodward and Bernstein publish their biggest story yet in the *Post*.

"FBI agents have established," it begins, "that the Watergate bugging incident stemmed from a massive campaign of political spying and sabotage conducted on behalf of President Nixon's re-election and directed by officials of the White House and the Committee for the Re-election of the President."

Election Day is now only twenty-seven days away.

With only twenty-two days to go, the *Post* exposes Donald Segretti as the chief saboteur, directed by Chapin, the President's appointments secretary, and paid by Herbert Kalmbach, the President's personal lawyer. Phone records also link Segretti with E. Howard Hunt.

"Not only fiction, but a collection of absurd lies!" a CRP spokesman insists. Chapin calls the story "fundamentally inaccurate." Segretti scoffs, "This is all ridiculous!"

McGovern demands that the American people be told the truth about Watergate before they vote. "Who ordered this act of political espionage?" he asks. "Who paid for it? . . . Who received the memoranda of the tapped telephone conversations?" And he warns, "History shows us it is but a single step from spying on the political opposition to suppressing that opposition."

The *Washington Post*'s exposés stir *The New York Times* and some other journals to begin digging seriously into the scandal. But it is too late to affect the election. A Harris poll shows that 62 percent of the American people dismiss the affair as "mostly politics," while only 25 percent believe that "White House aides ordered the bugging."

On October 16 Ziegler attacks the *Post* and other media now on the Watergate trail, declaring loftily, "I will not dignify with comment stories based on hearsay, character assassination, innuendo, or guilt by association. . . . That is the White House position; that is my position." Republican party chairman Robert J. Dole dismisses the charges as "garbage." Clark MacGregor, now head of CRP, insists that the Watergate Seven were "obvious volunteers."

The cover-up holds. Nixon's aides remain fiercely loyal. "It is important that Mr. Nixon win at all costs," Magruder explains to an associate, "to save the country."

The Administration is jubilant on October 17 when Judge John Sirica names November 15 as the earliest possible date for the Watergate trial—nine days *after* Election Day. CRP also seeks to delay another embarrassing trial: John Gardner, head of Common Cause, has filed a civil suit against CRP for violations of the campaign funds law. Stans wins a postponement until after November 7 by promising to reveal then the sources and amounts of all contributions.

With thirteen days to go, the *Post* hurls a new bombshell by identifying Haldeman as one of the Administration officials authorized to approve payments from a secret $350,000 espionage and sabotage fund. Responsibility has now been pinned on the President's own chief of staff.

"Shabby journalism!" cries Ziegler. ". . . A blatant effort at character assassination." He declares, "Mr. Dean informed me that there was no secret fund."

Next day the Nixon forces try to convince voters that the President is bringing peace and prosperity to the nation. Unable to force North Vietnam to yield to his demands, Kissinger nevertheless assures the American people, "We believe peace is at hand." McGovern calls this a "cruel political deception."

Farm votes are wooed by an Agriculture Department announcement that overstates farm income by over one billion dollars. Donald Paarlberg, director of the department's agricultural economics, later admits that this is a misrepresentation.

But the greatest deception of all is the cover-up of Watergate. The American people remain apathetic about the scandal. Administration spokesmen succeed in belittling it as just a routine political squabble.

In another context, the President later tells a *Washington Star* reporter, "The average American is like the child in the family." The *Nation* comments, "The implication was that the average citizen could easily be manipulated by Papa. It is, of course, a form of contempt for the common people."

In a campaign speech, Nixon pledges to "halt the erosion of moral fiber in American life and the denial of individual accountability for individual action." Tom Wicker of *The New York Times* calls the statement, in the light of Watergate, "obscene."

Nixon's devoted followers continue chanting his campaign slogan: "Four more years!" Many are in effect brainwashed into refusing to consider the facts or implications of Watergate by a gigantic campaign spending spree that costs well over $58,000,000—the greatest sum ever spent for a political candidate in any one year.

Despite Watergate, and despite the President's constant complaints of unfair treatment by the media, 93 percent of the newspapers who endorse any candidate support Nixon. CBS and ABC have assigned no correspondents to cover Watergate; NBC has only one. A few days before the election, CBS News broadcasts the first part of a report on the Watergate scandals.

Election night, 1972. Nixon and Agnew greet their supporters at the beginning of "four more years."

After a phone call from Charles Colson to CBS chairman William S. Paley, the second part of the report is cut in half.

The Administration persists in its claim that the media is "hounding" Nixon, hoping to suppress and discredit news breaking in the *Washington Post, The New York Times,* and *Time* magazine that dangerously incriminates the President and his men.

Shortly before Election Day CRP attorney Paul O'Brien begins receiving messages from William Bittman, Howard Hunt's lawyer, complaining that the money received from Kalmbach through Ulasewicz is insufficient. Hunt and the other defendants must have more.

On Election Day Nixon wins a landslide vote of 60.8 percent of the popular vote, 47 million votes compared to McGovern's 29 million, as well as 97 percent of the electoral vote. At the same time, however, on Election Day the turnout of eligible voters is the lowest since 1948—only 56 percent—indicating that almost half of the American voting public is unenthusiastic about either Nixon or McGovern. Nixon is actually re-elected by 31 percent of all Americans who are qualified to vote.

He nevertheless calls this a "clear mandate" from the people. He and his aides sigh in relief. All the hard work to cover up Watergate and its related scandals has paid off by winning a second term for the Nixon Administration.

But it is not to last the "four more years" they imagine they have won. The storms are only beginning to break, and Magruder is one of the first to realize it. He views the election as "a hollow triumph," admitting later, "I sensed that for me the fantasy was almost over."

Cover-Up of the Cover-Up

11

One week after the election, Hunt phones Colson demanding more money for himself and the Cubans. "The stakes are very, very high . . . ," he reminds Colson. "We're protecting the guys who are really responsible . . . but at the same time this is a two-way street. . . . the cheapest commodity available is money."

Colson informs Dean, who warns Haldeman and Ehrlichman that a new "cover-up of the cover-up" is now essential. On November 10, Dean flies to California to tape what Segretti has to say about Chapin's involvement in his dirty tricks. Next day he flies to Key Biscayne to play the tape for Haldeman and Ehrlichman. It is decided that Chapin must leave the White House. Ziegler denies to the press that Chapin's departure has anything to do with Segretti.

On November 15, Dean goes to New York City to get Mitchell to handle "all these problems." The chief problem is that there are now too many people who have dangerous information, and many are wary of being sacrificed to protect others. Past and present members of the Administration split into factions. Strategies are planned to ward off the threat of criminal prosecution.

On November 16 Ralph Nader files suit against Treasury Secretary George Shultz to recover for the public the salaries of Charles Colson and other White House staffers because they had spent all their time working for Nixon's re-election. "Never before has there been such an open, flagrant and large conversion of taxpayers' revenues and government facilities," Nader charges, "for a re-election campaign."

Colson announces on December 2 that he will resign.

According to Dean, Mitchell asks him to arrange a transfer of Haldeman's secret $350,000 cash fund to LaRue for paying off the Watergate defendants. Haldeman gives the money to Strachan, who takes it to LaRue's apartment. Since Ulasewicz has now quit as "bagman," along with Kalmbach, LaRue distributes it through Hunt's lawyer, Howard Bittman, and Hunt's wife, Dorothy. It is later estimated that the Watergate payoffs total close to half a million dollars.

On a wet and foggy December 8, 1972, a United Airlines jet suddenly nosedives and crashes during a landing in Chicago, killing forty-three passengers. One of the dead is Dorothy Hunt, and her purse is found to contain $10,000 in $100 bills. Besieged by reporters, Hunt insists that the money was intended for a business franchise his wife was planning to buy with her cousin.

The trial of the seven Watergate defendants in the U.S. District Court has to be postponed until January 8, 1973, because of the illness of Judge John J. Sirica. Before it opens, McCord finds himself under intense pressure from his lawyer to join the other defendants in claiming that the break-in was for CIA-connected national security purposes. He refuses. "I would not turn on the organization that had employed me for nineteen years," he tells his lawyer angrily.

On December 31 he writes an anonymous letter to John Caulfield, the security aide who originally got him the job at CRP: "If the Watergate operation is laid at the CIA's feet where it does not belong, every tree in the forest will fall. It will be a scorched desert. Pass the message that if they want it to blow, they are on the right course."

Another threat to the cover-up comes from Hunt. Depressed by his wife's death, he makes a new demand for more money on January 3, 1973, and insists upon the President's pledge to pardon him. Otherwise, according to McCord, Hunt threatens to "blow the White House out of the water" with "information which could impeach the President." Later Hunt defends his actions as only "bill collecting," insisting he had not been trying to blackmail the White House.

"Now what the hell do I do?" Colson asks Dean plaintively.

On January 8, the day the trial of the Watergate defendants opens, he tells the President that Hunt wants a guarantee he'll be released from jail within a year. The situation involving Hunt is "very desperate," Colson points out, because his information can be "very incriminating to us."

Nixon says that the problem can be handled by building up sympathy for Hunt's plight over his wife's death in a plane crash through public relations, then granting him clemency. "We'll build up that —— like nobody's business," he tells Colson. "We'll have [William F.] Buckley write a column and say, you know, that he should have clemency, if you've given eighteen years of service." It would be difficult, however, he feels, to grant clemency to the others.

"The others didn't know any direct information," Colson observes, adding, "See, I don't give a damn if they spend five years in jail. . . . They can't hurt us."

According to Dean, Nixon authorizes Colson to give Bittman "general assurance" of executive clemency.

The Watergate defendants are none too happy that the case is to be tried before Judge Sirica, an Eisenhower appointee known as "Maximum John" because of his stiff sentences. A hard-working, rock-honest jurist, Sirica prefers to cross-examine witnesses himself to get out the whole truth.

On January 10, two days after the trial opens, Hunt offers to plead guilty to conspiracy, burglary, and illegal wiretapping. He declares that no higher-ups were implicated "to my knowledge," and explains his switch of plea by low spirits over his wife's death.

When court closes for the weekend, McCord is phoned by the retired bagman Ulasewicz, who relays a message from Caulfield: "Plead guilty. One year is a long time. You will get executive clemency. Your family will be taken care of, and when you get out you will be rehabilitated and a job will be found for you." McCord, suspicious of this anonymous phone reassurance, insists upon talking to Caulfield personally.

Meanwhile, on January 11 Senator Sam Ervin announces his intention to hold Senate hearings on the Watergate affair, to

Judge John J. Sirica.

probe violations of the election laws by the Nixon campaign, and
to determine what new reform legislation is needed to prevent
any more Watergates.

Reporter Bernstein learns that Hunt has been visiting the
Cubans, urging them to follow his own example and change their
pleas to guilty. Hunt assures them that their families will be
cared for financially and that they can expect to receive pardons

after only a few months in jail. When they tell their lawyer, he warns them to stay away from Hunt. Instead they fire him and get a new lawyer who changes their pleas to guilty.

Judge Sirica is furious. Excusing the jury, he tells the Cubans sternly, "This jury is going to want to know . . . what purpose did you four men go into that Democratic headquarters for? . . . who, if anyone, hired you . . . if there are any other people . . . higher up . . . involved in this case. . . ."

All five insist they joined the break-in in the belief that they were helping to "liberate" Cuba from Castro. When Sirica demands that Barker reveal where they got the $100 bills found on them during the break-in, Barker professes ignorance: "I got the money in the mail in a blank envelope." Sirica snaps, "I don't believe you." When he asks Barker about the $114,000 in Nixon campaign checks deposited in his Miami bank account, Barker again has no idea where they came from.

In disgust Sirica insists that the Cubans reveal whether they have been pressured into remaining silent and pleading guilty by promises of money and executive clemency.

"No, Your Honor," they chorus.

They are led off to jail to await sentence. Defense attorneys protest Judge Sirica's direct questioning of witnesses as a usurpation of the prosecutor's role. He replies sharply, "The function of a trial court is to search for the truth."

Before seeing McCord on January 12, Caulfield consults Dean for instructions. Should he tell McCord that the offer of executive clemency comes directly from the President? "No," Dean replies, ". . . say that it comes from 'way at the top.' "

Meeting secretly with McCord at a Potomac River over-look, Caulfield says he's carrying a message "from the very highest levels of the White House." McCord is assured that if he follows the example of Hunt and the Cubans, he can expect the same deal. "I may have a message to you at our next meeting," Caulfield promises, "from the President himself."

But McCord is bitter at being expected to go to jail to cover up for higher-ups involved. "I have always followed the rule that if one goes, all who are involved must go," he declares. He adds firmly, "I want my freedom."

Caulfield consults Dean, who sends him back to appeal to

John J. Caulfield advised McCord to stick to the "game plan."

McCord's patriotism. "The President's ability to govern is at stake!" Caulfield pleads. "Everyone is following the game plan but you." McCord remains unmoved.

"I was involved in questionable activity," Caulfield later concedes, "but I felt that it was important for me to carry this message for the good of the President."

Meanwhile a second trial makes headlines in January—that of Daniel Ellsberg and his friend Anthony Russo for releasing the Pentagon Papers. When it opens on January 18 in Los Angeles before Judge W. Matthew Byrne, Jr., the government refuses to recognize Ellsberg's deed as a justifiable act of conscience. The defense argues that the government's "top secret" classification was improper, intended only to conceal the truth about the Vietnam War from Congress and the American people.

Supreme Court Justice William O. Douglas agrees, calling the Pentagon Papers in a 1972 decision, *Gravel v. U.S.,* "a chronicle of suppression of vital decisions to protect the reputations and political hides of men who worked an amazingly successful scheme of deception on the American people." And Judge Byrne learns of a government study that reports no harm done to the national defense by disclosure of the Papers. Sharply criticizing the prosecution for suppressing this information favorable to Ellsberg, he orders the study produced at once.

Judge Sirica is equally critical of the Justice Department for its feeble prosecution at the Watergate trial. Witnesses are asked no probing questions to discover who had planned and authorized the break-in. Baldwin is allowed to suffer a "lapse of memory" about the names of CRP officials to whom he delivered the Gemstone wiretap logs. Magruder lies about the amount and purposes of the money given to Liddy, and Porter compounds the perjury.

When the prosecution fails to question Sloan vigorously, Judge Sirica intervenes to demand who approved the payments to Liddy. Sloan names Stans and Mitchell. The prosecutors show little interest, however, in pursuing these leads to further indictments.

When Caulfield meets a third time with McCord on January 25, the latter reveals that he intends to tell all he knows before Judge Sirica hands down his sentence. Stunned, Caulfield warns, "You know that if the Administration gets its back to the wall, it will have to take steps to defend itself."

McCord later testifies, "I took that as a personal threat, and I told him in response that I had had a good life, that my will was made out." He prefers to risk what the powerful men in the White House can do to him rather than rot away in jail.

The Watergate trial ends after sixteen days, with Liddy and McCord found guilty on all counts. Judge Sirica is frustrated and angry because of the defendants' unwillingness to talk. Setting stiff bail bonds of $100,000 each for McCord and Liddy, pending their appeals, Sirica suggests that now the best hope of the American people to learn the whole truth about Watergate lies in a proposed Senate investigation.

Meanwhile he indicates his determination to keep the pressure on by the threat of imposing maximum sentences on the Watergate Seven, in the hope one will break ranks to earn a lighter sentence.

In a news conference on January 31, the President promises he will not try to prevent his aides from testifying at Senate hearings. "We are not going to use executive privilege as a shield for conversations that might be embarrassing to us but that really don't deserve executive privilege," he says. He declares that he has known nothing about Watergate or any cover-up because he has been too preoccupied with vital foreign policy matters— China, the Soviet Union, Vietnam.

This excuse is challenged later by Senator Lowell P. Weicker, Jr., Connecticut Republican, who demands, "How do you explain . . . your daily logs for June and July 1972 [which] show literally hundreds of meetings with principal Watergate figures, while only minutes were spent with . . . Dr. Kissinger?"

On February 7 the Senate votes 70–0 to set up a seven-man committee of four Democrats and three Republicans, headed by Senator Sam Ervin, Jr., of North Carolina, to investigate the Watergate break-in and related activities to sabotage the Democrats in the 1972 campaign. Two days later, Dean is summoned to California for two days of strategy meetings with Haldeman and Ehrlichman to cope with this new threat to their cover-up. They decide, Dean subsequently alleges, that "the White House will take a public posture of full cooperation, but privately will attempt to restrain the investigation and make it as difficult as possible to get information and witnesses. . . ." Since he has been so successful thus far, Dean is assigned the leading role in the obstruction.

Haldeman spells out White House strategy for justifying Watergate at the hearings in a February 10 memo to Dean: "We need to get our people to put out the story on the foreign or Communist money that was used in support of demonstrations against the President in 1972. We should tie all 1972 demonstrations to McGovern and thus to the Democrats as part of the peace movement. . . . We have to play a very hard game on this whole thing."

Compromised aides whose retention in the White House could make them an embarrassment as witnesses at the Senate hearings are transferred to good jobs elsewhere. Chapin has already become an executive at United Air Lines. Strachan becomes general counsel to the United States Information Agency. Egil Krogh becomes Undersecretary of Transportation, claiming at his confirmation hearing that he knew nothing about Watergate. Charles Colson is offered a partnership in a law firm that abruptly acquires the wealthy Teamsters Union as a client.

Dean warns Haldeman that Magruder is considering testifying before the Senate Watergate Committee that final approval of the Gemstone plan came from Haldeman, which would place it on the President's doorstep. Magruder indicates a change of mind when informed he will be appointed to a high government post. Sloan hears of this and angrily warns Dean that he will block this perversion of justice by exposing Magruder's perjury at a confirmation hearing on the appointment.

Subsequently, after Haldeman meets with the President, Magruder is appointed Director of Policy Development in the Commerce Department, the highest job available for which Senate confirmation is unneeded. Magruder's reward for perjury will be an annual salary of $36,000.

Reporter Bob Woodward's informant tips him off to another threat to the cover-up. Patrick Gray is allegedly complaining to the White House about "taking the rap" for limiting the investigation on Watergate, warning that "all hell could break

Dwight L. Chapin, former presidential appointments secretary.

loose" if he isn't appointed permanent FBI director to keep the lid on. Three days after Woodward is told this, Nixon sends Gray's appointment to the Senate for confirmation.

Fresh consternation breaks out at the White House when *Time* magazine reveals that it has information on the Administration's secret 1969–1971 wiretaps of newsmen and government officials and plans to publish the story. Ehrlichman, who has the logs and files of the wiretaps locked in his safe, tells Dean to have Ziegler brand the charges as false.

"We're going to stop these damn news leaks," Nixon fumes to his aides. "I don't care how much it costs!" On February 26, subpoenas are issued to reporters of *Time*, the *Washington Post*, and *The New York Times* to compel them to name confidential sources for their stories on Watergate or face jail terms. The strategy fails when the subpoenas are thrown out of court.

Nixon plans to try to keep his chief aides from being forced to testify before the Senate Watergate Committee on the grounds of executive privilege, claiming it would otherwise damage the ability of future Presidents to operate with an assurance of "confidentiality" in discussing problems with aides.

Dean warns Ehrlichman that this argument may not apply to White House counsel, even with the additional claim of the privacy of a lawyer-client relationship, because Dean so seldom sees Nixon personally. On February 27, after not seeing him for over five months, the President suddenly begins meeting with Dean almost daily, sometimes alone, sometimes with other aides present, and talks to him frequently over the telephone.

At the first of these meetings Nixon suggests a new strategy in the cover-up with Dean as a central figure. Since Haldeman and Ehrlichman are both "principals in the case," Dean can be "more objective" about Watergate. He is to keep tabs on the various investigations and report directly to Nixon.

The following morning Dean discusses with the President the question of clemency for Hunt and the other Watergate defendants. Nixon asks, "Do they expect clemency in a reasonable time?" Dean answers, "I think they do." Nixon: "You couldn't do it, say, in six months?" Dean: "No."

Worried about the Senate Watergate Committee hearings, Nixon says, "I wanted to talk to you about what kind of a line to take." He frets about a subpoena for Kalmbach's financial records, which might expose dubious transactions in Nixon's private affairs. He muses, "I suppose the big thing is the financial transaction they will go after him for. How does the money get to the Bank of Mexico, etc." Dean reassures him, "Oh, well, all that can be explained."

The President responds in surprise, "It *can?*"

Dean says he considered the Administration's position on the scandals "an impossible task to hold together until after the election . . . but we've made it this far and I'm convinced we're going to make it the whole road, and put this thing in the funny pages of the history books rather than anything serious." He assures the President that on *Time*'s wiretap exposé, "We are stonewalling [denying all] totally."

"Oh, absolutely," Nixon replies, and reminds Dean, "The main thing, of course, is also the isolation of the President [from any taint of Watergate]." Dean responds, "Totally true!"

The President orders him to talk to "our good friend Kleindienst. . . . Tell him we have to . . . work together on this thing." Mitchell's successor must save chief Administration figures from prosecution: "[The break-in] was done by the Committee to Re-Elect, and Mitchell was the Chairman, correct? . . . And Kleindienst owes Mitchell everything. Mitchell wanted him for Attorney General." Kleindienst, in other words, owes Mitchell an important favor.

Dean is also ordered to caution Senator Howard Baker, Republican vice-chairman of the Senate Watergate Committee, that Mitchell is vulnerable to "ruin" if the committee presses him too hard.

Half an hour after this conversation, the Senate Judiciary Committee begins confirmation hearings on the nomination of Patrick Gray as permanent director of the FBI. These hearings prove to be a disaster for the Nixon Administration. It is already obvious, because of Gray's injudicious campaigning for Nixon, that he is politically partisan. Under relentless questioning, he is forced to make a number of damaging admissions.

Yes, he refused to allow the FBI to interview Martha Mitchell about her threats to tell of "those dirty things that go on," out of "courtesy" to her husband, the former Attorney

General. Yes, he turned over FBI investigative reports to Dean, and permitted Dean to sit in on FBI interviews of White House principals involved in Watergate, thus keeping the White House posted on exactly what had been found out and letting Nixon's men tailor their alibis accordingly.

Yes, Gray knew that Charles Colson had sent Hunt to visit Dita Beard in a Denver hospital a year earlier, after which she repudiated her ITT memo as a forgery, and Gray had taken no action on it. Yes, Herbert Kalmbach told FBI agents two months after the Watergate break-in that Segretti was paid up to $40,000 on Chapin's authorization, yet Gray had not ordered the FBI to question Chapin's boss, Haldeman. Yes, Gray had discussed the FBI's investigation with Ehrlichman as well as with Dean.

Senator John V. Tunney, California Democrat, charges that Gray has also been derelict in failing to investigate Dean's conduct, since the FBI findings Gray gave Dean for the President's information were obviously leaked to key suspects in the Watergate affair. Tunney demands that Dean be summoned to testify at the hearings.

Senator Edward Kennedy wins an admission from Gray that following the Watergate arrests, there was a wholesale destruction of documents at CRP. Asked about the *Time* story, Gray testifies that he has checked FBI files and can find no record of the alleged wiretaps ordered by the White House.

Gray makes an urgent phone call to Ehrlichman, pleading that Dean and Ehrlichman keep secret the fact that Dean turned over to him documents from Hunt's safe. "I'm being pushed awfully hard in some areas," he laments, "and I'm not giving an inch, and you know those areas, and I think you've got to tell John Wesley [Dean] to be . . . very careful about what he says."

Ehrlichman tells Dean sardonically that in view of Gray's blabbing to the Senate Judiciary Committee, they ought to let him just hang there and "twist slowly, slowly in the wind."

"I was just with the boss this morning," Dean replies, "and that's exactly where he was coming out."

The ordeal for Gray grows steadily worse. He admits that before the election the FBI knew that Segretti was in frequent telephone touch with Hunt and Chapin, and that Kalmbach gave Segretti up to $40,000 out of campaign funds. He admits

L. Patrick Gray III, acting head of the FBI.

being aware that Dean lied to the FBI about not knowing whether Hunt had an office in the White House, yet still turned over to a perjurer all the FBI files Dean requested. After all, Gray pleads, "This man is counsel to the President."

The Senate Judiciary Committee demands that Dean and other aides testify. Nixon refuses to allow it, calling them "an extension of the Presidency." Although Colson's resignation takes effect in March, Nixon authorizes alteration of his severance papers to classify him as an "unpaid White House consultant" so that he, too, can escape the necessity to testify in Congress.

Nixon's aides suggest doing the same for Chapin. "That would be such an obvious fraud to have both of them as consultants," the President replies, "that that won't work."

He speculates with Dean how some of the other principals who have received subpoenas from the Senate Watergate Committee may fare. They worry that Sloan may implicate Kalmbach and Stans. "He's scared, he's weak," Dean says. "He has a compulsion to cleanse his soul by confession. We are giving him a lot of stroking [cajolery]." Dean isn't worried about Kalmbach. He reassures Nixon: "Herb is the kind of guy who will check, not once, not twice, on his story . . . but probably fifty to a hundred times. . . . There won't be a hole in it."

Strachan, he suggests, "is as tough as nails. . . . He'll go in and stonewall it and say, 'I don't know anything about what you're talking about.' He has already done it twice, as you know, in interviews."

"Yeah," the President observes, "I guess he should, shouldn't he . . . ?" He later records his Dictabelt impression of Strachan as a "courageous fellow."

When Dean speculates as to whether Mitchell and Haldeman actually knew about "this kind of operation" at CRP, Nixon scoffs, "You kidding?" The President is worried that Magruder might still be cornered into incriminating Haldeman. "That'll bring it right up to the White House, to the President," he frets. "We've got to cut that back." But he realizes the vast problems in keeping the cover-up nailed down, and at one point muses, "Is it too late to, frankly, go the hangout road [tell all]?" He answers himself, "Yes, it is. . . . The hangout road's going to have to be rejected."

He ponders the idea of letting part of the Watergate story be told and making it appear to be the whole truth. But Dean warns, "There is a certain domino situation here. If some things start going, a lot of other things are going to start going, and there are going to be a lot of problems if everything starts falling. So there are dangers, Mr. President. I'd be less than candid if I didn't tell you there are. There is a reason for not everyone going up and testifying."

"I didn't mean to have *everyone* go up and testify." Nixon explains: "I mean put the story out [through] PR [public relations] people: 'Here is the story, the true story about Watergate.' " When Dean observes that the Senate committee is unlikely to believe it, Nixon admits, "That's the point."

As preparation for its hearings, the Senate Watergate Committee has its staff interview witnesses who may be called upon to testify. But Nixon decides to take a hard line and on March 13 announces that he will not let any member of the White House staff appear as a witness, and that he is extending the claim of executive privilege to cover former members of the staff as well. In private he tells his aides that his stand on executive privilege is meant to avoid subjecting them to "a lot of tough questions by a smart goddamned lawyer."

The Senate Judiciary Committee is also denied the opportunity to question Dean at the Gray hearings. Gray knows now that he will not be confirmed.

Meeting with CRP attorney Paul O'Brien on March 16, Hunt complains that commitments to him have not been kept. He warns that he has done "seamy things" for the White House, and that unless he receives $130,000 more before March 23, when he is to reappear for sentencing before Judge Sirica, he may "review his options." This thinly disguised threat is relayed to Dean and Ehrlichman.

On March 17 Dean warns Nixon that Mitchell, Haldeman, Colson, and Dean are all vulnerable to the Watergate cover-up inquiry. Nixon suggests a blocking strategy: "I think what you've got to do, to the extent that you can, John, is cut her off at the pass."

But an even wilder firestorm is about to erupt. Determined to win a light or even a suspended sentence by cooperating with Sirica, McCord writes to the judge admitting that perjury was committed at the Watergate trial; that defendants were under "political pressure" to plead guilty and remain silent; that higher-ups were involved; and that "several members of my family have expressed fear for my life if I disclose knowledge of the facts of this matter."

He indicates that he wants to make a full revelation to Judge Sirica alone, without the FBI, the Justice Department, or other government officials present to leak what he says to the White House.

Sirica is elated. His trump card—the threat of imposing maximum sentences—has worked. He keeps McCord's letter secret until the day of sentencing, when he prepares to let Richard Nixon and his men know that the truth about Watergate is about to emerge.

12

Blackmailing the President

Unaware of McCord's defection, the President on March 20 asks Dean to concoct a statement for the Senate Watergate Committee. "Make it very incomplete," he orders. "I don't want too much in chapter and verse . . . just something general. Like 'I have checked into this matter; I can categorically [state], based on my investigation, the following: Haldeman is not involved in this, that and the other thing. Mr. Colson did not do this.' . . . Right down the line."

Dean is troubled, feeling that Nixon does not fully appreciate the extent of the peril he is in. Conferring with the President the following morning, he says, "I have the impression that you don't know everything I know." He warns Nixon bluntly, "We have a cancer within, close to the Presidency, that's growing. It's growing daily . . . because (1) we're being blackmailed; (2) people are going to start perjuring themselves very quickly. . . . And there is no assurance . . . that that [the cover-up] won't bust."

He reviews highlights of the cover-up that contained the Watergate investigation at the level of Liddy, saving the election. Dean explains that some credit belongs to Henry Petersen who "believes in you," and is grateful to the Administration for having made him Assistant Attorney General. Petersen has tipped Dean off "when we had problems, where we had problems. . . . he made sure that the investigation was narrowed down to the very, very fine criminal thing, which was a break for us."

But now explaining away the hush money paid the Watergate defendants is not going to be so easy "because (1) Bob [Haldeman] is involved in that; (2) John [Ehrlichman] is involved in that; (3) I am involved in that; (4) Mitchell is involved in that. And that is obstruction of justice."

Dean warns that the problem will get even worse: "This is going to be a continual blackmail operation by Hunt and Liddy and the Cubans. No doubt about it." He adds that "Colson has talked indirectly to Hunt about commutation [presidential pardon]. All of these things are bad."

Hunt is demanding another payment of $130,000 before he faces sentence by Judge Sirica in two days, Dean tells Nixon: "He says, '[Otherwise] I will bring John Ehrlichman down to his knees and put him in jail. I have done enough seamy things for he and Krogh, that they'll never survive it.' "

Dean suggests a cover-up angle in case Hunt talks about the break-in at Dr. Fielding's office: "You might put it on a national security grounds basis."

Nixon likes the idea. "National security," he muses. "We had to get information for national-security grounds . . . on a confidential basis. Neither [the FBI nor the CIA] could be trusted."

"I think we could get by on that," Dean agrees. But he warns that the chief problem is the continuous blackmail that will go on while the Watergate Seven are in prison. "It will compound the obstruction of justice situation. It will cost money. It is dangerous."

"How much money do you need?" the President asks.

"I would say these people are going to cost a million over the next two years."

"We could get that. . . . And you could get it in cash. I know where. . . . Your major guy to keep under control is Hunt . . . because he knows . . . about a lot of things."

"He knows so much, right. He could sink Chuck Colson."

The President is uneasy because Hunt's ultimatum gives them only forty-eight hours to meet his demands. "Don't you have to handle Hunt's financial situation . . . damn soon?"

"If this thing ever blows," Dean admits, "then we are in a cover-up situation . . . extremely damaging to you."

"Let me put it frankly: I wonder if that [blackmail] doesn't have to be continued." Nixon also muses about Colson's implicit promise to Hunt of a presidential pardon by Christmas.

"It may be just too hot," Dean warns. The President agrees it would be risky to grant it before the 1974 midterm elections. Dean: "It may further involve you in a way you shouldn't be involved in this." Nixon makes up his mind that it would be a mistake: "No, it's wrong, that's for sure." But he persists in urging prompt payment of new hush money to Hunt: "That's worth it, at the moment."

"That's worth buying time on," Dean says. "Right."

The President decides to "tough it through" rather than cooperate with the Senate hearings. Dean agrees, "Just hunker down, fight it at every corner, every turn, don't let people testify—cover it up is what we really are talking about."

Nixon suggests that they get Cabinet and congressional support by having Dean brief leading figures with assurances that no one of importance at the White House was involved.

"If we go that route, sir," Dean promises him, "I can give a show . . . just about like we were selling Wheaties."

When Haldeman joins them, he expresses concern about paying more blackmail because of the amount the Watergate Seven may demand tomorrow "and five years from now" for continued silence. But the President points out, "You've got no choice with Hunt. . . . Would you agree that . . . you better damn well get that done, but fast? . . . Well, for Chrissakes, *get it!*"

Later that day Haldeman phones Mitchell. Mitchell authorizes LaRue to make a payment of $75,000 to Hunt. LaRue puts the money in a plain envelope and has a courier deliver it that evening to the home of Hunt's lawyer, Bittman. Dean informs the President that Mitchell and LaRue are taking care of the matter.

At about this time Nixon tells Haldeman that in view of recent events any thought of granting Hunt a pardon by Christmas is out of the question. Haldeman suggests, "But if Hunt *thinks* that's what he's been promised—" Nixon finishes,

"—he'll shut up now." Haldeman: "But what do you do at Christmastime?" Nixon muses, "Yah, that's right. . . . You'd better find out from Colson what he *did* promise."

Later in the day, on March 21, Nixon meets with Dean, Haldeman, and Ehrlichman. Ehrlichman warns the President that Hunt expects Colson's promise of a presidential pardon to be kept. Nixon now acknowledges glumly, "He's got to get that by Christmas."

The four men work up a "scenario" all can use to explain away the incriminating facts of Watergate and related scandals that are likely to emerge at the Senate hearings. Nixon wants to beat the committee to the punch with a White House version.

Ehrlichman suggests an explanation for the break-in at Dr. Fielding's office. Liddy "was sent out to do an investigation on Ellsberg. And when we discovered what he was up to, we stopped them. . . . It was a national-security situation. The man exercised bad judgment."

They agree that it's impossible to concoct a cover-up story that will protect everybody involved. Dean suggests, "Draw numbers with names out of a hat to see who gets hurt."

At day's end the President confides his thoughts to his dictating machine: "What is causing him [Dean] concern is that . . . it will be each man for himself, and one will not be afraid to rat on the other. . . . Magruder would bring Haldeman down if he felt that he himself was to go down." He frets. "I hope that Mitchell will really put his mind to this thing and perhaps out of it all can come some sort of a course of action we can follow. . . . To hunker down without making any kind of statement is really too dangerous."

On March 22 he meets with Mitchell and his top aides to discuss further the "report" Dean is to write. According to later testimony by Dean and Ehrlichman, Mitchell indicates that Hunt is "a problem no longer." Mitchell suggests making a few minor admissions in Dean's report for the sake of credibility. Nixon points out, "All John Mitchell is saying is that we now use flexibility in order to get on with the cover-up plan."

He suggests the tenor of Dean's report: " 'As you directed, Mr. President . . . here are the facts with regard to the members of the White House staff, et cetera, which you asked from me. I have checked the FBI records; I have read the grand jury testimony and . . . here are my conclusions, chit, chit, chit, chit.' "

Ehrlichman says the report should be considered a "modified limited hangout." Dean observes, "What it's doing, Mr. President, is getting you up and away from it. And that's the most important thing."

Since Nixon now recognizes that it may not be possible to keep all his aides from testifying before the Senate Watergate Committee without convincing the whole country he is covering up Watergate, they discuss how to handle the hearings. Nixon assures his men that he will never abandon them the way President Eisenhower sacrificed his top aide, Sherman Adams, for accepting a bribe, and earlier almost had Nixon removed from the Republican slate as Vice-President. "That's all he [Eisenhower] cared about—'Be sure he's clean,' " the President says bitterly. ". . . But I don't look at it that way. . . . We're going to protect our people if we can."

Nixon praises the cover-up work of Dean who "put the fires out, almost got the damn thing nailed down till past the election." He acknowledges, "Some of it will come out [but] we'll survive it. . . . But I know we can't make a complete cave[-in] and have the people go up there and testify."

He tells his aides, "I don't give a —— what happens. I want you all to stonewall it . . . plead the Fifth, cover up or anything else, if it'll save the plan. That's the whole point." The new strategy is to offer the Senate Watergate Committee a few carefully chosen witnesses to testify in closed session, acknowledging only the most undeniable facts and disclosing as little damaging material as possible. "The purpose of this scenario is to clean the Presidency," Nixon explains.

Ehrlichman suggests, "Assuming that some corner of this thing comes unstuck, you are then in a position to say, 'Look, that document I published is the . . . report I relied on.' "

"That is what I was preparing to say," Nixon agrees. " 'This is everything we know, I know nothing more.' This is the whole purpose in that sense."

They discuss aides who must be sacrificed. Nixon asks, "Who do you let down the tube?"

Haldeman suggests that they try to hold culpability to the top level of Magruder. "It's the Justice Department that prosecutes that," he says, "so maybe we can control the prosecution."

The President indicates how Dean can justify his access to FBI files and interviews: "You were our investigator. You were directed by the President to get me all the facts. Second, as White House counsel you were on it to assist people in the Executive Branch who were being questioned. Say you were there for the purpose of getting information. That was your job." But he cautions Dean on being too specific.

To let Dean think through all the problems and come up with a detailed report, Nixon dispatches him to Camp David, the presidential retreat, for the weekend. He next phones Kleindienst to appoint him the Administration's "hand holder" to Senator Baker, to keep the Senate Watergate Committee from investigating too deeply.

"It is essential for him to stick to your guidance," Nixon orders. "You babysit him, starting in like ten minutes?"

On March 23 the seven Watergate defendants are brought before Judge Sirica for sentencing. Liddy wears a defiant, sneering smile. Petersen has reported to Nixon, "This man is crazy, Mr. President. He's burning his arms. He showed the prosecutor and said, 'I've made myself endure this to prove to myself that I can take anything. Jail will not break me.'" But Liddy's smile fades when Judge Sirica reads aloud McCord's letter.

The courtroom erupts in astonishment. In a few fatal moments the cover-up that had almost succeeded has exploded.

McCord's readiness to talk will force the men closest to the President before the grand jury, which will now be much more skeptical of cover-up stories. The Ervin committee is less likely now to spare members of the White House staff from testifying on Nixon's spurious claim of executive privilege.

Sirica continues to use his sentencing powers to pressure the other Watergate defendants into confessing as well. He first postpones McCord's sentence for three months, thus indicating that its leniency will depend on how well he cooperates in exposing Watergate. Calling the break-in at the Democratic

*James W. McCord later
published his story in a book
called* A Piece of Tape.

National Committee "sordid, despicable and thoroughly repre-
hensible," he imposes provisional maximum sentences of twenty
to forty years and fines of up to $50,000 each on Hunt and the
Cubans. If they change their minds and join McCord in agreeing
to tell the whole truth, they, too, can expect leniency. Liddy is to
be sentenced to a term of from six years, eight months, to twenty
years in jail and fined $40,000.

"What Judge Sirica has done," says Samuel Dash, chief

counsel for the Senate Watergate Committee, "has given us a greater opportunity to get information that might not be known." When Dash interviews McCord, McCord's information implicates Mitchell, Dean, Colson, Magruder, and Liddy in various wiretapping, bugging, and other illegal activities apart from the June 17 break-in.

"I have no doubt," McCord also states, "that Haldeman knew what was going on at the CRP." And if Haldeman knew, the implication is that the President must have known also.

McCord's revelations throw new suspicion on the Justice Department's efforts up to this point to get at the truth in its investigation and prosecution. Suspicion is deepened by McCord's insistence that he cannot "feel confident" in talking to FBI agents or Department of Justice attorneys. Earl Silbert quickly notifies Judge Sirica that he is reconvening the grand jury and will reopen the investigation to explore McCord's charges.

These sudden new developments create dismay at the White House. Patrick Gray receives a telephone call from the President, who reminds him of something he wants Gray to bring out in his testimony before the Judiciary Committee: "You will recall, Pat, that I told you to conduct a thorough and aggressive investigation."

The McCord bombshell also has its impact on John Dean at Camp David. He decides not to write the phony report the President wants, knowing that it can be used by Nixon and his top aides to claim innocence of any cover-up by virtue of relying upon it, while incriminating Dean himself for a wholesale obstruction of justice.

Without telling Nixon, Dean makes up his mind to hire a lawyer to try to make a secret deal with the Watergate prosecutors to reveal all he knows in exchange for immunity from prosecution. It is now, as Dean later testifies, "Every man for himself and devil take the hindmost!"

Mitchell, swarmed over by reporters for a statement, seeks to brazen out his own involvement. "I don't know what McCord is talking about," he growls.

The President seeks the help of Republican leaders to rally the party faithful to his defense. After Senator Hugh Scott is summoned to the White House, he emerges to quote Nixon as saying, "I have nothing to hide. The White House has nothing to hide . . . you are authorized to make that statement in my name." California governor Ronald Reagan objects to the description of the Watergate burglars as "criminals." "They were not criminal at heart," he explains. "Their only aim was to re-elect the President."

Unaware that Dean has decided to defect, Nixon attempts to defend him against McCord's charges. Ziegler issues a flat denial of them and tells the press that the President has "absolute and total confidence" in Dean.

Jeb Magruder joins Mitchell in "stonewalling" against McCord's accusations. But he is appalled when Herbert Porter and Magruder's former aide, Robert Reisner, decide they had better tell all they know to the Watergate prosecutors.

"My God, you are an ant!" Magruder fumes at Porter. "You are nothing! Do you realize the whole course of history is going to be changed?" Phoning Reisner, Magruder pleads, "I can't understand this . . . are you not going to be cooperative?"

Senator Lowell Weicker, one of the seven members of the Senate Watergate Committee, is asked by reporters, "Does the Watergate lead directly to the President?" He replies grimly, "*Somebody* had to start it. *Somebody* had to abet it."

Having made a career out of "hanging tough" through one political crisis after another, Nixon orders Ron Ziegler to exude calm assurance to the press, telling him, "Just get out there and act like your usual cocky, confident self."

The President and his aides confer to discuss plans for circumventing both the grand jury and the Senate Watergate Committee. Haldeman suggests setting up a time-consuming special investigation like the Warren Commission, which looked into the assassination of John F. Kennedy. Nixon wants Kleindienst to agree to the appointment of a special prosecutor, whom the White House would control.

Since the President and his men need to know what new facts about their crimes are surfacing to the reconvened grand jury, Ehrlichman is ordered to get Kleindienst to agree to leak these disclosures to the White House. Kleindienst is to be assured that all the top White House aides are innocent.

Ronald L. Ziegler, presidential press secretary.

Nixon coaches, "I think you've got to say, 'Look, Dick, let me tell you, Dean was not involved—had no prior knowledge; Haldeman had no prior knowledge; you, Ehrlichman, had none; and Colson had none.'"

They discuss handling revelations about the illegal wiretaps before Watergate. "I would put the national security tent over this whole operation," Ehrlichman suggests. The President agrees, "I sure would." The conspirators discuss ways to keep others with incriminating knowledge from joining McCord. Haldeman points out that once the 1974 elections are out of the way, Nixon will be politically free to give presidential pardons to any or all of the Watergate prisoners.

To keep Magruder from weakening and implicating Haldeman, Ehrlichman suggests that Haldeman should simply "stare him down on some of this stuff" and compel Magruder to corroborate Haldeman's story. If Magruder refuses, the President suggests, "Say that he is trying to lie to save his own skin." Ehrlichman agrees, "It'll bend him."

The President orders Ehrlichman to get Gray, who is a personal friend of Weicker's, to pump Weicker and find out what the Senate Watergate staff suspects or is trying to prove about White House involvement. At the same time Nixon wants his aides to make it appear that he is "out in front" in the Watergate investigation, cooperating fully with all probes.

"Ziegler is not sufficiently credible on this," Ehrlichman observes. The President agrees, "That's right."

So he takes to television with a campaign of speeches designed to win popular support, asserting that he is doing everything possible to discover and punish all Watergate wrong-doers.

"What really hurts in a matter of this sort," he tells the American people, "is not the fact that they occur. . . . What really hurts is if you try to cover it up."

In view of McCord's statement that Magruder committed perjury before the Watergate grand jury, Magruder flies to New York on March 27 to seek Mitchell's advice and help. Next day both fly to Washington to see Dean, asking him to back up their story that the only discussions at the Gemstone meetings in Mitchell's office were about the election law. Dean refuses.

It is obvious from McCord's testimony to the Senate Watergate investigators that the break-in at Dr. Fielding's office is going to come out. Dean asks Egil Krogh on March 28 if Ehrlichman, who was in charge of the Plumbers, had ordered it. Krogh replies, according to Dean, that he received his orders for the break-in "right out of the Oval Office." Dean later testifies, "I was so surprised to hear this that I said, 'You must be kidding.' And he repeated [it] again."

Ehrlichman tells Krogh that he has "had to dissemble . . . being less than candid" in an FBI interview, and suggests that Krogh and Young follow his example. "I don't think you should address the question of whether I talked to the President about it," he warns. Krogh subsequently insists that the break-in occurred without the knowledge of "any superior."

Dean refuses to perjure himself for Magruder and Mitchell.

According to Nixon, he learns on March 30 that Dean has been "unable" to write the assigned "report" at Camp David. It is now obvious to the President that Dean is not going to "play ball," and may be contemplating jumping ship to save his own skin.

Nixon tells Ehrlichman to take over the Watergate "inquiry" because "John Dean was in this thing up to his neck." Dean, out of fear that the whole Watergate cover-up may be pinned on him, decides to try to trade his testimony for immunity from prosecution.

13

Scapegoat Time

In the face of McCord's testimony to the Watergate Senate Committee investigators, those he implicates must either tell the truth to the grand jury or risk going to jail for perjury. On March 28, Hunt, in trouble enough already, reluctantly corroborates McCord's charges before the grand jury. LaRue lets it be known that he will admit helping to pay off the Watergate Seven. Nixon desperately invokes the principle of executive privilege to keep his aides from testifying, particularly Dean.

"Executive poppycock," scoffs Senator Sam Ervin on April 2. "The President is conducting himself in such a way as to reasonably engender in the minds of the people the belief that he is afraid of the truth. Divine Right went out with the American Revolution, and doesn't belong to White House aides."

Appearing on the CBS program, "Face the Nation," on April 1, Senator Weicker accuses Haldeman of knowing about the Watergate cover-up. "Now the time has come for the Chief of Staff to step forward and explain," Weicker insists. "I think it's absolutely necessary that Mr. Haldeman testify before the Select Committee."

Patrick Gray has continued to "twist slowly, slowly in the wind" at his now hopeless confirmation hearings before the Senate Judiciary Committee. He admits having notified the President, less than three weeks after the June 17 break-in, that

Nixon's closest aides were using both the FBI and the CIA to cover up the scandal. Kleindienst privately orders Gray to shut up. On April 5 Gray ends his ordeal by phoning Nixon to ask withdrawal of his nomination before he is further humiliated by having it rejected.

Nixon seeks to use the open post of FBI director to fend off several new dangers he now perceives. Witnesses may disclose his orders to Krogh to get something on Daniel Ellsberg; Ehrlichman's authorization of the break-in of Dr. Fielding's office; or the wiretaps ordered by Nixon which resulted in illegal eavesdropping on fifteen Ellsberg conversations. Any of these revelations could be explosive at the Pentagon Papers trial, unless Judge Byrne sees fit to exclude them as irrelevant.

The President has Ehrlichman invite Byrne to Nixon's San Clemente home. Ehrlichman asks the judge if he would be interested in becoming the director of the FBI. In the course of the conversation, Nixon drops in on them to shake Byrne's hand warmly, declaring that he's proud to meet such a fine jurist. Two days later Ehrlichman again meets with Byrne and repeats the offer.

Some members of the Senate Watergate Committee later brand these acts by Ehrlichman and the President, performed secretly in the middle of the Ellsberg trial, attempted bribery.

When Haldeman seeks support for the Administration from Republican leaders in Congress, he is asked if it is true that he directed a political intelligence-gathering operation during the 1972 campaign. Yes, he acknowledges, but nothing illegal was done.

On April 6, Dean talks secretly with the Watergate prosecutors. Unaware of the fact, Haldeman and Ehrlichman meet with him two days later to suggest that they are all in trouble because of trying to cover up for John Mitchell. Why not demand that Mitchell step forward and accept the blame? The public will be satisfied, and the Watergate clamor will die down. Nixon now wants Dean to tell the prosecutors about the Gemstone meetings in Mitchell's office in the Department of Justice.

At the same time the President orders Ehrlichman to tell Magruder not to answer any questions but to plead the Fifth

Amendment. Furthermore he instructs his aide, "We don't want Mitchell popping off."

With one cat after another jumping out of the bag, he has trouble persisting in his claim of executive privilege to keep his aides from testifying. "Can anybody tell me," demands Senator Weicker, "how the national interest is served by having these persons who are suspects *not* appear?"

Nixon sends Kleindienst to a Senate hearing to argue that no one in the President's employ, from senior staff aides to janitors, can be forced to testify before a congressional committee if the President forbids it. Amazed, Senator Muskie asks if that applies to 2,500,000 employees on the payroll of the executive branch of the government. It does, Kleindienst replies coolly, and if the senators don't like it they can either "cut off appropriations, impeach the President, [or] have another election." Kleindienst also warns Henry Petersen that Nixon does not want any White House aide granted immunity in exchange for his testimony before the grand jury.

Magruder, frightened of a jail sentence for perjury, tries to make such a deal without success. Lawrence Higby, Haldeman's aide, phones Magruder, taping the conversation without Magruder's knowledge. He gets Magruder to make a number of damaging admissions, then warns him that it isn't in his interest to blame the White House. Ehrlichman gleefully tells the President that the tape will "beat the socks off" Magruder if he ever "gets off the reservation."

But in desperation Magruder accepts his lawyer's advice to confess everything and plead guilty. On April 14, he tells Silbert about the Gemstone meetings, about receiving the wiretap logs of the DNC at CRP, about the payments of hush money and his having been coached by Mitchell and Dean to commit perjury. Coming on top of McCord's revelations, three weeks earlier, Magruder's testimony bursts the Watergate dam.

Mitchell retreats from his own earlier sworn denial that he knew in advance about the Watergate break-in. He now blames the White House for authorizing it. Dean implicates him, Haldeman, Ehrlichman, and Magruder in the cover-up, to Silbert.

"It's all over. . . . A lot of people are going to jail,"

*In May 1974, Jeb Stuart Magruder was sentenced to the Federal prison
at Allenwood, Pennsylvania.*

Magruder tells Porter dejectedly. "Mitchell, LaRue, Mardian,
myself, Dean, Colson, Strachan and maybe Haldeman. Silbert
may indict *you*."

"The Watergate, the Watergate," moans Republican Senator Barry Goldwater. "It's beginning to be like Teapot Dome. I
mean, there's a smell to it. Let's get rid of the smell."

Even hard-line Nixon loyalist Ronald Reagan admits, "Watergate is starting to hurt. People are disturbed."

On April 14 the President, Ehrlichman, and Haldeman hold anxious consultations. Ehrlichman reports that Colson wants Nixon to tell Liddy to talk: "He wants you to be able to say afterward that you cracked the case." New "scenarios" are discussed to explain away the incriminating evidence that the Watergate prosecutors and the Senate investigating staff are now hearing.

Nixon's aides suggest that payments were made to Hunt not to keep him silent but out of compassion for his motherless children. "That's right . . . ," agrees the President. "That's got to be the story."

Ehrlichman wants Mitchell told that "the jig is up" and that he must go to the prosecutors and accept responsibility for the Watergate break-in. Then a press release is to be issued stating, as Ehrlichman phrases it, " 'Charges of cover-up by the White House were materially dispelled by the diligent efforts of the President and his aides in moving on evidence which came to their hands . . . the previous week.' "

"I'll buy that," says the President.

He agrees with Ehrlichman's view that if a "big fish" is offered as a sacrifice, the demands for full disclosure may be quieted. Ehrlichman points out another useful purpose Mitchell's indictment would serve: "Mitchell's lawyers are going to somehow move to stop the Ervin hearing . . . on the point that they can't [otherwise] get a fair trial."

Segretti, who had surfaced after Election Day, is now scheduled to testify about his dirty-tricks campaign before a Florida grand jury. The President wonders whether it's better to "stonewall" Segretti's testimony or concede it. "Well," Ehrlichman points out, "we've got the option of caving [in] at any time."

Ehrlichman says that the President must convince the nation he didn't just sweep the truth about Watergate under the rug, but took action after having Ehrlichman investigate and report the facts. Nixon muses, "Now, in the scenario I sort of go out and tell people I have done this."

Summoning Mitchell from New York, Ehrlichman reveals that the President has decided he must step forward and make his admission to the prosecutors. But Mitchell demurs, "There is no way I am going to do anything except staying where I am because I'm too far out. . . . I got euchred into this thing by not paying attention to what those —— were doing."

He makes it clear that he has no intention of being the fall guy for the White House. He reminds Ehrlichman that he and Dean tried to keep the lid not only on Watergate but on "all the other things that were going on over here that would [if exposed] have been even worse." Pointing out that Haldeman's $350,000 cash fund was also involved, he reminds Ehrlichman that the "whole genesis of this thing"—the Plumbers—was in the White House, "as you're perfectly well aware."

"No," Ehrlichman replies coldly. "I didn't know that."

Mitchell also claims that Haldeman and Colson were actually running CRP through Magruder, "freezing me out of the operation." So why should he shoulder the blame?

Martha Mitchell gives *The New York Times* her view of the Administration: "They're lying from beginning to end. They're trying to hang this on my husband. . . . I won't let them. . . . I can name names." She fears an attempt to silence her.

Like Mitchell, Dean refuses to be made a scapegoat. On April 14 he tells Silbert that Hunt and Liddy, acting under White House orders, burglarized Dr. Fielding's office. He also implicates Haldeman, Ehrlichman, Colson, LaRue, Mardian, Mitchell, and Magruder.

Silbert reports this at once to Henry Petersen, who feels that the President must be warned, and tells Kleindienst. They go together to see Nixon, revealing Dean's charges. They warn that Haldeman and Ehrlichman are now so deeply compromised that it is essential for them to resign.

Upset, Nixon defends his top aides, suggesting that Dean and Magruder are simply trying to shift the blame. He insists that neither must be promised immunity from prosecution in return for testifying before the grand jury.

"It's embarrassing and all the rest," the President admits, "but it'll pass. We've got to just ride it through, Dick . . . do the best we can. Right?"

"Yes, sir," Kleindienst replies.

Nixon explains that previously he had always run his own

campaigns, but that in 1972 he was too busy with foreign affairs to pay attention to what was being done for him. Kleindienst observes that both Nixon and the office of the Presidency "have to be protected and preserved by the institution of justice." But since he is a political appointee, he suggests it might be wiser for him to step aside in Watergate and related matters, and let Petersen handle everything.

The President agrees, and the announcement is made on April 19, when Kleindienst disqualifies himself because of a "close personal and professional relationship" with some of the officials involved in the Watergate break-in.

On the evening of April 15 Nixon summons Dean to the White House. Dean later reports, "The President almost from the outset began asking me a number of leading questions, which made me think that the conversation was being taped," and that a record was being made to protect Nixon.

With a nervous laugh the President says that he had "of course, only been joking" when he talked about paying $1,000,000 in hush money to Hunt. During the meeting he gets out of his chair and paces to a corner of the room, possibly out of microphone reach, and mutters that he was probably foolish to have discussed clemency for Hunt with Colson.

In a conversation with Ehrlichman, he proposes that they abandon the pretext of having acted out of charity in giving money to the Watergate burglars as just too unbelievable. He suggests "a straight damn line that of course we raised money. Be very honest about it. But, uh, we raised money for a purpose that we thought was perfectly proper. . . . We weren't trying to shut them up, we just didn't want them to talk to the press."

Beginning that evening, Nixon phones Henry Petersen four times within the next twenty-four hours to give the impression of cooperating fully with the Justice Department investigation. At the same time he hints clearly that he is the boss and expects to be kept posted in advance of all developments.

"You know I am in charge of this thing," he tells Petersen. "You are and I am. . . . You know, I want to stay one step ahead of the curve." Petersen understands, and subsequently provides the President with full information on what Dean,

Magruder, and others are telling to the prosecutors and afterward to the grand jury.

While assuring Petersen that the information will go no further, Nixon passes his findings along to Haldeman, Ehrlichman, Colson, and Strachan to help adjust and synchronize White House "scenarios" accordingly. The President flatters Petersen by calling him the "White House counsel on Watergate," and hints at considering his appointment as director of the FBI.

Nixon boasts to Ehrlichman and Ziegler, "I've got Petersen on a short leash." Questioned later, Petersen admits that Nixon's tactics were "frankly . . . a little heavy-handed." He defends his actions to reporters by saying, "If you assume you can't trust the President, you're in trouble, and that's all there is to it."

In conference with his aides on April 16, the President asks them to invent scenarios that will let him claim credit for Magruder's decision to testify, explain why he removed Dean from the White House "investigation," and justify Haldeman's turning over $350,000 to LaRue for hush payments.

Ziegler warns that the *Washington Post* is preparing to crack the Watergate story wide open, implicating all of Nixon's top aides. He urges the President to beat the *Post* to the punch by persuading Petersen to let Nixon announce new results of "my investigation," to make it appear that the President is responsible for exposing the wrongdoing.

Hoping to save Haldeman and Ehrlichman, Nixon summons Dean and asks him to sign a letter of resignation which is a virtual confession. Dean refuses, insisting that if he resigns, so must Haldeman and Ehrlichman. When this ploy fails, Nixon tries to dictate what Dean will tell the grand jury.

"On this privilege thing," he tells Dean, "nothing is privileged that involves wrongdoing. . . . I am telling you that now, and I want you to testify . . . that the President told you that." He instructs further, "You are to say, 'I told the President first there was no involvement in the White House. . . . And the President said, "Look, I want to get to the bottom of this thing, period." ' See what I am driving at? . . . 'The President went out and investigated on his own. . . . And as a result of the President's actions this thing has been broken.' "

THE WHITE HOUSE
WASHINGTON

April 16, 1973

DESK COPY

Dear Mr. President:

You have informed me that Bob Haldeman and John Ehrlichman have verbally tendered their requests to be given an immediate and indefinite leave of absence from your staff. By this letter I also wish to confirm my similar request that I be given such a leave of absence from the staff.

Sincerely,

DESK COPY
Do Not Remove
From Senate Press Gallery

John W. Dean, III
Counsel to the President

Honorable Richard Nixon
The President of the United States
The White House
Washington, D. C. 20500

THE WHITE HOUSE
WASHINGTON

April 16, 1973

Dear Mr. President:

As a result of my involvement in the Watergate matter, which we discussed last night and today, I tender to you my resignation effective at once.

Sincerely,

The President
The White House
Washington, D. C.

John W. Dean refused to sign these letters of resignation and request for leave, but later offered them as exhibits to the Senate Watergate Committee.

But Nixon warns Dean not to say anything about wiretaps or reveal that he has disclosed to the President that White House aides were involved in Watergate in their talk almost four weeks earlier. Nixon cites executive privilege, national security, and the confidential lawyer-client relationship as grounds for Dean's silence on these points. In return, Nixon promises not to interfere with Dean's attempt to win immunity from the prosecutors for agreeing to testify.

Afterward, Nixon frets to his aides, "We have got to do something to restore the credibility of the Presidency." He adds with a sigh that once the press gets all the facts, "We are going to have one hell of a time."

He tries to stop the open Senate Watergate hearings that are scheduled to begin in a month by telling Petersen, "You've got to tell Senator Ervin that his continued investigation will jeopardize the rights of the defendants and also will jeopardize the possibilities of prosecution."

Pumping Petersen for new information from the prosecutors, the President repeats, "Of course, as you know, anything you tell me . . . will not be passed on." He learns that LaRue is pleading guilty to cover-up charges and that Dean has provided evidence linking Haldeman and Kalmbach to hush-money payoffs. Despite his pledge to Dean, Nixon presses Petersen not to let Dean become a witness for the prosecution in exchange for a promise of personal immunity.

Petersen is afraid that unless the prosecution names Haldeman and Ehrlichman as coconspirators with Magruder, "and it gets out, you know, it is going to look like a big cover-up again. . . . So we are trying to wrestle our way through that." If the Justice Department hasn't already done so, before Magruder testifies in court, "then we are all going to have a black eye."

Petersen also warns Nixon that newsmen have learned that "two or three people in the White House are going to be thrown to the wolves." Nixon says, "It's beginning to get out, yeah." The need to rush out a White House statement is imperative.

Knowing he can no longer save Haldeman and Ehrlichman from having to testify, the President tells Ehrlichman, "I think, frankly, let's get off the damned executive privilege." He decides to announce that all White House officials will appear before the Senate Watergate Committee in executive (private) session, but will reserve the right to refuse to answer some questions on grounds of executive privilege.

"At this point," Haldeman acknowledges, "the way we're in the soup, we can lose nothing by going."

On April 17 Nixon tells his two top aides that Colson is urging him to fire Dean. "I'm not ruling kicking him out," he declares. "But I think you got to figure—what to hell does Dean know? What kind of blackmail does he have? . . . He'd go out and say, 'Well, the President's covering up for Ehrlichman and Haldeman.' "

Haldeman is asked to keep Colson out of the Oval Office in the future because of Colson's links to the sleazy things being investigated. "I feel uneasy about that," Nixon admits.

He warns his aides to be careful not to commit perjury in any testimony they are forced to give. "I'm not talking about morality," he explains, "but I am talking about the vulnerabilities"—in other words, the dangers of being trapped in false testimony given under oath.

The three rehearse each other in the "scenario" answers they have agreed upon. They twist the President's discussion with Dean about hush money, so that Nixon's opinion it would be a tactical mistake to grant Hunt a pardon—"That would be wrong"—can be quoted instead as his response to the proposal to pay blackmail.

The President is hopeful they can ride out the storm. "If we handle it right," he observes, "the *Washington Post*'s stories on Watergate will soon be buried on page 19."

Heads Roll
at the White House

14

On April 17, when Petersen again talks to the President, Nixon warns him about granting immunity to Dean in exchange for his testimony. "The immunity thing scares me to death," he declares. Petersen admits, "It does me, too." Nixon asks, "What would you do if you were Mitchell?" Petersen replies, "I think I would probably go to Saudi Arabia."

Late that afternoon, hands trembling and looking wan, the President reads a televised statement to the press. He announces that he has changed his mind and will order his aides to testify before the Senate Watergate Committee because "on March 21st, as a result of serious charges which came to my attention, some of which were publicly reported, I began intensive new inquiries into this whole matter." Important facts have come to light about "which it would be improper to be more specific now, except to say that real progress has been made in finding the truth."

He insists, "I condemn any attempts to cover up in this case, no matter who is involved." Yet he opposes granting immunity from prosecution to any major Administration figure in exchange for his testimony against higher-ups. Reporters recall that in 1969 he had approved immunity for lower-rank criminals willing to squeal on bosses of the crime syndicate.

The President goes out of the room, leaving Ron Ziegler to

field questions from the press. His press secretary tries to put a bold front on the Administration's position toward what Ziegler once dismissed as a "third-rate burglary." He insists that there are no contradictions between the President's past statements and present announcement. Then which one, the reporters demand sarcastically, are they to believe and quote?

Ziegler swallows hard. "*This* is the operative statement," he finally replies. "The others are inoperative."

The newsmen are infuriated. Washington correspondent Clark Mollenhoff shouts, "Do you feel free to stand up there and lie and put out misinformation and then come around later and just say it's all *inoperative*? . . . You are not entitled to any credibility!"

When Ziegler doggedly insists that the President wants Watergate "thoroughly investigated," the reporters break out in derisive laughter. Their cynicism reflects the tide of disillusionment rolling across the country.

Next day Petersen phones the President to warn that the Senate Watergate Committee has called the FBI, asking to see FBI interview statements by Magruder, Porter, Sloan, and LaRue. The President groans, "Oh, my ——!" Petersen admits glumly, "I feel like I am sitting on a powder keg there."

What worries Petersen most of all is a statement by Dean implicating Hunt and Liddy in the break-in at Dr. Fielding's office. It is an obstruction of justice to conceal this information from Judge Byrne, because it is evidence vital to the trial of Daniel Ellsberg. When Petersen expresses this worry to Nixon on April 18, the President replies sharply, "I know about that. That's a national security matter. You stay out of that." He does not tell Petersen that this is the crime the White House has been paying Hunt blackmail to conceal.

Petersen relays Nixon's order to Silbert, who is told not to question Hunt about Dean's charge. But then Petersen anxiously consults Kleindienst, who agrees that they could all get in serious trouble by suppressing the Ellsberg information. They decide to see the President together and make him realize that Judge Byrne must be informed.

Sordid facts about the Watergate cover-up, leaking from grand jury testimony and the Senate Watergate investigators, multiply rapidly in the press, stunning the American people. The White House doggedly maintains that the President had known nothing about any cover-up by his aides.

"It is inconceivable to me," declares Republican Senator Edward Brooke on "Meet the Press," "that they would not have told the President about this matter [or] . . . asked for his approval or disapproval." A Jack Anderson column reveals that Strachan has testified that his boss Haldeman had controlled a secret cash slush fund of $350,000.

The Nixon Administration is in deep trouble. A Gallup poll reveals that 40 percent of the American people are now convinced that the President had known in advance about the plan to break into and bug the Democratic National Committee. Millions who believed in the integrity and abilities of Richard M. Nixon have had their confidence in him shaken.

How could their "law and order" candidate have permitted such behavior by his closest aides and associates? How could he have chosen such men as the leaders of his Administration? If he knew about the criminal acts going on around him and didn't stop them, shouldn't he be impeached? Or if he really didn't know, didn't that make him incredibly incompetent?

The revelations keep pouring out. The *Washington Post* reports that Colson warned the President about the cover-up in December 1972, four months earlier than Nixon has publicly claimed he knew. The *Post* also exposes the manipulation of public opinion by the White House and CRP to support Nixon's mining of Haiphong harbor in May 1972 by a fraudulent poll and telegram campaign.

Chairman George Bush of the Republican National Committee groans that Nixon and Watergate are ruining the party.

On April 19 Nixon expresses worry to Ehrlichman over what Dean is telling the prosecutors: "Don't know what the —— is going to say. That goddam Dean!" Ehrlichman suggests that they name Dean as the real mastermind of the cover-up and say that Nixon is the one who exposed him. "I suppose that really isn't true," the President replies, but agrees, "That's what we have to say."

Six days later Ehrlichman warns him, "It's entirely conceivable that if Dean is totally out of control and if matters are not handled adroitly that you could get a resolution of impeachment —" Nixon acknowledges, "That's right." Ehrlichman continues, "on the ground that you committed a crime." Nixon says again, "Right." Much depends on what Dean can prove was said in his meeting with Nixon in the Oval Office on March 21.

Ehrlichman, who later insists he didn't know that the White House was wired, suggests listening to a secret tape recording of that conversation. He tells the President that he had "better damn sure know . . . what your hole card is." Nixon gives the job to Haldeman. After listening to the tape, Haldeman reports that Nixon told Dean that Hunt had to be paid; that raising $1,000,000 in hush money would be easy enough, but granting clemency before the 1974 election "would be wrong"; and that the cap, in any case, had to be kept on the bottle.

Deeply worried, Nixon and his two chief aides devise a new scenario to explain these facts away. Haldeman suggests that the President had only been "drawing Dean out . . . smoking him out. . . . You're pumping him." Nixon replies "Yeah" to each suggestion, but then adds, "It's not a good story. Best we can. . . . Let me say, it's got to be you, Ehrlichman and I have got to put the wagons up around the President on this particular conversation."

Later on April 25, Nixon begins to worry that maybe while he was recording the conversation with Dean, Dean was secretly making his own recording with a miniature recorder hidden on his person. Perhaps he has already played that tape to the prosecutors. Nixon asks Haldeman if he can possibly check out this suspicion "surreptitiously or discreetly." Haldeman doesn't think so.

"That's a real bomb," Nixon worries. Haldeman believes the possibility is highly unlikely and that Dean would probably be testifying from memory. "Oh, well," Nixon says, "on that we'll destroy him. . . . It's his word against the President's." Nixon feels that the American people will want to believe him rather than Dean: "We'll survive. . . . There's still a hell of a lot of people out there, and from what I've seen . . . they want to believe. That's the point, isn't it?" Haldeman replies, "Why, sure. Want to, and do."

The Watergate dominoes continue to fall. On April 26 Jeb

Magruder is compelled to resign from the Department of Commerce, where it had been hoped to hide him away. On the same day Senator Lowell Weicker informs the press that Patrick Gray has confessed to burning the Hunt documents given him to destroy by Dean as "political dynamite." The scandal of the FBI acting director joining a White House conspiracy to conceal and destroy vital evidence for political reasons creates such an uproar that Gray is forced to resign next day.

Kleindienst and Petersen tell the President that he must notify Judge Byrne at once of the Ellsberg information, before it surfaces elsewhere and makes them all guilty of obstruction of justice. When Nixon balks, they threaten to resign. The President sulkily gives in.

On April 27 in Los Angeles, Judge Byrne reveals that the government has provided him with evidence of the Hunt-Liddy burglary of the office of Ellsberg's psychiatrist. He expresses indignation that this evidence in the Pentagon Papers trial has been concealed until now, and demands an investigation.

Ehrlichman is forced to admit to FBI agents on the same day that he ordered a "secret investigation" of the leak of the Pentagon Papers on the President's orders, which resulted in the break-in at Dr. Fielding's office. Ehrlichman denies any prior knowledge of either the break-in or the cover-up, but his affidavit implicates Egil Krogh as head of the Plumbers.

Petersen warns the President that he had better do something fast to convince the country he had nothing to do with the Watergate cover-up. He reports his assistants in the Department of Justice suspect him of revealing the evidence they uncovered to Nixon. He reassures the President that he told them, "We have to draw the line. We have no mandate to investigate the President. We investigate Watergate."

Nixon expresses concern over press reports that Dean is planning to implicate him personally in the cover-up.

"We've got to head them off at the pass," he warns Petersen, "because it's so damned dangerous to the Presidency. . . . If there's one thing you have got to do, you have got to maintain the Presidency out of this." He adds bitterly, "I sometimes feel like I'd like to resign. Let Agnew be President for a while. He'd love it." Nixon orders Petersen to tell him everything Dean says about him to the prosecutors, because he needs to know. "Yes, sir," says Petersen.

He reports back that Dean's lawyers are threatening to involve the President unless Dean is promised immunity. Nixon replies angrily, "All right. . . . Do it. . . . but boy, I am telling you—there ain't going to be any blackmail!"

But the prosecutors and Dean's lawyers can't agree on how much immunity he should be given, so Dean prepares to tell all. Petersen warns Nixon to lose no more time in getting rid of Dean, Haldeman, and Ehrlichman.

The President decides to gamble on a bold nationwide television broadcast. He must find phrases that will persuade the American people that he is innocent of all wrongdoing; that whatever crimes were committed were done without his knowledge; and that he is cooperating fully with every effort to bring out the whole truth.

On April 30 he sets the stage at his desk with a bust of Lincoln on one side, a picture of his family on the other, and the American flag behind, symbolizing his virtues as a disciple of Lincolnian honesty, a family man, and a patriot.

Speaking over all networks simultaneously, he promises, "Justice will be pursued, fairly, fully and impartially, no matter who is involved." He announces that he has accepted the resignations of "two of my closest associates in the White House—Bob Haldeman, John Ehrlichman—two of the finest public servants it has been my privilege to know."

He also announces the resignation of Richard Kleindienst— "a distinguished public servant"—as Attorney General, to be replaced by Elliot Richardson, who will have the power to appoint a special prosecutor for Watergate should he deem one is needed. And the President adds the curt statement, "The Counsel to the President, John Dean, has also resigned."

He insists again that in his preoccupation with foreign affairs he left campaign decisions and operations to others. It would be "cowardly," he asserts, to blame Watergate on "people whose zeal exceeded their judgment, and who may have done wrong in a cause they deeply believed to be right." The President then accepts a vague "responsibility" as the "man at the top."

He pledges to bring all the guilty to justice, and to see that such misdeeds never again occur.

He has not been trying to cover up the truth, Nixon insists, but only to learn it. He conducted his own "investigation" to learn if any White House members were involved, and he believed "repeated assurances that there were not." So, "I discounted the stories in the press that appeared to implicate members of my Administration or other officials of the campaign committee." He claims not to have learned the facts until Dean told them to him on March 21, at which time he ordered a new investigation, directing all White House and CRP officials to tell the truth.

To appear credible, Nixon is forced to admit what everyone now knows—that the truth about Watergate has emerged primarily because of two forces he has bitterly assailed in private, "a courageous judge, John Sirica, and a vigorous free press." He ends by appealing to his listeners' religious and patriotic emotions: "I love America. . . . God bless America, and God bless each and every one of you."

In many respects the speech is a replay of the Checkers speech, which rescued him from disaster in 1954. But this time he badly disappoints his believers who hoped he would settle all their doubts. The President has answered no questions about Watergate and has told nothing of what he knows about it. Forced to accept the resignation of his two top aides, he has dismissed them with words of ringing praise.

It is not lost on the American people that the list of banished knights from the Nixon court now includes Mitchell, Chapin, Mardian, Colson, Sloan, LaRue, Magruder, Haldeman, Ehrlichman, Kleindienst, and Dean. Can so many of his trusted intimates have been touched by scandal, leaving the President alone wholly innocent?

Yet in his speech he asks the American people to believe, "There had been an effort to conceal the facts both from the public—from you—and from me."

Afterward, the President is heard to mutter a tearful aside: "It wasn't easy." He then appears in the White House press room to humble himself before those he has so often denounced. "We have had our differences in the past," he tells reporters meekly, "and I hope you give me hell every time you think I'm wrong."

Vice-President Agnew follows his lead by admitting that maybe he had been too "abrasive" in his attacks on the press. A glum Ron Ziegler apologizes publicly to Bob Woodward and Carl Bernstein for having reviled them and their disclosures about Watergate in the *Washington Post*. The news media has been vindicated in its charges that the Administration was deeply involved in criminal acts, had systematically lied about it, and had tried to persuade the public that the whole Watergate affair was the invention of reporters biased against the President. The Administration's accusations of "slanted news" will no longer work.

A Gallup poll taken after the speech shows that public confidence in the President is crumbling fast. Fully 50 percent are now convinced that he took part in the cover-up, and 30 percent believe that he ought to be impeached.

"Right now," admits Senator Robert Dole, former Republican national chairman, "the credibility of the Administration is zilch, zero." Dole blames the arrogant, power-mad aides with whom Nixon chose to surround himself.

Among those shocked by the revelations of White House conversations is jailed Howard Hunt, who determines to turn on Nixon and "come clean." He later testifies against the President's top aides at the Watergate cover-up trial. "I read the President's contemptuous references to those of us who had gone to prison as 'idiots' and 'jackasses.' I realized that there had been a wild scramble going on for months in the White House to protect themselves and very little thought had been given to our plight."

On May 1 the Senate, indicating lack of faith in the investigation conducted by the Justice Department, approves a resolution drafted by Illinois Republican Charles Percy that a special prosecutor be appointed to probe Watergate. The Senate Judiciary Committee makes it clear that Richardson's appointment as Attorney General will not be confirmed unless he agrees and guarantees total independence to the special prosecutor.

More heads roll at the White House. On May 9 the two original chiefs of the Plumbers, Egil Krogh and David Young, resign along with Gordon Strachan, Haldeman's aide. Donald Segretti is indicted in Florida for illegal dirty tricks that sabotaged the 1972 Democratic primary campaigns in that state.

Dean charges that his one-time White House colleagues are "out to get me." He gives Judge Sirica the keys to his safe-deposit box, which contains nine secret documents on Watergate he had removed from White House files to prevent their "illegal destruction." The White House rushes out a regulation forbidding the publication of classified information.

Nixon tries to restore respectability to his discredited Administration by naming new aides untainted by Watergate. Dean is replaced by Leonard Garment, a lawyer with liberal credentials. General Alexander Haig, Jr., takes over Haldeman's job. Former Treasury Secretary John B. Connally, who has recently become a Republican, joins the staff as special adviser. J. Fred Buzhardt, Jr., is appointed White House special counsel for Watergate matters. The public is given the impression that the President will no longer be isolated by a palace guard like Haldeman and Ehrlichman but will run an "open administration."

On May 9 the investigation of the government's handling of the Pentagon Papers case, ordered by Judge Byrne, compels the government to admit that FBI wiretaps had illegally monitored some Ellsberg phone conversations. Byrne immediately halts the trial and orders that the FBI produce the wiretap records to determine how many of the government's charges are based on illegally gathered evidence and whether anything on the wiretaps indicates Ellsberg's innocence.

Petersen lamely explains that the wiretap logs have disappeared from FBI files. Outraged, Judge Byrne dismisses all charges against Ellsberg and codefendant Anthony Russo on May 11, because of "improper government conduct." One hour later Ehrlichman informs FBI agents that the wiretap records, delivered secretly to the Oval Office at the President's direction, can be found in Ehrlichman's White House safe.

It is now too late for them to become part of the public record, revealing the political nature of the wiretaps which the President had ordered for "national security."

Alexander M. Haig, Jr. (left) succeeded H. R. Haldeman as White House chief of staff, and J. Fred Buzhardt (right) was appointed special counsel for Watergate matters.

"The President has led a conspiracy . . . against the American people," Ellsberg charges, and announces that he intends to file a multimillion-dollar civil damage suit.

To make the President's cup even more bitter, the annual

Pulitzer Prize award had been bestowed on the *Washington Post* for the remarkable, relentless exposure of Watergate by its two young reporters, Carl Bernstein and Bob Woodward.

"People are saying this is the finest hour for investigative journalism," Woodward had told a cheering throng, "but there's much more the press should have done, and so much more to do." All the news media are now ready to do it as the Senate Watergate Committee begins its televised public hearings with a dramatic cast of Watergate witnesses.

Daniel J. Ellsberg and his wife, Patricia, at the Federal Courthouse in Los Angeles after charges against Ellsberg and Russo are dismissed.

During the thirty-seven days the hearings dominate the news of the nation, they are followed daily on television by an estimated twenty-five million Americans.

"White House Horror Stories"

15

$\mathbf{F}$or many weeks now the legal staff of the Senate Watergate Committee, the Select Committee on Presidential Campaign Activities of 1972 as it is officially named, has been interviewing witnesses in closed session, preparatory to the public hearings in Room 315 of the Old Senate Office Building. While the public hearings go on, the staff continues to question later witnesses behind the scenes.

Chairman Sam Ervin, who likes to call himself "just an old country lawyer," gavels the first public televised hearing to order on May 17, 1973. The Watergate Committee consists of four Democrats—Chairman Ervin, Daniel Inouye of Hawaii, Joseph Montoya of New Mexico, and Herman Talmadge of Georgia; and three Republicans—Howard Baker, Jr., of Tennessee, Edward Gurney of Florida, and Lowell Weicker, Jr., of Connecticut.

Ervin begins by underscoring the gravity of the hearings, pointing out that those responsible for Watergate have been "stealing not the jewels, money, or other property of American citizens, but something much more valuable—their precious heritage, the right to vote in a free election."

The first witness, former CRP office manager Robert Odle, reveals that the White House gave CRP most of its orders, relayed through Haldeman's aide Strachan. Odle states that

171

Sam J. Ervin, Jr., and Howard H. Baker, Jr., chairman and ranking Republican member of the Senate Watergate Committee.

Mitchell made major campaign decisions while still Attorney General, which Mitchell has denied under oath.

James McCord testifies on the Watergate burglary and bugging operations. He says, "I felt the President of the United

May 17, 1973. The first day of public hearings of the Senate Watergate Committee.

The first witness, Robert C. Odle, displays an organizational chart of the CRP.

States had set into motion this operation." Describing John J. Caulfield's attempts to bribe him into silence after the arrests, he says he was told that the offer came "from the very highest levels of the White House."

On May 18 Elliot Richardson names Professor Archibald Cox of the Harvard Law School as special Watergate prosecutor. Nixon consents, confident that he can control and limit Cox, just as he manipulated the Justice Department under Mitchell and then Kleindienst. Richardson guarantees that Cox will have total independence and immunity from dismissal except for "extraordinary improprieties."

Cox makes it clear that *his* investigation will be thorough, honest, and impervious to White House influence. "Somehow," he tells the press, "we must restore confidence in the honor, integrity, and decency of government."

John Caulfield follows McCord as a witness before the Senate committee. Senator Montoya asks him how he interpreted Dean's assignment to carry an offer of cash and clemency to McCord from "way at the top." Caulfield replies, "In my mind I believed he was talking about the President."

White House spokesmen insist that the President is ignoring the hearings, but subsequently admit that he keeps his television set on constantly, giving full attention to crucial testimony. On May 22 he issues a statement intended to counteract damaging evidence emerging against him. "At no time did I attempt, or did I authorize others to attempt, to implicate the CIA in Watergate matters," he asserts. But, he concedes, "With hindsight it is apparent that I should have given more heed to the warning signals I received along the way about a Watergate cover-up and less to the reassurances." He acknowledges that he ordered a series of wiretaps between 1969 and 1971, but insists that these were only to prevent leaks of secret information on foreign policy.

Henry S. Ruth, deputy special prosecutor, with a chart of the Special Watergate Prosecution Force.

He concedes approving the Huston plan to spy on and burglarize domestic radicals, but claims he rescinded it after J. Edgar Hoover opposed it. He admits having set up the Plumbers to stop such leaks as publication of the Pentagon Papers, but denies having given Krogh authority to break into Dr. Fielding's office.

The press quickly points out inconsistencies in the President's statement. If, as he claims, he needed his own private spy system because the FBI under Hoover was undependable, why did he continue to keep Hoover in office? If Nixon was concerned enough to create the secret Plumbers unit, why later was he so little concerned as not to ask what it was accomplishing?

Why had the President concealed the evidence of the Ellsberg break-in from Judge Byrne for over a month while tempting Byrne with the FBI directorship in the midst of the trial? Why did the President try to get Gray to stop FBI agents from investigating the Mexican money-laundering operation, stating that it might compromise CIA operations, without even asking Helms and Walters if this were so?

"The President found it necessary to issue a few thousand words of cover-up rhetoric," observes former Senator Wayne Morse of Oregon, "in an attempt to fool the American people into believing that he must have been running his office in a fog so thick he did not know that Ehrlichman, Haldeman, Dean, Mitchell, Stans, Colson, Kleindienst, Krogh, Magruder, Young, Hunt, Liddy, Kalmbach—yes, and Kissinger, too—were using police-state surveillance methods on many persons to accomplish his political ends."

Bernard L. Barker, leader of the Cuban Watergate burglars, testifies in the Senate that Hunt, whom he reveres as a leader, told him the Ellsberg and Watergate break-ins were "a matter of national security." He is asked, "Whom did you think you were working for?" Barker replies plaintively, "Sir, I was not there to think. I was there to follow orders, not to think."

Alfred Baldwin, the Watergate lookout, is asked by Senator Weicker why he did not question the legality of the break-in of the DNC. Baldwin explains that since he was working for the White House and the former Attorney General, he assumed the operation must be legal.

Nixon's popularity is dropping sharply. By late May the Gallup poll shows his public support down to 45 percent, the lowest rating since he took office in 1968. At a Republican fund-raising dinner Nixon reminds the party faithful that he is used to crises and always rises above them: "The finest steel has to go through the hottest fires."

But Republican Senator Charles Percy now leads a movement to divorce the party from the President and Watergate. He tours the country telling crowds that Watergate "is an outrage to decent men everywhere . . . and I am one of them." Nixon fights back by inviting top Republican leaders to the White House.

On May 30 Justice Department prosecutors tell Silbert that they have new evidence to justify calling the President himself before the grand jury. Ziegler quickly announces that Nixon will not answer any prosecution questions about Watergate because it would be "constitutionally inappropriate."

The New York Times and the *Washington Post* report that between late January and April, Dean had numerous discussions about Watergate with the President. The White House retaliates by stating that the press is trying to discredit Nixon by "innuendo, distortion of fact, and outright falsehood. . . . We categorically deny the assertions and implications of this story."

On June 4 the President spends a full twelve hours listening privately to ten tape recordings of his conversations with Dean, made without Dean's knowledge, to see what might be compromising.

The next Ervin committee witness is Sally Harmony, Gordon Liddy's former secretary. She admits typing up wiretap conversations on Gemstone stationery; seeing photos of private Democratic National Committee documents; forging the name of Gary Hart, McGovern's campaign director, on a pass to McGovern headquarters; and shredding all her notebooks at Liddy's order.

Magruder's former aide, Robert Reisner, testifies that Magruder discussed Gemstone wiretaps with Mitchell before the June 17 break-in at Watergate. Hugh Sloan, the former treasurer of CRP, implicates Mitchell and Stans in the payments to Liddy for Gemstone, and Magruder in the attempt to get Sloan to

Hugh W. Sloan, Jr. (right), with his lawyers.

commit perjury on the amount and purpose. Sloan reveals that he told all this to the prosecutors soon after the Watergate arrests, but they simply ignored his disclosures.

Sloan says of the Nixon Administration, "There was no independent sense of morality there. I mean if you worked for someone, he was God, and whatever the orders were, you did it—and there were damned few who were able to make, or willing to make, independent judgments."

Herbert Porter, CRP's former scheduling director, admits that at Magruder's instigation he lied to the FBI, the grand jury, and the Watergate trial jury about how the money given to Liddy was spent. Asked by Senator Baker why he had done this, Porter replies that he was afraid not to be a "team player." "I was not the one to stand up in a meeting and say that this should be stopped. . . . I kind of drifted along," he says.

Maurice Stans, who has been indicted with John Mitchell on May 10 on charges of conspiracy and perjury in the Vesco affair testifies in the Senate hearings on June 9 that he was neither curious nor suspicious when $114,000 in back-door campaign contributions were found to have been funneled through Barker's Miami bank account or when Sloan told him of Magruder's demand that Sloan join Porter in lying about the Liddy payments.

"I did not have time for any curiosity," Stans explains. He claims he was unaware of these payments, and he "cannot recall" a request from Kalmbach for a large sum of cash after the Watergate arrests. Stans also insists that his destruction of some CRP financial records after the break-in had nothing to do with any cover-up.

"So you think it is kind of normal . . . to destroy those records," Senator Ervin demands, "after five men are caught in an act of burglary with money that came from the committee in their pockets?"

Jeb Magruder, the next witness, tells the whole story of Gemstone from its approval by Mitchell up to the attempted cover-ups. Involving almost everyone at the top of the Nixon Administration, his testimony conflicts with that of Stans, confirms that Mitchell knew of the Gemstone plot as Attorney General, and identifies Dean as the general director of the cover-up. Magruder reveals that he informed Haldeman all about the cover-up in January 1973, two months earlier than Haldeman admits to knowing about it, and that he told Haldeman he intended to lie to the grand jury.

"So Mr. Haldeman knew that perjury was going to be committed?" asks Senator Weicker.

"Yes, I think that would be correct."

By this time the ability of the government to function is clearly impaired by Watergate. Former Defense Secretary Melvin Laird, brought out of retirement to replace Ehrlichman, laments, "Government in some quarters is at a standstill. This cannot be allowed to continue." Nixon supporters demand that the Watergate hearings be cut short in the national interest.

But the latest Gallup poll, one year after the Watergate break-in, shows that two out of three Americans now believe that

Jeb Stuart Magruder and his wife listen as Maurice Stans testifies.

the President either knew about Watergate in advance or about the cover-up. More and more cars pass by the White House bearing bumper stickers that read HONK IF YOU THINK HE'S GUILTY. Comedians, once fearful of blacklisting if they satirized Nixon, no longer abstain. Black comic Dick Gregory sends the President a telegram thanking him "for not having any blacks in his administration."

On the floor of the House of Representatives, liberal Republican Paul N. McCloskey, Jr., proposes that the House consider impeachment of the President.

A haggard Nixon seeks to fight back by making public appearances before carefully selected audiences in the South and Midwest, where he feels he still has strong support. In Orlando, Florida, he urges Americans "to talk about what is right about this country," not what is wrong with it. His supporters argue that all politicians do crooked things and that Nixon's trouble was simply that he and his crowd got caught. Some call Nixon a good President "who got mixed up with the wrong people."

The Senate Watergate Committee suspends the hearings for a week, during the visit of Soviet party leader Leonid Brezhnev, so that the President will not be embarrassed by them during important foreign policy consultations.

On June 25 John Dean finally appears in public hearings. Like Magruder, he has been granted immunity from prosecution for any testimony he gives before the Senate Watergate Committee but not before the grand jury. In thirty hours of testimony he delivers the most damning indictment yet. He begins by reading a six-hour statement, pausing only occasionally for a sip of water. Describing the cover-up conspiracy in great detail, he drones out names, dates, and places.

Dean testifies that Watergate resulted from a "siege mentality" that pervaded the White House, stemming from a highly insecure President's dread of antiwar and anti-Nixon demonstrations. Nixon, Dean alleges, was prepared to go to all lengths to stifle opposition. Obsessed with proving that the demonstrators were sponsored by either foreign governments or the Democrats, the President became infuriated with the FBI and CIA for not finding a "scintilla of viable evidence" to justify his suspicions of a master plan against him.

Dean reveals that Nixon had an excessive concern about news leaks to the media, and was convinced that only a private White House force could gather the needed intelligence against his foes. So he set up his own secret group, the Plumbers, to conduct clandestine political operations.

The nation is even more shocked when Dean produces the White House "enemies list" of eminent Americans in business, the academic world, politics, the arts, labor, the media, and civic betterment, and describes the President's attempts to punish them illegally through misuse of the FBI and IRS.

As far as Dean knows, Nixon took part in the cover-up for eight months, despite constant public denials. Dean flatly contradicts seven statements made by the President about Watergate, the cover-up, the Fielding break-in, and wiretaps. He

June 25, 1973. John W. Dean III begins his thirty hours of testimony.

denies that Nixon ever ordered him to make a real investigation of wrongdoing in the White House and CRP. His assigned role, Dean reveals, was only to find out what the FBI and Justice Department were discovering, so that plausible "scenarios" could be invented to cover up the truth.

Ziegler is forced to admit to the press that Nixon had never directly ordered or received an in-house investigation of Watergate or the cover-up from Dean, despite his two previous statements to the American people that he had. Now Ziegler tells reporters that Nixon had made this request to Ehrlichman, who subsequently told the President that Dean had cleared the White House staff of any complicity.

Dean's damning testimony as former counsel to the President is not without its vulnerabilities, despite a stack of documents and memoranda he introduces to support it. He sets the date he told Nixon of Hunt's demand for hush money as March 13, 1973, eight days too early. And he is compelled to confess that he dipped into campaign cash to finance his honeymoon, although he claims to have replaced it at the time with his personal check.

On June 27, special White House counsel J. Fred Buzhardt sends the Senate Watergate Committee highly detailed questions for a "cross-examination" of Dean. Senator Daniel K. Inouye agrees to ask them. Dean's answers are so prompt, firm, and documented that the Buzhardt attempt to discredit him turns out, in *Newsweek*'s term, "a near disaster." Nixon at once announces that he never approved it, nor does it represent his position on either Dean or Watergate.

Senator Ervin asks Dean whether Nixon wanted him, Haldeman, or Ehrlichman to testify before the committee. Dean replies, "He certainly did not." Ervin then points out, "And this was . . . about a month *after* Mr. Buzhardt says that the President was anxious for all the facts to be revealed. Do you know how facts can be revealed except by people who know something about those facts?"

Senator Weicker denounces the Administration for committing "illegal, unconstitutional and gross acts." Such behavior, he declares, is a total violation of his party's principles. "Republicans do *not* cover up, Republicans do *not* threaten, Republicans do *not* commit illegal acts. And God knows, Republicans don't view their fellow Americans as enemies to be harassed!" The spectators at the hearing burst into forbidden applause.

Later Colson visits Weicker's office to dispute the senator's charges that the White House had tried to intimidate him. Weicker snaps, "You make me sick, and I don't even want you in here. You can just get . . . out of my office!"

On June 27, Frederick LaRue, Mitchell's former senior assistant at CRP, pleads guilty to a single count of felony on a conspiracy charge, having agreed to turn state's evidence. Asked whether Mitchell rejected the Liddy Gemstone plan at Key Biscayne "out of hand," as Mitchell claims, LaRue tells counsel for the Senate Watergate Committee, "Not to my recollection, no sir."

Senator Lowell P. Weicker, Jr.

The Watergate hearings have so weakened the President's prestige that his support in Congress slips badly. On July 1 Congress votes to deny him the use of any funds for bombing in Cambodia and Laos. It is the first time in the nation's history that Congress has ever used its powers to stop a President from waging an undeclared war.

This spillover of Watergate into foreign policy handicaps Special Advisor Henry Kissinger in his negotiations with other countries. Not only does he represent a President whose conduct is under suspicion, but an angry Congress is showing it may reject his foreign-policy measures.

Nixon's public image is further damaged by the admission of the General Services Administration (GSA) in late June that it erred in its estimate that only $39,525 of taxpayers' money had gone into improving the President's lavish estate at San Clemente, California. The real figure, the GSA now concedes, was $703,367, with another $1,200,000 spent on his Key Biscayne home. These figures are later revised again to a total of $20,000,000, including the cost of security installations.

After the Dean testimony, some conservative columnists feel they can no longer continue to support Nixon.

"To continue to believe that President Nixon was wholly innocent of any involvement in the Watergate cover-up," Stewart Alsop writes, "requires, by this time, a major act of faith. . . . If Dean was lying, his lie was the most complex, the most detailed, the most carefully prepared, in the long history of lies. . . . If the Buzhardt memorandum is the President's best defense, then the President has no defense. . . . The picture of the inner Administration that emerges from the testimony . . . is a picture of a nest of vipers."

Both Senator Ervin and Special Prosecutor Cox ask the President to permit access to presidential papers necessary to the investigation. Ervin also wants him to testify before the Senate Committee. Nixon refuses, insisting that either course would "violate my constitutional responsibility to defend the office of the Presidency against encroachment by other branches." Three months earlier he promised the American people, "We will cooperate fully with the Senate . . . [in] the Watergate matter."

But at the same time he places in the hands of a private citizen the evidence he will not disclose to Congress. Even though Haldeman is no longer a government employee, Nixon has him listen secretly at home to several tapes of the President's conversations with Dean. Neither the Senate Watergate Committee nor the special prosecutor, nor Judge Sirica nor the grand jury nor the public suspects that such evidence exists.

When John Mitchell testifies on July 10, he makes constant, emphatic denials of charges against him: "In no way, shape or manner of form whatever, no sir!" He insists that he never authorized the Liddy Gemstone plan or the Watergate break-in nor ordered incriminating documents destroyed. He refers to all the illegal and unsavory things that went on in the Nixon Administration as "White House horror stories," and indicates that others, not he, were responsible.

He explains his failure to expose or stop the cover-up by the fact that 1972 was an election year: "It occurred to me that the best thing to do was just to keep the lid on." He implicates Haldeman and Ehrlichman but declares that Nixon had not known about the cover-up. Committee counsel Samuel Dash asks

Mitchell why, as Nixon's old friend, law partner, Attorney General, and then manager of his campaign, he hadn't informed the President. Mitchell replies that if he had, Nixon might have "lowered the boom" on his aides, and the resulting scandal would have doomed the President's re-election.

Hadn't the President asked Mitchell *anything* about the conspiracy, even after Dean told Nixon that Mitchell was

John N. Mitchell pauses in his account of the "White House horror stories."

involved? No, Mitchell claims, but if the President *had* asked him, he would have recited "chapter and verse."

"If the cat hadn't any more curiosity than *that*," drawls Sam Ervin, "it would still be enjoying its nine lives—all of them!"

Mitchell's testimony contradicts that of half a dozen earlier witnesses, and his own word under oath elsewhere. Dash asks him bluntly, "Since you may have given false testimony under oath on prior occasions, is there really any reason . . . to believe your testimony before this committee?"

Mitchell admits that he had listened to Liddy propose the Gemstone plan in his office while he was still Attorney General. Dash asks why he hadn't thrown Liddy out of the office. Mitchell growls that "in hindsight" he "should have thrown him out the window." But he is unable to explain why Liddy's plan was brought back to him two more times, or who had authorized it if he hadn't.

Senator Talmadge asks if Mitchell hadn't placed winning re-election for Nixon above his obligation to inform the President that top aides were involved in crime, perjury, and obstruction of justice. "Senator," Mitchell replies blandly, "I think you have put it exactly correct."

To explain his earlier statement to the FBI that he had known nothing about Watergate, Mitchell says it was the policy of those in the cover-up "not to volunteer anything." Dash puts it more bluntly: "If you do not volunteer an answer to a direct question . . . actually you are lying." Weicker compels Mitchell to admit that he also violated his oath as a lawyer and former Attorney General by failing to report his knowledge of the break-in of Dr. Fielding's office.

As Mitchell finishes his testimony, he mutters bitterly, "It's a great little trial being conducted up here, isn't it?"

16

The President's Secret Tapes

Another cover-up by the Nixon Administration is exposed on July 13 at a different Senate hearing before the Armed Services Committee. Former Air Force Major Hal Knight, Jr., testifies that on Nixon's orders, the United States Air Force violated Cambodia's neutrality by conducting 3,630 bombing raids and filing false reports about them that were used to deceive the Senate and the American people. Knight admits that 102 U.S. servicemen listed as killed in South Vietnam actually lost their lives in the illegal raids on Cambodia and Laos.

An outraged House of Representatives passes a bill to restrict the presidential power to wage war in the future without the prior approval of Congress.

Reporter Bob Woodward gets a tip from his White House source that Alexander P. Butterfield has highly important secret information about his former job as Haldeman's assistant, and ought to be interviewed by the Ervin committee investigators. Woodward informs chief counsel Samuel Dash, and Butterfield is questioned in executive session on July 13.

Republican counsel Donald Sanders is curious about the exact quotations from conversations between the President and Dean used in the memo Buzhardt sent to the Senate Watergate Committee for use in cross-examining Dean. How could Nixon's memory of talks that took place months ago be so precise?

"Is there any validity," he asks Butterfield casually, "to Dean's public speculation that the President was trying to avoid being overheard by a tape recorder when he supposedly took Dean off to a side of the room to talk about discussing clemency with Colson?"

"I was wondering if someone would ask that," Butterfield replies unhappily. He reveals that the President has had installed a system of bugging and taping all phone calls and personal conversations, in his Oval Office, the office in the Executive Office Building, the Lincoln Room in the White House, and Camp David, preserving the tapes as an oral record.

The electronic eavesdropping system was installed by the Secret Service in mid-1970 and has been maintained and checked regularly ever since. The recording devices are started automatically by the sound of voices. Their existence is known only to Butterfield and his replacement, Stephen Bull; Haldeman and Haldeman's former aide Lawrence Higby; a few Secret Service men; Alexander Haig; and the President of the United States.

"I realize . . . the fantastic significance of the information I have given you," Butterfield tells the Ervin committee investigators. "If you had it before, fine. If you haven't had it before, I hope you handle it awfully carefully." The amazing news is relayed to Senator Ervin, who orders that Butterfield must give his testimony in the public hearings.

"I won't appear," Butterfield insists. When Ervin is told, he raises his distinctive white eyebrows and observes, "If he isn't in my office at 12:30, I will have law-enforcement officers come and get him."

Butterfield testifies. His revelations stun Congress, the nation, and the world. Everyone now knows that for three years every caller on the President, and everyone speaking to him on the phone—American official or foreign head of state—has had what he assumed to be a private conversation recorded on tape without his knowledge.

The Ervin committee and Special Prosecutor Archibald Cox at once ask access to certain tapes for proof of—in Senator Baker's words—"what the President knew, and when he knew it." It is now clear that Nixon has been deliberately sitting on

Alexander P. Butterfield,
assistant to Haldeman, revealed
the existence of the White House
tapes.

hard evidence vital to the investigations of the Senate Watergate
Committee and the grand jury.

The President refuses to turn over any of the tapes, insisting that this would violate his constitutional duty to protect the executive branch of government from encroachment by the legislative and judicial branches. The press suggests a less lofty reason: the tapes may bear out Dean's charges. Both the Ervin committee and Cox issue subpoenas for them.

Surprisingly, Nixon is not alarmed into destroying the tapes. One reason is that he prizes them as "an oral history for the Nixon Library" of his years in the White House. Carefully screened and edited later, they will help historians of the Nixon Administration. Besides, his tax lawyers advise him that selected tapes can be donated later to the national archives, with huge deductions for them taken off his income tax. Finally, Nixon is confident of keeping the tapes in his own custody as his "own property," as well as on grounds of "presidential confidentiality."

This fatal mistake, compounded of vanity, greed, and miscalculation, is to prove the President's undoing.

Herbert Kalmbach, the next witness, testifies on July 16 that under instructions from Dean he raised $220,000 for the seven Watergate defendants and distributed it through Ulasewicz. Admitting that he now recognizes this to have been "an improper, illegal" act, he says that when it first dawned on him he was serving as a conduit for paying blackmail, it was "just as if I had been kicked in the stomach. . . . I feel that I was used."

Ulasewicz tells about his role as "bagman," relating that he suggested to Kalmbach that they quit when Hunt's wife began to demand more and more money for herself, Hunt, and the other defendants. Although Ulasewicz provokes laughter by his droll description of his activities, Senator Weicker is not amused. He compels Ulasewicz to admit that his investigations for the White House included snooping on the drinking and sexual habits, domestic problems, and social activities of Nixon's political opponents.

"I think what we see here," Weicker observes somberly, "is not a joke, but a great tragedy."

Frederick LaRue testifies that he believed that authority for the Watergate break-in had come from "some high level." He admits having taken over distribution of the payoffs from Kalmbach, giving out $230,000 more, and checking the final payment with John Mitchell.

Robert Mardian tells the Senate Watergate Committee on July 19 that Liddy told him authorization for the break-in at Dr. Fielding's office came from the President. He verifies that Mitchell approved a $250,000 budget for Liddy's Gemstone operation.

Senator Ervin observes that the testimony he has heard so far reveals a definite conspiracy "to pollute justice." He expresses outrage that "men upon whom fortune had smiled benevolently, and who possessed great financial power, great political power and great governmental power, undertook to nullify the laws of man and the laws of God for what history will call a very temporary political advantage."

The outbreak of applause that greets the chairman indicates that his handling of the Watergate hearing is making him a new folk hero. "Uncle Sam" Ervin fan clubs begin springing up all over the country. He is seen as a wise, honest, and decent American dedicated to upholding the Constitution and the Bill of Rights, in sharp contrast to the lawless and conspiratorial behavior of the President and his men.

Gordon Strachan testifies that he reported Mitchell's approval to Haldeman a month before the first Watergate break-in. He admits destroying this memo and other political intelligence documents right after the arrests on Haldeman's orders. Haldeman says subsequently he "cannot recall" either allegation. Strachan also indicates his belief that Haldeman would have promptly reported any knowledge he had of the break-in to Nixon.

Many Watergate witnesses acknowledge that "in hindsight" they realize their actions were wrong. Senator Ervin sighs, "Sometimes I wish that people were not like lightning bugs, which carry their illumination behind them."

John Ehrlichman testifies belligerently, denying every allegation of wrongdoing on his part and defending the President as totally innocent. When he cannot explain away an incriminating fact, he "stonewalls" by saying firmly, "I have no such recollection of that."

Forced to admit that he ordered Kalmbach to continue payoffs to the Watergate Seven, he shrugs off such payments as "a commonplace of American life." Denying that either he or

Nixon authorized the Dr. Fielding break-in, he insists the order would nevertheless have been within the President's constitutional authority in protecting "national security."

Senator Ervin recalls a statement by William Pitt about the sanctity of the poorest man's home against government invasion: "It may be frail, the storm may enter, the rain may enter, but the King of England cannot enter." Ervin adds dryly, "And yet we are told here today that what the King of England can't do, the President of the United States can."

Senator Talmadge asks Ehrlichman whether the President's power to protect national security might also extend to other crimes, including murder. Ehrlichman replies coolly, "I do not know where the line [to be drawn] is, Senator."

His answers are so evasive that committee counsel Samuel Dash tells him in exasperation, "If the answer is no, say no. If the

John N. Ehrlichman is sworn in.

answer is yes, say yes." But when the committee tries to draw
Ehrlichman out on the operations of the Plumbers, he refuses to
reply on grounds of executive privilege. He defends Nixon's right
to have ordered the FBI not to investigate this "sensitive" area of
"national security."

Ehrlichman sees nothing wrong in the White House's spying
on political opponents for "dirt," insisting that the public has a
right to know about the morals of candidates. He denies that
either he or the President had any intention of bribing Judge
Byrne with the FBI directorship at a time when they knew Dean
was about to expose the break-in at Dr. Fielding's office.

He denies ever discussing clemency for Hunt with the
President, pressuring the CIA into stopping the FBI investigation
of laundered Mexican money, or conspiring to make Mitchell
the "fall guy" for Watergate.

At one point his denials, in the face of overwhelming
previous testimony to the contrary, are too much for Senator
Inouye, who mutters to an aide, "What a liar!" This remark is
picked up by a live microphone to Inouye's embarrassment, and
he apologizes for it. But Senator Talmadge tells Ehrlichman,
"It's hard to believe that a man of your intelligence could have
been involved in so much complicated complicity and know
nothing about it."

In his five days of testimony before television cameras at the
public hearings, Ehrlichman makes statements under oath that
sharply conflict with those of other key figures—Dean, Walters,
Helms, Kleindienst, Petersen, Mitchell, Magruder, Mardian,
and Kalmbach.

Ehrlichman is followed as a witness by Nixon's former chief
of staff, the short-haired, quiet-mannered H. R. Haldeman. He
supports Ehrlichman's claim that the President is innocent and
was "badly misled" by Dean. Stating that he has listened to the
tape of the conversation on March 21 in which Dean told Nixon
about Hunt's demand for hush money, Haldeman asserts that
the President replied, "There is no problem in raising a million
dollars; we can do that, but it would be wrong."

Like Ehrlichman's, Haldeman's memory is selective. He
evades dangerous questions by answering "I can't remember" or
"I don't know" some 150 times. He "doesn't recall" seeing a

*Senator Daniel K. Inouye
questions Ehrlichman, whose
calendar is in the background,
and then mutters, "What a liar!"*

memo prepared for him on how to use the Internal Revenue Service as a weapon against Nixon's enemies. He denies that Magruder told him the truth about Watergate early in 1973 and that he knew in advance of Magruder's intention to commit perjury.

Admitting that he authorized the expenditure of $90,000 for "black projects" directed by Charles Colson, he maintains he had no idea what these were all about. But he acknowledges that as an Administration counteroffensive in February 1972, he ordered propaganda spread that foreign or Communist money was behind the antiwar demonstrations, McGovern, and the Democratic campaign. When Senator Weicker asks what facts there are to support such a contention, Haldeman confesses, "I don't know."

All the conversations in the White House about Watergate, Haldeman maintains, represented only attempts to learn the truth. But Senator Montoya says bluntly, "It is patently clear that you people were trying to fabricate a situation, and not develop the facts." Senator Inouye tries to question Haldeman about the political dirty tricks he and Nixon were guilty of in the 1962 California campaign for governor, but Haldeman's lawyer blocks this line of inquiry.

Next to appear is Marine Corps Commandant Robert E. Cushman, former CIA deputy director, who states that in 1971 Ehrlichman authorized him to give Hunt spy paraphernalia, then asked him to alter a memo to conceal this fact.

Cushman's superior at the CIA, Richard Helms, and Helms's deputy, Walters, testify that Haldeman and Ehrlichman both tried to maneuver the CIA into blocking the FBI investigation of the laundered Mexican money, even after Helms had repeatedly told them that the CIA was in no way involved.

Patrick Gray acknowledges that he let Dean sit in on all FBI interviews with members of the White House staff and gave Dean batches of FBI investigative material. He also grimly admits destroying secret files from Hunt's safe, on orders given by Dean in Ehrlichman's presence. Relating that three weeks after Watergate, he told the President that his top aides were involved in obstructing justice, Gray adds, "I frankly . . . expected the President to ask some questions." Nixon had not.

As more and more implications of the President's guilt surface at the Senate hearings, he angrily assails those who would "wallow in Watergate." At a White House dinner for the prime minister of Japan, he declares, "Let others spend their time dealing with the murky, small, unimportant, vicious little things—we have spent our time and will spend our time in building a better world."

Former Attorney General Richard G. Kleindienst testifies on August 7 that he and Assistant Attorney General Petersen

H. R. Haldeman.

cracked the Watergate case in April but found no evidence
linking Nixon to the cover-up. He concedes, however, that they
warned the President on April 15 that the cover-up conspiracy
involved senior officials in the White House and CRP. Admitting
he once explained to Ehrlichman and Dean how presidential
pardons work, he declares he warned Ehrlichman about the risk
Ehrlichman was running of being charged with obstruction of
justice.

Henry Petersen concedes that he had narrowed down the
scope of the Watergate investigation under pressure from the
White House. He also admits having permitted top Administration officials to escape testifying before the grand jury. But he

expresses indignation that the investigation was taken out of the hands of the Justice Department and turned over to Special Prosecutor Archibald Cox.

On August 15 a nervous and haggard Nixon tries to improve his image with another televised address to the nation. He delivers a plea to be let alone and given a chance to govern the country. He offers no proof that he is innocent except his own word. "Not only was I unaware of any cover-up," he maintains, "but I was unaware that there was anything to cover up."

He blames Watergate on a few "overzealous" aides who, he insists, had been provoked into extreme reactions by the extreme behavior of the antiwar movement. "One excess begets another," he says. He promises that his Administration will now be cleaned up "to a new level of political decency and integrity in America." And he urges, "The time has come to turn Watergate over to the courts, where the questions of guilt or innocence belong. The time has come for the rest of us to get on with the urgent business of our nation."

Another sour smell of financial corruption wafts from the White House when it is reported in the press that a Federal grand jury in Baltimore has evidence that Vice-President Agnew has taken bribes from contractors, both as a Maryland official and as Vice-President. Other charges against him include extortion, tax fraud, and conspiracy. Denying all, Agnew vows that he will fight to prove his innocence.

The multiplying crises take their toll on the President's temper. In full view of a CBS-TV camera on August 20, Nixon wrathfully shoves his faithful press secretary, Ron Ziegler. When the White House denies the incident, it is screened that evening on television newscasts. The act looks so irrational that many Americans worry that the President may be losing his mental balance over Watergate.

Nixon decides to call a news conference two days later to show himself in full possession of his faculties and to persuade the public that the commotion over Watergate really represents a vendetta being waged against him by the news media. His answers to reporters' questions are elusive.

Why didn't he ask Mitchell what he knew about Watergate? "I was expecting Mr. Mitchell to tell me in the event that

Television cameras recorded Nixon's shoving of Ziegler.

he . . . or anyone else is involved." What about Dean's charges that he authorized raising hush money for the Watergate defendants? He maintains that Haldeman had quoted him correctly in saying he had turned down the proposal as "wrong."

He no longer insists that he personally ordered the FBI and Justice Department to redouble their efforts to investigate Watergate, because Gray, Kleindienst, and Petersen have all denied receiving such orders from him. He tries to dismiss the Watergate affair as "water under the bridge."

CBS reporter Dan Rather asks how he feels about having increasing numbers of his former supporters calling for his resignation. Nixon replies that he will never resign and denies all wrongdoing.

Didn't he think it was bribery to offer Judge Byrne the FBI directorship in the middle of the Ellsberg trial? No, he had decided that Byrne would not be compromised by being interviewed for the post at that time. Though admitting that he erred in stating earlier that he had not heard of the Dr. Fielding break-in before April 1973, he claims he was informed of it only a month earlier. Since this still makes him guilty of having withheld vital evidence for thirty-nine days of the Ellsberg trial, he charges that previous Democratic administrations had also bent the law for national security reasons, citing as an example the "burglarizing" of foreign embassies.

Nicholas de B. Katzenbach and Ramsey Clark, former attorney generals under President Johnson, promptly deny this charge and demand that Nixon document it. He fails to do so.

By now about twenty different investigations of Watergate and related matters are going on. In Los Angeles the grand jury hands down indictments against Ehrlichman, Krogh, Young, and Liddy on charges of burglary and conspiracy to commit burglary, arising out of the break-in at Dr. Fielding's office. The Watergate prosecutor permits Magruder to plead guilty to a one-count conspiracy charge, in return for his becoming a government witness.

When the staff of the Senate Watergate Committee interviews Charles Colson in executive session on September 19, he refuses to answer any questions, pleading the Fifth Amendment. He asks that this fact not be made public, but his request is refused.

On September 24 a new round of Senate Watergate hearings spotlights the Administration's campaign of political dirty tricks. Pat Buchanan, the President's acidic speech writer, admits to having participated in White House strategy to sabotage Muskie's campaign and get McGovern nominated as the weakest Democratic candidate. But he denies that this amounted to rigging the 1972 elections.

He minimizes Segretti's dirty tricks as having had no more impact than "the weight of a feather." CRP, he concedes, ran deceptive ad campaigns using false names as a front. He also admits having urged the White House to use the IRS against what he considers to be "leftist" institutions and foundations on Nixon's enemies list.

The Common Cause lawsuit forces Maurice Stans to reveal

a list of wealthy contributors to Nixon's 1972 campaign. It shows that Stans raised at least $8,000,000 more than he has admitted. Almost $1,500,000 was in cash, much of it from corporations barred by law from making campaign contributions. Large personal contributions came from men who were, or who became soon afterward, ambassadors.

Campaign contributions were used to pay Segretti, Caulfield, and Ulasewicz among others, and $50,000 went to Haldeman's brother-in-law for helping to arrange the purchase of Nixon's San Clemente estate. But Stans angrily denounces as "rubbish" a congressional report that the funds were mishandled.

A fresh shock is handed the public by *New York Post* disclosures that during the President's first term, he ordered the Secret Service to wiretap the phone of his younger brother Donald, out of fear that Donald Nixon's financial dealings might embarrass the re-election campaign.

The President calls another press conference at which he blames television commentators for the loss of public confidence in his Administration. His efforts to solve the country's problems of inflation and energy, he complains, are being hampered by the continuing Watergate crisis.

Hunt claims in his testimony before the Senate Watergate Committee on September 24 that imprisonment has ruined his health and finances. "I am crushed," he complains, "by the failure of my Government to protect me and my family in the past, as it has always done for its clandestine agents." He denies that his demands for money from Colson amounted to blackmail or that he insisted upon a promise of executive clemency as price for his silence.

He admits that he faked the Kennedy cables; helped plan the Plumbers' burglaries, which ended at Watergate; directed spy "Fat Jack" to steal papers from Muskie's headquarters in 1972; and plotted with Liddy to commit other political burglaries. But he feels he is being too harshly punished.

Segretti testifies on October 3 to all the acts of forgery, libel, burglary, and character assassination he performed to get Nixon re-elected. "My activities were wrong," he admits. "They have no place in the American political system." He says that he worked under and reported to Chapin, who warned him top secrecy was essential, "so that I would never prove an embarrassment to the President."

Robert Benz, one of Segretti's agents, tries to defend their dirty tricks by equating them with Democratic tactics. Angered, the Democratic members of the committee demand he offer proof of this charge. He admits that he has none. He then suggests that he and Segretti were "somehow" justified because their dirty tricks spotlighted the need for campaign reforms.

"You believe," Senator Ervin demands indignantly, "that the way to clean up politics is to make it more filthy?"

On October 9 political spies "Fat Jack" (John R. Buckley) and "Sedan Chair II" (Michael McMinoway) admit having stolen information from Muskie headquarters.

Frank Mankiewicz, McGovern's campaign director, tells the Senate Watergate Committee on October 11 that the dirty-tricks campaign seriously sabotaged the Democrats' chances of winning the 1972 election by making each presidential candidate believe that the dirty tricks were the work of his fellow Democrats. This tactic created such bitterness within party ranks that the Democrats could not unite behind McGovern.

Mankiewicz's testimony brings to an end the televised Watergate hearings. A new Gallup poll shows that 52 percent of Americans approve of the Senate Watergate Committee's attempt to get the facts in the open as "a good thing for the country." The poll also indicates that only 31 percent approve of Nixon, the lowest rating for any President in two decades. An Oliver Quayle survey shows that if the 1972 elections were now being held, McGovern would defeat Nixon.

No one can bring an end to all the Watergate probes quicker than the President, by simply turning over the White House tapes that contain the evidence of what was actually said and done about Watergate, of who was guilty, and of what. But he persistently refuses, insisting "the confidentiality of conversations between a President and his advisers" is "absolutely essential to the conduct of the presidency."

The President's refusal to let the evidence of the tapes be heard soon leads to the uproar known as the Saturday Night Massacre.

The Saturday Night Massacre

17

There is one drawback to the validity of the tapes as evidence. The President had the advantage of knowing that his conversations were being taped, while those he talked with did not. He could have therefore at any time made self-serving statements for the record, which could later be produced, if absolutely necessary, to exonerate him. Nixon's aides who know about the tapes, however, state that most of the time he either forgot about or paid no attention to them.

The President tries to ward off a storm of criticism by claiming that Kennedy and Johnson used taping systems, too. Newsmen learn that this is true; the former Presidents taped a few conversations on special occasions. But they did not routinely bug their offices as Nixon did. Two days after Butterfield exposes the existence of the taping system, the White House announces that the President has decided to discontinue taping his conversations and phone calls.

He rejects the Senate Watergate Committee's request for tapes to check against conflicts in witnesses' testimony. "The tapes are entirely consistent," he declares, "with what I . . . have stated to be the truth. However . . . they contain comments that persons with different perspectives and motivations would inevitably interpret in different ways. . . . Accordingly, the tapes which have been under my sole personal control will remain so." *203*

Senator Ervin dryly suggests that if he yields the tapes, "The Constitution would not collapse and the heavens would not fall, but the committee might be aided by the President in determining the truth of his involvement."

Archibald Cox has also requested that the President turn over the tapes of eight conversations to the special prosecutor's office, because they may be essential as legal evidence in criminal indictments now being prepared. When Nixon refuses, arguing that Cox's intention to use the tapes in the courts would violate Constitutional safeguards ensuring the separation of powers, Cox obtains a show-cause order from Judge Sirica directing Nixon to explain by August 7 why he should not be compelled to release the taped conversations.

Special Prosecutor Archibald Cox.

The President is caught in a perilous dilemma. Giving up the tapes may be suicidal, because of conversations that incriminate him as an early conspirator in the Watergate cover-up. He is also worried because of the profane and cynical language he and his former aides used in private. If made public, he knows the tapes will deeply offend millions of his supporters. Yet if he does not surrender the tapes, the country will correctly surmise that he is concealing conclusive evidence of his guilt.

His refusal to release them sends public confidence in him, measured by a Harris poll, to a new low of 21 percent. In his appeal to the nation of August 15, he compares his right to keep the tapes secret to the right of confidentiality between lawyer and client, priest and penitent, husband and wife. Significantly he omits the example of doctor and patient, since he has violated this confidentiality in ordering Ellsberg's medical file burglarized.

Nixon's defenders rush to his support, arguing that the public is weary of Watergate and wants the whole matter ended. Representative Glenn R. Davis, a Republican from Wisconsin, acknowledges, "My constituents say they're tired of it." He adds, "But they still want the guilty brought to justice."

That can be swiftly done, Senator Ervin points out, if the President will release the tapes which can establish the innocence or guilt of all those involved. Meanwhile public suspicion grows that the White House may be busy splicing, erasing, scissoring, or otherwise doctoring key tapes to destroy all evidence damaging to Richard Nixon.

In his press conference of August 22, Nixon is asked why he had allowed Haldeman to listen to the tapes after Haldeman had resigned. "To be sure," he replies, "that we were absolutely correct in our response to Dean's allegations."

On August 29 Judge Sirica orders President Nixon to turn the eight subpoenaed tapes Cox needs over to the district court, and he will listen to them personally to screen out any matters dealing with national security. "The court fails to perceive any reason," Sirica declares, "for suspending the power of courts to get evidence . . . in criminal matters simply because it is the President of the United States who holds the evidence." He cites Chief Justice John Marshall's ruling that there is "no exception whatsoever" in the right of a grand jury to have every man's evidence.

Refusing to obey, Nixon instructs White House lawyers to take the case to the United States Court of Appeals. On September 13 the court urges the special prosecutor and Nixon's attorneys to try to reach some form of out-of-court agreement, but a week later both sides report that they have been unable to do so.

Some news analysts suspect that Nixon's strategy in refusing to give up the tapes includes a "super cover-up" of the whole Watergate affair. Many Watergate defendants are now having their lawyers call upon the White House to make the tapes available for their trials. All can then move for a dismissal of charges on grounds that they cannot get a fair trial, being denied evidence they need to defend themselves.

The Gallup poll shows that 61 percent of Americans believe Nixon should turn over the tapes to Judge Sirica, and 72 percent believe him guilty of Watergate involvement. Only 31 percent approve of his conduct in office. His unpopularity is worsened by revelations that he paid only a $792 Federal income tax in 1970, $878 in 1971, and no California state taxes at all since 1969, on an income of well over $200,000 for each year.

As Federal prosecutors prepare evidence in the Agnew bribery case for a Baltimore grand jury, the Vice-President bitterly accuses Henry Petersen of trying "to reinstate his reputation as a tough and courageous and hard-nosed prosecutor" at Agnew's expense, because Petersen bungled the Watergate investigation. In a speech to Republican women in Los Angeles, Agnew vows emphatically that if he is indicted, he will not resign but fight and prove his innocence.

Nixon, relieved to have the press spotlight on someone else's misdeeds for a while, does not come to the Vice-President's assistance. For one thing, he knows that Congress will be more hesitant to impeach him if the next in line of succession to himself is under criminal indictment. But the case against Agnew is too overwhelming to allow him to remain in office long.

The Vice-President's bold front quickly collapses as the evidence makes it clear that he faces certain conviction and a stiff jail term. Bitter at Nixon for failing to defend him, Agnew resigns

Spiro T. Agnew resigns.

under fire on October 10, in return for a deal whereby he escapes imprisonment. Prosecuted only for income tax evasion, he is fined $10,000 and sentenced to three years on probation. "I've never seen a stronger case of bribery and extortion," says Chicago's United States Attorney James R. Thompson, a Republican racket buster involved in the case. "If it had gone to trial, I'm sure he would have been sent to jail. He was simply a crook. The country is well rid of him."

To add to his disgrace, Agnew is later disbarred as unfit to practice law because of "deceitful and dishonest" conduct and "moral turpitude." Americans who once cheered his attacks on intellectuals and the media are crestfallen. The "law-and-order" candidates they voted for have turned out to be themselves shocking violators of the law. Even those Americans who still believe in Nixon are dismayed by the appalling judgment he showed in choosing his closest aides. Many disillusioned voters feel cynical about not only Nixon and his aides but *all* politicians.

On October 12 Nixon names the House Republican minority leader, Gerald R. Ford of Michigan, to replace Agnew as Vice-President. Because of Ford's popularity with the Congress,

Nixon obviously hopes he will be of help in warding off growing demands the President's impeachment.

As Agnew departs from the Administration, Nixon tells Attorney General Richardson, "Now that we have disposed of that matter, we will get rid of Cox."

On October 12 the Court of Appeals upholds Judge Sirica's order to the President to surrender the eight tapes within a week, holding that "he is not above the law's commands."

Nixon, afraid he will again lose if he carries the issue to the Supreme Court, now decides to try to evade the verdict by a "compromise" compliance. On October 18, the day before the tapes are due, he offers to give Cox "summaries" of the subpoenaed conversations. They will be audited and verified by Democratic Senator John Stennis of Mississippi. In exchange, Cox must demand no further tapes or documents.

Cox rejects this transparent ruse, insisting that the original tapes alone are competent evidence. He further enrages the President by letting John Dean plead guilty to only one count of conspiracy to obstruct justice, in exchange for his evidence at all Watergate-related trials.

At a staff meeting on October 18 Nixon proposes to fire Cox and appoint Richardson and Petersen to take over the Watergate investigation. Appalled, Richardson warns that the public would never stand for it. He reminds Nixon of their promise to the Senate Judiciary Committee that Cox would have total independence to investigate and prosecute the case. But Nixon's aides agree with the President. Richardson recalls later, "I wondered whether I was the only sane man in the room."

Richardson doesn't realize that Nixon is desperate because he now has no alternative. If he gives Cox the raw tapes, his guilt will be exposed and impeachment will follow. On October 20, preparing to "tough out" the hue and cry he knows will result from dumping the special prosecutor, Nixon orders Richardson to fire Cox. Richardson refuses.

Haig phones him a little later and flatly repeats the President's order. Richardson again refuses and resigns. Haig then demands that Deputy Attorney General William D. Ruckelshaus fire Cox. Ruckelshaus also refuses.

"Your Commander-in-Chief [Nixon] has given you an order," Haig tells him coldly. "You have no alternative."

Ruckelshaus, too, resigns, and rebuffs Haig's demand that he fire Cox before he does. The President finally gets the reluctant Solicitor General, Robert Bork, to carry out his order. The whole affair astonishes and appalls the nation. The press labels it "the Saturday Night Massacre."

In just twenty-four hours Nixon has fired the special prosecutor and his staff of ninety and driven out the Attorney General and the Deputy Attorney General. Nixon orders the FBI to seal off all their offices, permitting no files to be removed. Cox declares somberly, "Whether ours shall continue to be a government of laws and not of men is now for the Congress and ultimately the American people to decide."

It is now obvious to most Americans that the President has

Gerald R. Ford becomes Nixon's new Vice-President.

taken these extraordinary and desperate measures to keep incriminating tapes out of the special prosecutor's hands. The Saturday Night Massacre provokes what Haig gloomily terms a "firestorm" of protest. Over one million telegrams and letters flood into the capital, demanding the President's resignation or impeachment. Nixon's popularity in a Gallup poll sinks to a new low of 27 percent.

The conservative *Chicago Tribune*, which has always supported the President, charges him with "the worst blunder in the history of the Presidency." Another former supporter, the *Colorado Springs Sun*, declares, "He has discredited his leadership, dishonored his office and betrayed the trust of those who elected him." Calls for his resignation come from *Time, The National Review*, and *The New York Times.*

"Gestapo tactics!" snaps Senate majority whip Robert Byrd. Representative Jerome Waldie, California Democrat, calls for the President's impeachment, charging that he "in one wild move, has removed the few remaining men of integrity in the Administration." Senator Edward Brooke, Massachusetts Republican, agrees that there is now "sufficient evidence . . . to begin impeachment proceedings." Senator Edward Kennedy charges that it is now "obvious that Mr. Nixon is bent on maintaining the Watergate cover-up at any cost." Representative John B. Anderson, Illinois Republican, grieves that the President has "precipitated a constitutional crisis."

The president of the American Bar Association, Chesterfield Smith, accuses Nixon—whom he has twice supported—of "an intolerable assault upon the most rudimentary and basic principles of justice." Harvard Law School professor Raoul Berger, an authority on impeachment, warns, "Democracy cannot survive if a President is allowed to take the law into his own hands."

On October 22 the AFL-CIO convention approves by acclamation a resolution by its head, George Meany, calling on the President to resign or face impeachment. It declares: "We believe that the American people have had enough. More than enough." Charging the President with showing signs of "dangerous emotional instability," Meany, who supported him against McGovern, now calls the Nixon Administration "the most corrupt in our history."

House Democratic leaders agree that an inquiry should be begun by the Judiciary Committee as to whether there are grounds for impeaching the President.

Shaken by the intensity of the public fury over the Saturday Night Massacre, the President is forced to reverse himself on the subpoenaed tapes. On October 23 he agrees to hand them over to Judge Sirica.

Nixon's credibility is now so low that when Kissinger announces a U.S. military alert on October 25 to counter Soviet movements in the Middle East, millions of Americans suspect it is a phony crisis manufactured by Nixon's men to rescue him from Watergate. "It is a symptom of what is happening to our country," Kissinger laments, "that it could even be suggested that the United States would alert its forces for domestic reasons."

Fearful of impeachment proceedings, Nixon holds a news conference on October 26, in which he tries to depict Cox as the real villain of the piece for having refused the Stennis "compromise" Nixon offered. "I had no choice but to dismiss him," he pleads. He also announces that he will appoint a new special prosecutor.

Outspoken Clark Mollenhoff of the *Des Moines Register* asks bluntly how he can explain "a law-and-order Administration covering up . . . evidence of high crimes and misdemeanors?" The President doggedly repeats his assertion that he is innocent of all charges. He blames the press for the nation's anger against him. "I have never," he rages, "seen such outrageous, vicious, distorted . . . frantic, hysterical reporting."

When CBS correspondent Robert Pierpoint asks why he is so worked up, the President replies with a cold, contemptuous smile, "Don't get the impression that you arouse my anger. You see, one can only be angry with those he respects."

In a desperate attempt to turn the tide of public opinion, Nixon orders an all-out White House counterattack on the media. CBS newsman Walter Cronkite and other television reporters are assailed for giving too much time to the President's accusers. Julie and David Eisenhower, Nixon's daughter and son-in-law, go on NBC's "Today" show to charge that the media are unfair to the President. *The New York Times* is accused of publishing "distorted and unfair news"; *Newsweek,* of presenting "false and irresponsible news."

Unfortunately for the President's credibility, Senator Weicker releases White House memos, turned over as evidence by Dean, proving that Nixon, from the very beginning, has sought to suppress all criticism of him by the media. The conservative *Wall Street Journal* now calls the President "a pitiful giant . . . [who] has no one to blame but himself."

His standing in the Gallup poll remains low—only 28 percent approving his handling of the Presidency. At Nixon's alma mater, Duke Law School, 350 out of 400 law students petition to have his portrait removed from its place on the school's walls.

Kleindienst is no help when on October 29 he admits that he lied at Senate hearings that no one from the White House had interfered with him on the ITT case. He now concedes that the

Indignation over the "Saturday Night Massacre" leads to demonstrations at the White House.

President emphatically ordered him to drop the antitrust prosecution.

The next day the Judiciary Committee of the House of
Representatives sets in motion its inquiry into grounds for
impeachment and gives Chairman Peter W. Rodino, Jr., the
power to subpoena evidence, which a hundred staff members will
compile.

Nixon's prestige plummets even lower that same day with
the shocking new revelation, made to Judge Sirica by White
House lawyers, that an important two of the nine subpoenaed
taped conversations are "missing." At this Barry Goldwater
declares that the President's credibility has reached "an all-time
low from which he may not be able to recover." "Incredible,"
says the *Los Angeles Times*. "Unbelievable."

Demands continue to mount from the public and press for
Nixon's resignation, from Republicans as well as Democrats.
"The nation," declares House Speaker Carl Albert somberly, "is
now in the midst of the gravest crisis in its history."

The measure of Nixon's desperation is so great that on
November 1 he feels it necessary to appoint as his new Attorney
General, Senator William Saxbe of Ohio, who only weeks earlier
had said that the President and his men should be measured for
clown suits, and that Nixon is "through, finished." As for the
President's claim to have known nothing about the Watergate
cover-up, Saxbe observed, "It sounds like the fellow who played
the piano in a brothel for twenty years, and insisted that he
didn't know what was going on upstairs."

Saxbe appoints a conservative Texas Democrat, Leon
Jaworski, as the new special prosecutor, with a presidential
pledge that he will have a totally free hand, and cannot be fired
without the consent of Congress.

But the cry for the President's resignation or impeachment
has become a rolling thunder throughout the land. Nixon
retreats into deepening seclusion at Camp David and Key
Biscayne.

18

"I'm Not a Crook!"

Off-year elections cause tremors throughout the Republican party in November. Republican candidates are resoundingly defeated for state and local offices. In New Jersey Brendan Byrne, a Democrat who has never before run for state office, is elected governor with a 68 percent plurality—the biggest in the state's history. He has run on the anti-Watergate slogan: "One Honest Man Can Make a Difference."

Many leading Republicans now feel that they must get Nixon out of office before the 1976 presidential election if the party is to stave off political disaster. Beleaguered, Nixon starts a desperate counteroffensive to stay in office.

"I want the facts out," he insists in a televised address, "because the facts will prove that the President is telling the truth. . . . I will do everything I can to cooperate." Rejecting demands for his resignation, he says doggedly, "I have no intention whatever of walking away from the job I was elected to do."

By this time Watergate has taken a terrible toll of the nation's affairs. Government is almost paralyzed. The President is so preoccupied with surviving in office that it is almost impossible to get White House decisions on policy. Many officials are disgusted with the Nixon Administration and want to leave Washington.

Congress is in revolt against the President. Having sustained eight bills over his veto, Congress now passes a ninth curbing presidential power to wage undeclared war. Nixon pleads with Republican congressmen not to turn against him.

"If you cut the legs off the President," he warns, "America is going to lose." But Senator Howard Baker tells him bluntly, "You're in trouble, and we're in trouble." Senator Brooke insists he ought to resign rather than put the nation through the traumatic experience of impeachment. "That would be the easy way out," Nixon replies doggedly, "I won't resign."

Senator Robert Packwood, Oregon Republican, tells him that he has broken faith with Congress and the people, and so has forfeited the capacity to lead the country. Perhaps the only man who has ever called a President in office a liar to his face, Packwood tells Richard Nixon bluntly, "Your problem is credibility."

New revelations in the media and in congressional hearings worsen the President's image almost daily. The *Wall Street Journal* publishes documents revealing that Nixon had been told of the dairy industry's huge campaign contributions, had expressed his gratitude, and two days later had given them highly profitable price-support increases.

Corporation officials testify that they were blackmailed into giving large illegal contributions to the Nixon re-election campaign. Gulf Oil Corporation vice-president Claude C. Wild reveals that he was made to understand if his firm refused, it would end up on "a blacklist or bottom of the totem pole" when it came to government contracts or favors.

On November 9 the six remaining Watergate defendants are sentenced. Eight days later, Nixon launches a frantic "Operation Candor," promising that he will disclose critical evidence he has heretofore suppressed, answer the charges against him conclusively, give Jaworski whatever tapes or documents he needs, and "let it all hang out." The President admits that the last seven months have been "pure hell" for him.

His aides arrange a series of televised speeches before business audiences who can be counted on to applaud politely rather than boo. At a convention of Associated Press managing editors, however, he is stung by a pointed question about his dubious financial transactions and low tax payments.

"People have got to know whether or not their President is a crook," he replies angrily. "Well, I'm not a crook!" He claims only to have followed the example and advice of President Johnson in taking a huge tax deduction for donating his vice-presidential papers to the National Archives. He does not reveal that Johnson had thought better of it and had not done so. Nor does he reveal that a deed turning over his papers for this purpose had been falsely backdated a year, to get around a new law prohibiting such deductions.

At a conference of Republican governors on November 20, the President assures them that he will vindicate himself of all charges. Oregon Governor Tom McCall asks frankly whether Republicans are going to be stunned "by any more bombs" dropping in the Watergate affair. Nixon assures the governors, "If there are any more bombs, I'm not aware of them."

Next day a new "bomb" explodes when his counsel, Fred J. Buzhardt, informs Judge Sirica about an 18½ minute buzz that blots out a crucial discussion about Watergate between Nixon and Haldeman on a key June 20, 1972, tape. Outraged, Sirica demands an explanation.

Rose Mary Woods, the President's longtime secretary, testifies that she made a "terrible mistake." According to her story, she was transcribing the tape for Nixon at Camp David when her phone rang. Reaching for it with one hand, with the other she mistakenly pushed the "record" instead of "stop" button on her recorder, while keeping her foot on the operating treadle, and so set in motion the erasure mechanism.

To demonstrate how the "accident" occurred, she has to assume such a grotesque position as to make the explanation wholly absurd. A panel of technical experts is selected jointly by the White House and the special prosecutor to study the erasure. The panel later reports that someone made at least five separate, deliberate *hand* erasures of the tape.

Who erased the 18½-minute Nixon-Haldeman conversation? Only three people had access to the tape—Rose Mary Woods, the President, and his aide Stephen Bull. The White House quickly issues a statement insisting that the President did

J. Fred Buzhardt delivers the
tapes to Judge Sirica.

not personally alter the tape. When General Haig is called to testify, he suggests with a straight face that the erasures might have been caused by "some sinister force." The matter is never cleared up.

A new Gallup poll shows that as a result of the President's

Rose Mary Woods demonstrates how the 18½-minute gap might have been caused.

behavior during the Watergate investigation, only 24 percent of registered voters now say they will vote for a Republican congressional candidate. The party is stunned.

The President worsens matters by refusing to turn over three more tapes on grounds of executive privilege. And two days later his lawyers admit to Judge Sirica that there are still more gaps on other subpoenaed tapes. Two out of three Americans, the Gallup poll shows, are convinced that all incriminating tapes have already been doctored.

"It's a sad, sad day when Americans cannot believe their President," declares AFL-CIO chief George Meany, adding, "Mr. Nixon's relentless resistance to full disclosure has left the people with only one avenue to the truth . . . impeachment."

Special Prosecutor Leon Jaworski demands additional tapes. Ziegler insists that the nineteen already delivered under subpoena should be enough for "reasonable men," and charges the special prosecutor's staff, which Jaworski took over from Cox, with having "an ingrained suspicion and visceral dislike for the President."

Egil Krogh pleads guilty on November 30 to violating the civil rights of Dr. Fielding, acknowledging now that the break-in at his office had nothing to do with national security but had been a "terrible mistake" and "repulsive conduct." He is later sentenced to six months in prison.

In December the White House now orchestrates "Support the President" rallies around the country, at which speakers attack the media for causing Nixon's troubles by biased news reporting. This claim is checked out by the American University School of Journalism in a special study; it finds that the press has been fair and carefully balanced overall.

The Senate Watergate Committee issues subpoenas for almost 500 White House tapes and documents on December 9. Nixon flatly refuses to surrender any more evidence because it could be "misinterpreted" and "could lead to confusion in the minds of the American public." He determines to dig in for a long court battle to hold on to the tapes on grounds of "presidential confidentiality" and the separation of governmental powers.

A Roper poll shows that 79 percent of the public now believes the President guilty of one or more of the most serious charges against him. The AFL-CIO distributes eight million leaflets demanding his impeachment.

Congressmen return home over the Christmas recess to sound out how their constituents feel about impeachment. They find citizens angered not only about Watergate and the cover-up, but also about the President's income taxes, the taxpayers' money spent on Nixon's homes in San Clemente and Key Biscayne, the milk-price boosts, the ITT case, and the Administration's failure to do anything to stop inflation, fuel shortages, and soaring gas prices.

Fourteen senators dispatch a letter to Nixon, asking why he is letting the oil companies "raise prices and make record profits at a time when the average citizen is being told to turn down his heat [and] slow down his car."

In an attempt to fend off angry criticism of Nixon's tax payments, the White House challenges critics to make their own tax returns public as the President has been compelled to do. Senators Ervin and Weicker promptly do so, revealing that they have paid triple the amount in taxes that Nixon has on gross incomes which are only a quarter the size of the President's.

Congressmen come back to Washington convinced that the President has lost the confidence of the country, which no longer believes him. Barry Goldwater notes, "I hate to think of the old adage, 'Would you buy a used car from Dick Nixon?', but that's what people are asking around the country."

In January 1974 the President replaces Buzhardt, his chief Watergate defense counsel, with James St. Clair, a Boston trial lawyer with a reputation for winning controversial cases. "There is a time to fly and there is a time to fight," Nixon tells a group of Republican congressmen, "and I'm going to fight like hell."

The President turns his annual State of the Union message into a fight for political survival. Praising his own accomplishments in office, he vows to resist all attempts to impeach him. He will cooperate with the House Judiciary Committee, but only in ways that do not hurt the doctrine of "presidential confidentiality." In other words, he alone will decide what evidence Congress may have in assessing the need for his impeachment.

"One year of Watergate is enough," he states. Ron Ziegler, following orders to pursue a tough line, curtly tells reporters he will answer no more questions on Watergate.

The President gets Hugh Scott, the Senate minority leader, to defend him by showing him some "digests" of taped Nixon-Dean conversations that purport to prove Dean lied about the President. Scott dutifully proclaims this conviction to the press. But Jaworski's special prosecutors certify in court and on national television that evidence they possess proves that Dean told the truth in his testimony.

Congressmen greet Nixon after his State of the Union message.

Upset, Scott bitterly tells friends that he feels he has been "used" by the White House, and will make no further defense of the President without hearing the tapes themselves. He publicly advises Nixon to "pull a truck up to the White House and pile it with every damn document relevant to the investigation."

On February 6 the House of Representatives votes 410 to 4 to extend its impeachment inquiry, giving the Judiciary Committee power to subpoena anything and everyone, including the President himself. By this time over fifteen Republican congressmen have decided not to seek re-election, considering a crushing defeat for the party almost inevitable in November.

On Lincoln's Birthday Nixon makes a television speech in front of the Lincoln Memorial, saying of the Great Emancipator, "He was very deeply hurt by what was said about him and drawn about him, but . . . Lincoln had that great strength of character never to display it." His obvious comparison of himself with "Honest Abe" does not sit well with most Americans.

"When Abraham Lincoln ran for Congress in 1846," observes Senator Alan Cranston, California Democrat, "his supporters raised $200 for his campaign. He won—and gave back $199.25, saying, 'I did not need the money.'" Nixon's attempt to wrap himself in Lincoln's mantle is too much for lifelong Republican James Lemon of Falls Church, Virginia, who pays over $1,000 of his $11,000 salary for a newspaper ad announcing that he is taking back his vote for Nixon. "It's a wonder," Lemon marvels, "that Lincoln's statue didn't topple over."

On March 1, 1974, the grand jury hands down a 50-page indictment of Haldeman, Ehrlichman, Mitchell, Colson, Strachan, Mardian, and Kenneth W. Parkinson on a total of twenty-four counts of conspiracy, perjury, and obstructing justice to hinder the investigation of the Watergate burglary in June 1972. Haldeman is also charged with perjury in stating that the President had raised moral objections to the payment of hush money to Hunt.

The grand jurors also want to indict Richard Nixon for having participated in the conspiracy, but Jaworski informs them that they cannot indict a sitting President. So instead the grand jury gives Judge Sirica a sealed report that is to be forwarded to the House Judiciary Committee, along with a locked briefcase full of supporting evidence. By a vote of 19–0 the grand jury has named the President an "unindicted co-conspirator." Although this sealed report is secret, the startling news leaks out.

His back to the wall, Nixon takes a political gamble to keep Republican congressmen on his side in the event of a vote for impeachment. Trying to prove that his support is valuable to them, he goes to Michigan to campaign personally for a Republican representative. In a district that has sent Republicans to Congress for forty straight years, the Democratic candidate campaigns on one issue alone—Watergate—and wins on March 5.

"Watergate killed us," laments the Republican state chairman of Michigan. Humiliated and repudiated, Nixon is now regarded by many Republican candidates who are facing re-election as a millstone around their necks. More and more call for his resignation to save the party, especially after the Republicans lose three more out of four special elections.

In another televised press conference on March 6, Nixon again protests his innocence of any wrongdoing, but now acknowledges for the first time that Dean told him during their conversation on March 21, 1973, that payments had been made to keep the Watergate burglars quiet. Nixon also admits that tapes of that day's conversations with Haldeman and Ehrlichman are subject to different "interpretations" than his own.

But he takes issue with those who consider his conversations with Dean incriminating. "*I* know what I meant," he insists, claiming that what he meant was that hush money should *not* be paid to the Watergate Seven.

James St. Clair, Nixon's counsel, argues that his client cannot be impeached except on proof that he personally violated criminal statutes. Constitutional experts disagree, pointing out that the Founding Fathers considered "abuses of Constitutional duties" sufficient grounds and that President James Madison considered a President impeachable for the offenses of his subordinates if he "neglects to superintend their conduct, so as to check their excesses."

A Harris poll shows that almost three fourths of the American public want President Nixon to face impeachment proceedings. Nixon quickly organizes an anti-impeachment campaign, using Vice-President Ford as its spearhead.

On March 12, the House Judiciary Committee demands forty-two more tapes and many more presidential documents while Jaworski demands sixty-four more tapes. Nixon flatly rejects the special prosecutor's demand and offers the HJC only what he has already felt compelled to supply to Jaworski—nineteen tapes and seven hundred documents.

Some congressmen fear that impeachment will tear the country apart; others worry that rioting may break out if the President *isn't* impeached. Politicians of both parties grow increasingly uneasy. "The Democrats don't want to look like a lynch mob," observes *Newsweek* columnist Henry Hubbard, "and the Republicans don't want to look like apologists for the White House."

Senator Jacob Javits, New York Republican, is convinced that impeachment is inevitable: "It's a juggernaut. It can't be stopped." Conservative columnist George F. Will notes, "The disgrace is permanent. There are not going to be any Richard M. Nixon high schools, parks, highways, stadiums." On March 19

New York's Conservative senator James Buckley calls on the President to resign for the good of the country.

Vice-President Ford is warned by advisers that he is hurting himself politically by defending Nixon, and he begins putting some distance between himself and the President. He declares that *he* would have notified the Justice Department the moment he was told of hush-money demands and payments. He also suggests that the President ought to surrender the subpoenaed tapes. Nixon soon summons him to indicate concern that the Vice-President is "working too hard at the job." Ford subsequently takes a more fence-sitting position.

The President's problems multiply on April 2 when the Joint Committee on Internal Revenue Taxation investigating his tax returns during his first term in office discloses that he used every tax dodge and loophole to escape paying $432,787 in income taxes. The revelation comes at a time when the nation's taxpayers are painfully filling out their own tax forms, many of them forced to pay higher taxes on a worker's salary than the President with his annual $200,000 paycheck.

By a 9 to 1 vote the report shows that Nixon grossly understated his total income and vastly inflated his deductions. He claimed a $482,018 deduction for donating his pre-presidential papers and charged the government over $90,000 in personal expenses that included $5,000 for a "masked ball for Miss Tricia Nixon."

The President hastily promises to pay the taxes he has evaded; he pleads that the "errors" on his returns were caused by tax experts without his knowledge or approval. One of his tax lawyers angrily calls the statement "ridiculous," reporting that he went over the tax reports with Nixon himself page by page. Testimony by a former Justice Department tax expert, Fred Folsom, indicates that if Nixon's tax returns had been "the case of an ordinary taxpayer, on the facts as we know them in this instance, the case would be referred for presentation to a grand jury for prosecution."

Struggling against impeachment, Nixon insists that he is not trying to protect "the man, Nixon," but the office of the Presidency. "Dragging out Watergate drags down America," he

Rejecting demands that he resign, Nixon tells the National Association of Broadcasters on March 19 that he will "stand and fight."

warns. ". . . The time has come to get Watergate behind us and get on with the business of America."

He begins flying around the country seeking conservative and business audiences to whom he appeals for support. Anti-Nixon demonstrators are kept away behind a line of patrolmen and police dogs.

*The "masked ball for Miss Tricia Nixon" was a presidential deduction
that especially annoyed average taxpayers. Among the guests were the
daughters of former President Johnson. (Left to right) Pat and Luci
Nugent, David and Julie Eisenhower, Tricia Nixon, Barry Goldwater,
Jr., Charles and Lynda Robb.*

Dwight Chapin, Nixon's former appointments secretary, is
found guilty on April 5 of two counts of perjury in connection
with Segretti's dirty-tricks campaign. He goes to jail followed
shortly after by Herbert Porter. By now thirty-five men have
been either indicted or convicted in the Watergate scandals.
Seven are top corporate executives who have paid fines for
making illegal contributions to the Committee to Re-elect the
President.

When lawyers for the defendants in the trial for the Dr.
Fielding break-in ask for dismissal on the grounds of national
security, Judge Gerhard Gesell rejects the motion. "What this
case is all about," he declares, "is respect for law and government. . . . My concern is with the wisdom of creating a

precedent which allows individuals who are not law enforcement officers . . . on their own notion of what is good for the country, [to] bust into the homes and residences of honorable citizens."

19

The President Stonewalls It

On April 11 the House Judiciary Committee votes 33 to 3 to subpoena tapes and records of over forty more presidential conversations. A few days later, Jaworski subpoenas sixty-four for his prosecution.

It is no longer possible to stall off the multiplying demands for evidence. Nixon decides on a new scheme to pretend compliance while still keeping the White House tapes under lock and key. He offers to give the House Judiciary Committee and also make public forty-six transcripts of the subpoenaed conversations, supposedly edited only for national security precautions or to screen out "irrelevant" discussions. Actually the omissions and changes made in the transcripts conceal or obscure his most damaging remarks.

In a television speech on April 29, 1974, before delivering the transcripts to the House Judiciary Committee, Nixon tries to persuade the American people that he is cooperating fully. He appears on television with volumes of the transcripts stacked beside him in expressive bulk. He acknowledges that they will subject him to embarrassment, "even ridicule," and agrees that they are open to interpretations that may be "drastically different" from his own.

He is making the transcripts public, he says, because he is confident that the record as a whole will prove he was ignorant of the Watergate cover-up until John Dean told him of it on March

April 29, 1974. President Nixon announces the release of the transcripts.

21, 1973. Then he "had to find out more about what they were before I could decide how they could best be made public." He insists, "Whatever the potential for misinterpretation . . . my actions and reactions . . . show clearly that I did not intend the further payment to Hunt or anyone else be made."

Five hours before the transcripts are released, a 50-page White House summary "interpreting" the transcripts in the President's favor is issued to grab early headlines away from the detailed contents of the transcripts. John Dean is represented as having skirted the truth, while remarks by the President that suggest his guilt are explained away as "taking the role of devil's advocate" or "merely thinking out loud."

Nixon is gambling that very few Americans will have the

patience to wade through—let alone analyze—the censored quarter million words about Watergate in the White House transcripts. They are widely reproduced in newspapers, magazines, and "instant books," and quoted on television and radio newscasts. As the reaction sets in, the reverberations shake the White House.

Carefully edited and laundered though they are, the transcripts still show sharp contradictions between what Nixon claimed was the truth and what actually took place in presidential conversations. They prove that both Nixon and Haldeman lied in quoting the President as saying "it would be wrong" to pay hush money, a remark made only about granting clemency, and then in a context of tactics, not morality.

They show the President returning to the discussion of hush

Paperback editions of the transcripts become instant best sellers.

money at least ten times subsequently, declaring, "This is why the Hunt problem is so serious. . . . It has to do with the Ellsberg case." They reveal Nixon assuring his aides that it is safe to have a faulty memory before a grand jury, adding, "Perjury is a hard rap to prove."

The legal staff of the House Judiciary Committee compares the altered transcripts with nine original tapes sent them by the Watergate grand jury. The comparison reveals significant differences. The tapes, notes Congressman Jerome R. Waldie, California Democrat, "were incredibly more incriminating." The transcripts are garbled by almost two thousand omissions from significant conversations, indicated by such terms as "expletive deleted," "unintelligible," "inaudible," and "material unrelated to Presidential actions deleted."

In a March 13, 1973, taped conversation with Dean, Nixon says, "The hangout road is going to have to be rejected." In the White House transcript his remark reads only, "The hangout road (inaudible)." A March 21 transcript has him wondering, "Is it too late to go the hangout road?" But it omits his decision on tape, "Yes, it is." His taped remark, "I did know about it," becomes in the transcript, "I didn't know about it." His taped remark about using flexibility, "In order to get on with the cover-up plan," becomes in the transcript, "In order to get off the cover-up line."

The President's remark that Hunt must get executive clemency by Christmas is transferred in the transcript to Dean. And a March 22 transcript omits 16 minutes of a taped conversation with his aides in which the President said, "I don't give a —— what happens. I want you all to stonewall it . . . plead the Fifth, cover up or anything else, if it'll save the plan. That's the whole point."

Perhaps most shocking of all to those of the President's followers who are religious are the 146 deletions marked "expletive deleted," most of them obscenities used in Nixon's remarks, suggesting a far different image from the President of highly publicized White House "prayer breakfasts."

The House Judiciary Committee does not consider the laundered transcripts a satisfactory response to its subpoena for the tapes. "Quite candidly," declares chief counsel John Doar, "these transcripts are not accurate." The members of the committee again vote that the President must turn over the tapes themselves.

The self-portrait that emerges from the transcripts appalls millions of Americans whom Nixon has convinced that he is a resolute, decisive, able leader. The Nixon of the private conversations is revealed to be highly insecure, rambling in thought and speech, indecisive, submissive to his aides.

He displays a persecution complex. "Nobody is a friend of ours," he gloomily warns Dean. "Let's face it."

The President is shown never to question the morality of any decision but to be absorbed only in how it will "play in Peoria"—whether, that is, it will persuade the unsophisticated general public. He is shown spending endless hours with Haldeman, Ehrlichman, and Dean trying to invent "scenarios" to explain away incriminating Watergate evidence.

Senator Ervin charges that the transcripts prove, "The plan was to pretend to cooperate but at the same time to do everything possible to impede and obstruct our work."

"Nowhere in . . . even these defective records," notes a *New York Times* editorial, "is there any indication that the President wanted to speed the process of full disclosure."

Former Nixon speechwriter William Safire writes that the transcripts "illuminate a dark side of Richard Nixon," revealing him as having a "moral blind spot." They "add up to as damning a document as it is possible to imagine."

The *Chicago Tribune* calls for Nixon's impeachment, declaring, "We have seen the private man and we are appalled." Labeling him immoral, devious, vacillating, profane, and unprincipled, the *Tribune* admits, "There can no longer be a charge that he was railroaded out of office by vengeful Democrats or a hostile press."

The *Kansas City Times* asks sadly, "Can the end-product of the men who gathered nearly two centuries ago to frame the Constitution be a band of knaves who talk of advantage, revenge and adroit maneuver, and never of what is right or wrong, or what is good for the country?"

Conservative publisher William Randolph Hearst calls the transcripts, "As damning a document as it is possible to imagine short of an actual indictment. . . . I have never heard anything as ruthless, deplorable, and ethically indefensible as the talk on those White House tapes."

Senator Hugh Scott labels them, "Deplorable, disgusting, shabby and immoral." Reminded that he insisted that the whole Watergate story should be aired, Scott replies, "That's right, but I didn't have the slightest inkling it was anything like *this!*" Even Nixon's close friend, the Reverend Billy Graham, calls reading the transcripts, "A profoundly disturbing and disappointing experience. We have lost our moral compass."

Nixon is stunned by his catastrophic plunge into disgrace. He had failed to foresee the extent to which Americans would be shocked by the revelations of what he and his aides said and did in private, in contrast with the high moral tone they always assumed in public. Telegrams to Republican congressmen are running 60 to 70 percent against him, demanding his impeachment.

James St. Clair insists that the President can be impeached only on specific charges of criminal misconduct. On May 11 Julie Nixon Eisenhower tells reporters that her father will "fight impeachment to the end if there were only one Senator who believed in him." Ziegler declares that the President "will not be driven out of office by rumor, speculation . . . or hypocrisy."

Nixon retreats into solitary brooding to work out his strategy of survival. He finds himself between the devil and the deep. On May 31 the Supreme Court agrees to decide, on Jaworski's appeal, whether the President has the right to withhold evidence of possible crimes from the special prosecutor. If Nixon relinquishes the subpoenaed tapes, he will be exposed, impeached, and convicted. If he fails to yield them, especially after a Supreme Court order, he will be impeached and convicted for that offense. And if he resigns and becomes a private citizen, he will not only be forced to give up the tapes but will then be vulnerable to a criminal indictment and trial.

On June 7 Judge Sirica lifts the secrecy from the court papers of the grand jury naming Nixon as an unindicted coconspirator.

His only hope, Nixon feels, is to use delaying tactics, while seeking to win back enough public support to block a two-thirds vote for conviction on the impeachment charges in the Senate. On June 12, after sending Kissinger to the Middle East to arrange a cease-fire between the Arabs and Israelis, he quickly arranges a five-day mission to the Middle East and the Soviet Union to take the headlines away from his critics.

"The President's evident eagerness to be airborne even before the ink was dry on the ceasefire agreement is embarrassing . . . ," notes the *Nation*. "A prime motive for the President's hasty departure from Washington was his evident desire, at this critical juncture in the impeachment proceedings, to escape

President Nixon and Henry A. Kissinger aboard Air Force One, bound for NATO talks in Brussels and a summit meeting with Soviet leader Brezhnev in Moscow. The President's legs are raised to ease a recent attack of phlebitis.

mounting political pressures for his removal, and if possible brighten his soiled image through the cooperation of the media which he has long maligned and threatened."

Nixon returns home on June 19 hoping that he has restored his image as an active President negotiating foreign-policy triumphs, instead of as a target of criminal proceedings.

The Senate Judiciary Committee summons Henry Petersen to answer questions about the failure of the Justice Department to uncover the Watergate cover-up until after the 1972 presidential elections. "If you mean we accepted the lies of all those who lied to us," Petersen says lamely, "I guess we did—we were snookered."

On June 21 Charles Colson is sentenced to from one to three years in prison by Judge Gesell, after pleading guilty to obstruction of justice. The former White House "hatchet man" claims to have had a sudden religious conversion which has made him repent his misdeeds in the White House. He admits that the break-in at Dr. Fielding's office was not a national security matter, but a political attempt to get scurrilous information about Ellsberg to influence his trial, destroy his reputation, and smear the Democrats along with him.

"I lost my perspective," he declares, "to a point where I instinctively reacted to any criticism or interference with what I was doing or what the President was doing as unfair and as something to be retaliated against. . . . I never really questioned whether what he wanted done was right or proper."

He labels Nixon as the mastermind behind the conspiracy against Ellsberg: "The President on numerous occasions urged me to disseminate damaging information about Daniel Ellsberg . . . and others with whom Ellsberg had been in close contact." Colson also informs the staff of the House Judiciary Committee that it was Nixon who had ordered an FBI investigation of CBS newsman Daniel Schorr.

When the Senate Watergate Committee issues its final three-volume report in July 1974, it describes the Nixon re-election campaign of 1972 as "characterized by corruption, fraud and abuse of power," but does not assign individual responsibility. "Some people draw a picture of a horse and then write 'horse' under it," Chairman Sam Ervin explains dryly. "We just drew a horse." The report recommends thirty-seven changes in the law to lessen the risk of ever having a future Watergate.

Among the hundreds of incriminating disclosures in the report is the revelation that Nixon's friend Bebe Rebozo, using laundered bank accounts, had channeled $50,000 in campaign funds to the President's private use. The money had paid for a swimming pool, fireplace, putting green, and pool table at his private home in Key Biscayne. Another $4,562 had gone into the purchase of diamond earrings for the President's wife.

In a separate report Senator Weicker charges Nixon and his aides with 370 distinct violations of the law and the Constitution in connection with the Watergate scandals.

At the House Judiciary Committee, chief counsel John Doar, after careful study of all the evidence with his staff, concludes that Nixon is guilty of "this terrible deed . . . this enormous crime in the conduct of his office," and should be impeached. He tells the committee that he has come to this conclusion reluctantly, declaring, "Reasonable men acting reasonably would find the President guilty." Republican minority counsel Albert E. Jenner, Jr., concurs in this judgment.

Doar finds that Haldeman did nothing on his own initiative, acting always to carry out the President's orders. He finds that the President has constantly issued untrue statements to the press and public, such as crediting Dean with an "investigation" that had cleared everybody in the White House, while telling Dean privately, "You handled it just right—you contained it." Even though Nixon has refused to honor the Judiciary Committee's subpoenas for tapes, providing only forty censored transcripts and a miscellany of censored documents, Doar's 200-page brief of evidence for the committee contains sufficient facts to justify having the Judiciary Committee draw up and vote upon charges of impeachment.

The brief states that the President "encouraged and approved" actions against victims "whose sole offense was their constitutionally protected political views." He ordered defamatory intelligence gathered on the peace movement, Ellsberg, and the Democrats, leading to the break-ins at Dr. Fielding's office and the DNC. He directed the cover-up of Watergate to cut off the trail to his other secrets—the illegal wiretaps, the Plumbers, the dirty-tricks campaign, the laundering of illegal campaign funds, the enemies list, the abuse of the tax system, the ITT affair, the milk fund, his private financial irregularities.

"For all this," the Doar report concludes, "Richard M. Nixon is personally and directly responsible."

The President sends Ziegler before newsmen to denounce the House Judiciary Committee as a radical "kangaroo court" determined to destroy the President with a "calculated public-relations campaign."

As the committee deliberates on the evidence, six hundred believers in Richard Nixon hold a prayer fast for him on the Capitol steps. But the Gallup poll shows belief in the President at an all-time low of 24 percent. "He's gone," declares House majority leader Thomas O'Neill. "He's had it."

James St. Clair is permitted to plead Nixon's case before the House Judiciary Committee. The White House transcripts compel him to admit that the President knew about the cover-up at least by March 13, 1973, eight days before Nixon previously insisted he first learned about it. But St. Clair maintains that Nixon didn't get "substantially all the details" until Dean reviewed the whole story on March 21.

St. Clair also insists that there is no solid evidence that Haldeman informed the President about the Dr. Fielding break-in; or that Nixon authorized payments of hush money to Hunt; or that he had favors done for ITT and the milk industry in return for large campaign contributions. His setting-up of the clandestine Plumbers is defended on the grounds of national security.

St. Clair tries to limit the basis for impeachment to a single issue—the payments of hush money to Hunt, which he argues were set in motion by John Dean, not Nixon. He emphasizes occasional remarks of the President, such as objecting that continuing the payments would "look like a payoff," while ignoring Nixon's final order about raising the money for blackmail—"Well, for Chrissakes, *get it!*"

Democrats on the committee point out that St. Clair's brief on behalf of the President "ignores 95 percent of the evidence." One member finds the excuse that Nixon approved payments to the Watergate Seven only because he was moved by their plight

*Presidential attorney James D.
St. Clair.*

hard to swallow. "If you're going to be magnanimous," he says
skeptically, "why do it with cash, in paper bags, in the dark of
night?" Another points out that to prove a crime it doesn't
matter who set the payoff train in motion, but whether the
President climbed aboard.

When it is noted that St. Clair quotes only from the
sanitized White House transcripts, he is asked whether he himself
has heard the tapes and can vouch for the accuracy of the
transcripts. St. Clair admits that he has heard only one or two
tapes in a "spot check" but is satisfied that the transcripts are
true records—a confidence not shared by the majority of
members on the Judiciary Committee nor by Doar's staff.

St. Clair's case is so weak that even the Republican minority
counsel on the Judiciary Committee, Albert Jenner, favors

impeachment. At the insistence of diehard Nixon defenders on the committee, he is replaced by Samuel Garrison, who argues that Nixon's guilt must not be inferred from his refusal to surrender the tapes. Garrison also urges the members of the committee to consider, regardless of the evidence against the President, "whether the best interests of the country would be served by his removal."

Many Americans are shocked by this suggestion that Nixon, if found guilty of criminal conduct that would put any other citizen in jail, should be judged above the law and allowed to remain President of the United States.

St. Clair insists that the Judiciary Committee can only recommend impeachment if it finds clear and direct evidence that the President personally committed a serious crime—evidence as conclusive as "a smoking gun." He has no idea that the withheld tapes contain exactly such evidence.

Judge Sirica orders Nixon to obey Jaworski's subpoenas for sixty-four more tapes. Nixon now insists that St. Clair appeal this decision directly to the Supreme Court, hoping that his four appointees on the court will remember by whose favor they sit upon the bench of the nation's highest tribunal.

On July 24, 1974, Chief Justice Warren Burger announces the unanimous decision of the Court in the case of "United States v. Richard M. Nixon." The President alone cannot be allowed to be judge of what evidence is sufficient for the prosecution of crimes charged to him and his aides, the Court rules, and cannot withhold evidence on grounds of executive privilege.

"Without access to specific facts," the Chief Justice points out, "a criminal prosecution may be completely frustrated." The Supreme Court also decides that the Watergate grand jury acted properly in naming the President an "unindicted co-conspirator," since it could not ignore the evidence against him and a President does not possess the immunity of a king.

The Supreme Court's order that the President must surrender the subpoenaed tapes and documents deals a final and fatal blow to Nixon's long struggle to conceal his crimes. He begins to slide from power over a period of fifteen days as his two-year fabrication of lies and deceit starts crumbling around him.

*Special Prosecutor Leon Jaworski leaves the Supreme Court after the unanimous decision
that the tapes must be released.*

When news of the Court's decision reaches the Nixon estate,
in San Clemente, panic sets in. His chief of staff, Alexander Haig,
hesitates for forty minutes before telling the President.

Nixon at once calls an extraordinary seven-hour strategy
session to help him "stonewall" to the last possible moment. He
tries to convince St. Clair that he has a Constitutional right and
duty as President to declare himself immune to orders of the
Supreme Court. But St. Clair warns if he refuses to obey, he will
surely be impeached in the House and swiftly convicted in the
Senate.

Besides, St. Clair says firmly, unless the President follows his
advice and obeys the Court, he will feel compelled to withdraw
as Nixon's defense counsel. Nixon is trapped, recognizing that St.
Clair's resignation would destroy his last shreds of credibility. He
gives in and St. Clair announces on television that the President
will obey the decision of the Court.

Appearing in court before Judge Sirica, St. Clair indicates

that sorting the subpoenaed tapes will be a "time-consuming process," and suggests that they may not all be available in time for a vote on impeachment by the full House of Representatives. At Jaworski's request, Sirica orders St. Clair to deliver a first batch of tapes within one week.

The impeachment deliberations of the Judiciary Committee, held in open session, are broadcast over the television networks. At least fifteen million Americans watch history being made as the thirty-six men and two women on the HJC, acutely aware that their own political careers may rest on how they vote and why, seek to justify their actions to their watching constituents back home.

Tension is high in the country when Chairman Peter W. Rodino, Jr., New Jersey Democrat, opens the dramatic proceedings. "The Judiciary Committee," he declares, "has for seven months investigated whether or not the President has seriously

A formal portrait of the House Judiciary Committee. John M. Doar (left) and Albert E. Jenner (right) are in the foreground.

abused his power. . . . We have deliberated, we have been patient, we have been fair. Now the American people . . . demand that we make up our minds."

Nixon has roughly ten hard-core defenders on the committee. They seek to split the vote along party lines, so that a recommendation of impeachment can be attacked before the full House as a Democratic plot to oust a Republican President. The President's last hope of surviving in office depends upon the success or failure of their effort.

The "Smoking Gun"

20

$\mathbf{S}$ix Republican members of the House Judiciary Committee, agonized by the incriminating evidence, are torn between party loyalty and conscience.

"Is the office of the Presidency being operated in the manner intended by the Constitution," asks Robert McClory of Illinois, "when, under the guise of national security, dissatisfaction with the head of the FBI or personal animosity to enemies, we experience burglaries, wiretaps, bugging, shredding and concealment of evidence, misuse of the CIA, FBI, IRS and a host of other misdeeds . . . ? I ask myself, is this any way to run a White House, or a country?"

"It is not easy for me," declares Representative Lawrence J. Hogan of Maryland, "to align myself against the President, to whom I gave my enthusiastic support in three Presidential campaigns. . . . [But] my President has lied repeatedly . . . concealed and covered up evidence. . . . approved the payments of what he knew to be blackmail. . . . Richard M. Nixon has beyond a reasonable doubt committed impeachable offenses."

"Watergate is our shame," says Representative M. Caldwell Butler of Virginia. ". . . It is a sad chapter in American history, but I cannot condone what I have heard, I cannot excuse it, and I cannot and will not stand still for it."

"Some of my people say that the country cannot afford . . . to impeach a President," declares Representative Tom Railsback   *243* of Illinois. "[But] . . . if the young people in this country think we are . . . not going to really try to get to the truth, you're going to see the most frustrated . . . turned-off . . . disillusioned people, and it's going to make the period of LBJ in 1967–1968 . . . look tame."

"It has been said that impeachment proceedings will tear this country apart," says Representative William S. Cohen of Maine. ". . . I think what would tear the country apart would be to turn our back on the facts. . . . If we are to have confidence in the concept of even-handed treatment under the law, then we simply cannot condone this kind of conduct."

Representative Harold V. Froehlich of Wisconsin points out, "The President is shown to be a man concerned with detail, with the salad at the banquet table . . . the pictures on the wall . . . yet a man [who] we are asked to believe did not demand or receive a clear and true picture of the real situation."

Committee Democrats are equally scathing. Representative Jack Brooks of Texas declares angrily, "Never in our 198 years have we had evidence of such rampant corruption in government."

"Impeachment is the one way," points out Representative Robert Kastenmeier of Wisconsin, "in which the American people can say to themselves that they care enough about their own institutions, their own freedom and their claim to self-government, their national honor, to purge from the presidency anyone who has dishonored the office."

"Refusal to impeach," warns Representative William Hungate of Missouri, "would be a decision as momentous as impeachment itself. . . . The evidence against Mr. Nixon is in his own words—made public at his own direction. There can no longer be a charge he was railroaded out of office by vengeful Democrats or a hostile press."

Representative John F. Seiberling of Ohio observes that the President "was obsessed with the preservation and extension of his own personal power. In the name of protecting his associates and himself, President Nixon was willing to use the powers of the government to destroy anything which he considered an actual or potential threat to his power."

"I am overwhelmed by the stark contrast this [evidence]

presents to the President's words and actions," declares Representative Elizabeth Holtzman of New York. "Nowhere in the thousands of pages . . . does the President ask: 'What does the Constitution say? What are the limits of my power? What does my oath of office require of me? What is the right thing to do?' "

Republicans on the House Judiciary Committee attack the proposed Doar articles of impeachment as too broad and imprecise. Ranking Republican Edward Hutchinson of Michigan argues that they "leave the defendant . . . groping around trying to find out what he's accused of." Representative Charles Wiggins of California demands specific proof of when, where, and how the President was supposed to have set the cover-up in motion: "Simple theories are, of course, inadequate. That is not evidence."

Representative Charles Sandman of New Jersey demands "specificity" of the charges, tying the crimes of his aides directly to the President. Representative David Dennis of Indiana shouts angrily that he will join in no "political lynching": "You cannot tear the Constitution up and throw it away, and that's what you're doing!" Representative Delbert R. Latta of Ohio warns that impeachment could set a dangerous precedent "which could have a far greater impact . . . than any mortal man can foresee."

Nixon's defenders demand to be shown hard evidence—the "smoking gun" in the President's hand. Republican Hamilton Fish of New York replies, "They are not going to find it because the room is too full of smoke." Representative Hungate evokes laughter by observing, "If a guy brought an elephant through the door, some of the doubters would say, 'You know, that's an inference. That could be a mouse with a glandular condition.' "

Soft-spoken Jerome R. Waldie, California Democrat, points out, "Common sense tells you that a President of the United States does not condone the payment of over $400,000 to seven people occupying a District of Columbia jail cell because they have committed a burglary, unless he wants something from them. That is not compassion. . . . That was cover-up."

Nixon merits impeachment, says Representative George Danielson, California Democrat, whether he directed hush-money payments or just agreed to them. "He's the chief executive officer with the responsibility for seeing that the laws are enforced. He should have beat on the table, kicked the wastebasket, called the marshal and sent the people who suggested it to jail."

On July 27, 1974, the thirty-eight men and women of the House Judiciary Committee prepare to vote "Aye" or "No" on Article I of the Bill of Impeachment. This specifies that the President has obstructed justice by covering up the Watergate break-in, interfering with the FBI, withholding evidence, encouraging perjury, approving hush money, using the CIA as a cloak, using confidential FBI information to help his aides avoid criminal prosecution, and deceiving the American people.

Suspense runs high across the nation. How many Republicans will break ranks to vote with the Democrats to impeach a Republican President?

Eleven Republicans hold to the party line, but six—Railsback, Fish, Hogan, Butler, Cohen, and Froehlich—join the Democrats in a 27 to 11 vote for Article I.

Article II specifies that the President has abused his powers by misusing Federal agencies, including the FBI, CIA, and IRS; by violating citizens' rights through wiretaps and plots of the Plumbers; and by violating his oath to see that the laws are faithfully executed. The House Judiciary Committee votes for this article by an even higher vote—28 to 10—with seven Republicans supporting this ground for impeachment.

Article III specifies that the President is guilty of contempt of Congress by refusing to produce the tapes and documents subpoenaed as needed evidence. This article passes by the much slimmer margin of 21 to 17.

Two articles, accusing Nixon of infringing on congressional war powers by secretly bombing Cambodia and of tax fraud, are defeated; Representative Railsback describes them as "political overkill." Impeachment by a majority of the House, and conviction by two thirds of the Senate, on any one of the three approved charges is sufficient to oust the President from office.

The Bill of Impeachment concludes, "In all of this, Richard M. Nixon has acted in a manner contrary to his trust as President and subversive of constitutional government, to the great prejudice of the cause of law and justice, and to the manifest injury of the people of the United States. Wherefore Richard M. Nixon, by such conduct, warrants impeachment and trial and removal from office."

The American people are greatly impressed by the fairness and earnestness of the House Judiciary Committee deliberations they have watched on television. The Harris poll shows a favorable opinion of the legislators by a 65 to 29 margin. The six Republican votes for Article I, and the seven for Article II, ruin any hopes of Nixon's supporters being able to discredit impeachment proceedings as a Democratic vendetta.

Representative Latta of Ohio desperately seeks to head off a certain impeachment vote by the House. He circulates a petition to substitute instead a vote of censure of Nixon for "negligence and maladministration," but this transparent maneuver to keep Nixon in office has few supporters.

The hearings of the House Judiciary Committee win applause abroad. "This debate was a lesson in democracy," observes West Germany's *Stuttgarter Zeitung*. Tokyo's *Mainichi Shimbun* declares, "We are deeply impressed by the basic soundness of the American political system and the political consciousness of the American people underlying the impeachment drama."

Day after day Nixon sits brooding in his isolated Executive Office Building office, listening to sixty-four more tapes he must surrender to the special prosecutor. He knows that his support is eroding fast, both in his own party and among the Southern Democrats who were his allies. With the Senate already preparing for his trial, there is growing doubt that President Nixon can count on a third of the Senate vote to block impeachment.

Bad news increases his gloom. His former Treasury Secretary, John Connally, is indicted for taking a $10,000 bribe from the milk industry to influence Nixon in granting a price hike, perjury, and conspiracy to obstruct justice. And Judge Gesell sentences Ehrlichman to a term of from twenty months to five years in prison for the Dr. Fielding break-in—"this shameful episode in the history of our country."

When James St. Clair appears in court on July 26 to arrange a turnover of the first batch of tapes, Judge Sirica asks whether as Nixon's counsel he has personally listened to them.

St. Clair says that he has not. "You mean to say," Sirica asks incredulously, "the President wouldn't approve of *your* listening to the tapes?" Flustered, St. Clair promises to familiarize himself with each tape submitted to Jaworski.

Nixon now has no choice but to let St. Clair hear the damning evidence he has suppressed for so long. There is no longer any possibility of more mysterious erasures. By court order the Secret Service has removed the erase button from the White House tape recorder. Besides, there are now duplicates of the subpoenaed tapes with accurate transcripts.

Among the first thirteen conversations subpoenaed by Jaworski that St. Clair listens to are the President's talks with Haldeman on June 23, 1972, only six days after the Watergate break-in. To the lawyer's astonishment he hears Haldeman informing Nixon that the burglars' money had come from CRP campaign funds, and the President ordering Haldeman to use the CIA to stop the FBI from pursuing the investigation. *The "smoking gun!"*

Shocked, St. Clair tells Chief of Staff Haig. Both agree that once the truth becomes known—as it now must in Jaworski's hands—the President's impeachment and conviction will be swift and automatic. Haig tells Kissinger, who agrees that there is now no way the President can cling to his office.

On August 1 Haig has two meetings with Ford at which he warns the Vice-President that new taped evidence has come to light which can have "devastating, even catastrophic" consequences for Nixon, and advises Ford to be ready "to assume the Presidency within a very short time." Ford is stunned. Haig mentions the possibility of "a pardon to the President should he resign." Ford asks what powers of pardon a President has. Haig replies that they are broad enough to pardon a man even before any charges have been brought against him. Ford later denies that these discussions were in any way a deal or agreement, with the understanding that if he becomes President he would protect Nixon from prosecution by granting him a pardon.

Taking a trip south, on August 3 Ford tells a Republican luncheon, "I still think the President is innocent of any impeachable offense." Next day a Harris poll shows that 66 percent of the American people believe the House should vote to impeach Nixon. Ford later explains that he did not want to seem to be trying to force Nixon out of office by turning on him suddenly.

St. Clair, Haig, and Kissinger set about convincing the proud, stubborn Nixon to resign and spare himself and the country the humiliation of impeachment, trial, and removal from office. They try to persuade him that his cause is hopeless and let him reach by himself the decision to resign. But Nixon doggedly argues that the June 23, 1972, evidence is "inconsequential."

St. Clair, however, warns that it must be made public at once. By releasing it first, Nixon can cushion some of the shock with a self-serving statement to put it in the best possible light. When Nixon balks, St. Clair again indicates he will resign if his advice is ignored. A despondent Nixon mutters, "What's done is done. Let it go."

St. Clair and Haig seek to keep Nixon from changing his mind by spreading the secret to Congress. On Friday, August 2, St. Clair phones Charles Wiggins, Nixon's chief defender on the House Judiciary Committee, and asks him to "come over and talk." Wiggins goes to the White House, where St. Clair and Haig show him the transcript of the Nixon-Haldeman conversations.

Wiggins is dismayed by the "smoking gun" he and his colleagues had demanded to see before voting for impeachment and angered that until now this information has been withheld from the House Judiciary Committee. He warns that unless the President makes this damning evidence of cover-up public by Monday, he will.

Copies of the June 23, 1972, transcripts are hastily prepared, along with a Nixon statement admitting that he has withheld vital evidence. These are circulated among party leaders before they are made public. Representative John Rhodes of Arizona, Republican minority leader of the House, takes one look at the evidence and decides it is "so overwhelming there was no way the President could stay in office."

On Monday afternoon, August 5, St. Clair meets with eight of the ten Republicans on the Judiciary Committee who voted against impeachment and gives them copies. Representative Latta of Ohio says afterward, "We were just dumfounded. We'd put our trust in the President. We felt he was telling us the truth. . . . It was a terrible, let-down feeling." Representative Henry P. Smith of New York declares, "We all felt we had been betrayed." St. Clair says he, too, feels betrayed.

The following day all the members of the committee who voted against impeachment decide to change their vote, making the recommendation to the full House unanimous. The reason is quickly clear to the American people when Nixon's statement is released.

The President admits that when he had made public the first set of White House transcripts in April, he had not been truthful in assuring the American people that they would "tell it all" with respect to what he personally knew and did about Watergate. He acknowledges that because he had kept the June 23, 1972, taped talks with Haldeman a secret from both James St. Clair and the House Judiciary Committee, the committee's members had "information that was incomplete and in some respects erroneous . . . a serious act of omission . . . which I deeply regret."

Nixon acknowledges that the new tapes are "at variance with certain of my previous statements." Admitting that he did not tell the truth in his May assertion that he ordered his aides to stop the FBI investigation for "national security reasons," he admits that the tapes show "I also discussed the political aspects of the situation, and that I was aware of the [election] advantages" of the cover-up.

Trapped in his own web of deception, he urges that the evidence against him "be looked at in its entirety and . . . in perspective." He pleads, "I am firmly convinced that the record, in its entirety, does not justify the extreme step of impeachment and removal of a President."

His guilt is now plain to the millions of Americans who believed in him and whom he betrayed by persistently lying to them. The President's liaison staff warns him that his Senate support is crumbling fast; he cannot count on the thirty-four votes he needs to prevent an impeachment conviction. Senator Robert P. Griffin, Republican whip, tells reporters that Nixon's resignation would be in the best interests of the nation.

On the presidential yacht *Sequoia,* members of the Presi-

dent's family urge him not to resign but to fight this seventh—
and worst—crisis of his political career. They assure him it will
soon fade away, like the uproar over the Saturday Night
Massacre. Resisting the growing cry for him to get out of the
White House, Nixon insists that he is not guilty of "high crimes
and misdemeanors."

His defenders argue that the President is not bound by the
same laws that apply to ordinary citizens; that impeaching him
will hurt the office of the Presidency; that other Presidents have
also committed crimes but were not caught; that our nation's
foreign policy requires that Nixon remain in office; that the
whole Watergate scandal has been overplayed and ought to be
put aside for the "greater good of the nation."

On Tuesday, August 6, Nixon summons his Cabinet to rally
their support. Insisting that he has no intention of resigning, he
tries to convince them that Watergate occurred because he was
too busy with foreign affairs to keep tabs on what his aides were
doing.

The New York Stock Exchange, August 6, 1974. Hope that the
Watergate affair is nearing a climax sends the market soaring.

When Senator Goldwater is informed, he says testily, "There are only so many lies you can take, and now there have been one too many. Nixon should get . . . out of the White House *today!*" He receives a phone call from Haig, who asks how many senators will stand by the President in impeachment proceedings. Goldwater estimates a maximum of fifteen—less than half the number Nixon needs to survive—but privately doubts that the President can count on even nine.

Meanwhile the new White House tapes are being played as evidence for members of the full House of Representatives preparing to vote on the Judiciary Committee's bill of impeachment. Representative Ronald V. Dellums, California Democrat, exclaims, "It sounds just like a Gestapo meeting!" Representative Peter Peyser, New York Republican, marvels, "You begin to realize the conniving—the things you wouldn't think a President would be dealing with."

Haig gets Henry Kissinger to point out to Nixon on August 6 that a prolonged Senate trial would have a "devastating" effect on foreign policy. Kissinger indicates that resignation is the only way out.

Republican leaders decide to send a three-man delegation to the White House to force the President to face reality. Senators Scott and Goldwater and Representative Rhodes secure an appointment with Nixon on Wednesday, August 7. They avoid using the word "resignation," fearful it will only make him more stubborn, but they let him know that of the 435 members of the House, about 425 intend to vote for his impeachment, while at the Senate trial he will be unable to count on even a dozen of the thirty-four senators he needs to prevent conviction.

Senator Scott calls the situation gloomy. "Damn gloomy," Nixon admits. Goldwater adds, "Hopeless." Nixon sighs, "I just wanted to hear it from you." He adds bitterly, "I campaigned for a lot of people. Some were turkeys, but I campaigned for all of them." And now that he needs them to save him, they are voting instead to impeach him.

Cornered and isolated, the President finally surrenders.

Summoning Gerald Ford on August 8, he notifies the Vice-President that within twenty-four hours Ford will be

August 7. Nixon and Ziegler on the way to the meeting with Senators Goldwater and Scott and House Republican leader Rhodes.

President. Rumors spread like wildfire, and crowds gather outside the White House fence. Anti-Nixon signs appear, and voices cry, "Jail to the Chief!" When a few last-ditch Nixon defenders protest this lack of "patriotism," a conservative Republican replies, "Nixon represents only Nixon—*not* the country!"

At eight o'clock that evening the President meets with forty-six of his most loyal supporters in Congress to thank them. His behavior is strange, as though he is verging on a breakdown.

August 7. The first family poses for the White House photographer. Left to right: Edward and Tricia Cox, President and Mrs. Nixon, Julie and David Eisenhower.

Noting that this will be his last meeting in the Cabinet Room, he suddenly laughs loudly. He talks distractedly about his early years in college sports, then laughs again.

"I don't know when I'll come back to Washington," he says forlornly, "if ever." Overcome with emotion, he sobs and is forced to say, "Wait a bit," before he can continue. Many of his followers weep with him. A President in disgrace, he now seems a pitiful figure. Representative Elford A. Cederberg, Michigan Republican, describes him as "pretty much a broken man."

Half an hour later, his composure recovered, Nixon goes on television to announce with controlled calm that he will resign the next day. He declares, "It has become evident to me that I no longer have a strong enough political base in Congress" to stay in office, as though he had simply lost a political battle instead of being faced with certain impeachment and conviction for high crimes and misdemeanors.

"I have never been a quitter," he continues. "To leave office before my term is completed is opposed to every instinct in my body. But as President I must put the interests of America first.

. . . I would say only that if some of my judgments were wrong—and some were wrong—they were made in what I believed at the time to be the best interests of the nation."

His sloughing-off of criminal acts and abuses of power as errors of judgment only, with no acknowledgement of guilt, and his use of the speech for self-serving eulogy, angers millions of Americans. His absence of contrition and failure to apologize to the millions of Americans he has betrayed and deceived outrages Republican Senator Edward Brooke of Massachusetts, who has introduced a Senate resolution urging Jaworski not to prosecute Nixon as a civilian if he resigns. Brooke states that he will not support his own resolution.

On Friday morning, August 9, 1974, a perspiring, red-eyed Richard Nixon gathers his staff and Cabinet to bid them farewell in a maudlin and distracted speech, recalling his childhood,

Crowds gather outside the White House as rumors spread.

August 8, 1974. The President announces his resignation.

struggles, and accomplishments. With unconscious irony the President whose White House operated under a siege mentality of "us against them," in an atmosphere of spite and hatred, counsels his listeners never to be petty or to hate those who hate them because to do so is self-destructive.

At one point he breaks down and sobs—a bewildered man, ruined by his own deeds, filled with self-pity and wonder that a mere lack of moral principles could have tumbled him from the highest office in the land to the pit of resignation under fire and disgrace.

There are consolations. Resignation preserves his $60,000 annual pension, an expensive staff paid by government funds, and his expectations of over $1,000,000 a year to sustain him at San Clemente. It also permits him to escape the stigma of becoming the first President ever removed from office by House impeachment and Senate conviction.

The President has received urgent requests from Haldeman and Ehrlichman that he pardon them before handing in his own resignation. They suggest a "package deal" to make the pardons appear part of a general act of clemency, by also granting amnesty to Vietnam draft evaders and deserters in exile and jail.

Nixon refuses, resenting the requests as "blackmailing" in tone. He knows, besides, that the pardons would raise a new storm of fury against him for a final act of cover-up, preventing the trial of his aides which is expected to air his own guilt in court. Out of office he will no longer be immune to indictment as a Watergate coconspirator. He dares not flout the public opinion that he hopes will save him from the final ignominy of criminal prosecution.

On Friday morning, August 9, 1974, at 11:30 A.M., he

August 9, 1974. Vice-President Ford and his wife escort the Nixons to the waiting helicopter on the White House lawn.

dispatches a formal letter of resignation to Secretary of State Kissinger as senior Cabinet member. He and Mrs. Nixon are seen off by the Fords as they board the helicopter taking them to the silver and blue presidential jet, *Spirit of '76*, to return home to California.

While the plane is over Missouri, heartland of the Middle America Nixon claimed as his constituency, Gerald Ford takes the oath of office as the thirty-eighth President of the United States, and Richard M. Nixon flies on into retirement as a private citizen.

AUGUST 9, 1974

Office of the White House Press Secretary

THE WHITE HOUSE

The following letter was delivered by General Alexander M. Haig Jr.
to the Secretary of State in his White House office at 11:35 a.m. today:

The White House
Washington

August 9, 1974

Dear Mr. Secretary:

I hereby resign the Office of President of the
United States.

Sincerely,

/s/ Richard Nixon

The Honorable Henry A. Kissinger
The Secretary of State
Washington, D.C. 20520

\# \# \#

As the President's plane is airborne, his letter of resignation becomes effective.

21

Out of the Crisis

At his inauguration Gerald Ford eschews the Nixon love of pomp by asking the band *not* to play "Hail to the Chief." He declares, "Truth is the glue that holds governments together. . . ." He acknowledges that this bond has been stained by "the internal wounds of Watergate, more painful and more poisonous than those of foreign wars. . . ." But he tells his fellow Americans, "Our long national nightmare is over. Our Constitution works. Our great Republic is a government of laws and not of men. Here, the people rule." Promising to be the President of *all* Americans, he vows to run an open, candid, and honest Administration.

There is rejoicing in the big cities, and students celebrate on college campuses. New Yorkers flock to Times Square as though it were New Year's Eve. Jubilant San Franciscans square-dance in the streets. Most Americans, however, are simply vastly relieved by Nixon's resignation and hope that the new President will be able to attend to such urgent national problems as inflation, growing unemployment, and fuel shortages.

Reaction to the resignation abroad is highly favorable. Italy's *La Stampa* headlines the news: AMERICA HAS WON; NIXON RESIGNS. West Germany's *Vorwärts* calls it a "deliverance." London's *Daily Telegraph* sees it as "an unconscious act of cleansing and renewal, with Richard Nixon as the ritual sacrifice, embodying all the less reputable aspects of [America's] rambunctious democracy."

American liberals are disappointed, however, that Nixon has taken the "easy way out" by resigning—an act he repeatedly swore he would never consider—instead of facing an impeachment trial. They wanted his guilt clearly spelled out as a warning to future Presidents tempted by the arrogance of power.

On August 10 the American Constitutional Rights Committee files a $25,000,000 class-action suit against Nixon and CRP, and asks that the 1972 presidential election be declared null and void because of "fraud and corruption." The Democratic party agrees to settle its civil suit against CRP over the Watergate break-in for $775,000. Lawrence O'Brien announces that he will return his portion of the settlement—$400,000—to the Democratic party, to be used in a program "to re-enlist the confidence of the American people in our two-party system."

A new dilemma faces Americans. The Watergate grand jury named the former President as an "unindicted co-conspirator." Now that he is a private citizen, should he not be indicted, just as his former Vice-President, Agnew, was?

Many of Nixon's former supporters, sad and depressed in their disillusionment, feel that his resignation in disgrace is punishment enough. They wince at the idea of forcing a former President to stand trial on criminal charges and perhaps even end up in jail.

But the American Bar Association points out that under American law, all men are equal; none is above the law, which must be applied impartially "regardless of the position or status of any individual alleged to have violated the law." Because of Nixon's cover-up of Watergate, over thirty of his aides have been indicted, many of them convicted and sent to jail. Can justice be said to be served if the hirelings go to prison to protect their master while the chief conspirator himself goes free?

Columnist Garry Wills refers to Nixon as a "guy who sent all his troops out to be shot before he finally dragged out himself." The *Cleveland Plain Dealer* argues against clemency because Nixon's resignation speech has shown "no humility, no admission of the real abuse of power spread on the record." The

Los Angeles Times demands that Nixon's Federal pension be denied him so that he does not receive a "reward for malfeasance."

As the special prosecutor deliberates over the question of indicting the former President, Georgia state representative Julian Bond points out that Nixon denied amnesty to dissenters who resisted the draft out of conscientious objection to the Vietnam War and were punished by prison or forced into exile. Bond adds caustically, "The prisons of Georgia are full of people who stole $5 and $10, and this man tried to steal the Constitution of the United States."

Meanwhile a new tone in the White House is quickly made manifest by its genial, popular new occupant. Gerald Ford declares, "I've had lots of opponents, but no enemies that I can remember." An unassuming, informal man who toasts his own English muffins for breakfast and works in the Oval Office in his shirt sleeves, he sends a gust of fresh air through the White House with a festive dinner party to which liberal Democrats and even a *Washington Post* reporter are invited.

When Ford's son publicly declares that Nixon owes the American people a "total confession," the President merely remarks, "All my children have spoken for themselves. . . . I expect that to continue."

Congressmen, senators, governors, mayors, and labor leaders of both parties, who have not set foot in the White House in six years, are now cordially welcomed there. Ford is acclaimed by old friends when he addresses a joint session of Congress to pledge a new era of "communication, conciliation, compromise and cooperation."

He tells Congress, "I do not want a honeymoon with you—I want a good marriage. . . . I intend to listen to the people themselves. . . . My office door has always been open, and that is how it is going to be at the White House." Hailing the press for its role in preserving democracy, he promises, "There will be no illegal tappings, eavesdropping, buggings or break-ins in *my* administration." The chamber rocks with applause.

"The sun is shining again," says Mike Mansfield, Democratic leader of the Senate. A Gallup poll shows that 71 percent of the American people believe in the integrity, honesty, and candor of the new President. Almost overnight the tarnished office of the Presidency has regained its prestige.

Republicans who despaired of their chances in the 1972 and 1974 elections see new hope that Watergate may finally be put behind them. For a month Ford's moves win applause from Democrats and Republicans alike, as well as from the press. A Midwest conservative, he wins the support of the Eastern liberal wing of the Republican party and many Democrats by selecting ex-Governor Nelson Rockefeller of New York to be his Vice-President, although some are disenchanted when questionable acts by Rockefeller surface at congressional hearings on his nomination.

He mends fences with black voters by making personal calls to neglected black leaders in Congress. When sixteen big-city mayors ask whom they can deal with on urban problems, Ford replies, "Start with me." Using soft words, first names, and a conciliatory approach, he dissolves the fear and hatred the Nixon Administration has left in its wake. To "bind America's wounds," he announces his intention of setting up a board to study amnesty for Vietnam draft resisters and deserters.

Suddenly on September 8, 1974, after church on a quiet Sunday morning, President Ford stuns the nation by a television and radio announcement. He begins by stating that he has had a change of mind brought about by his conscience and prayers. He now feels that someone must write "The End" to the tragedy of Richard Nixon and his family, out of mercy and concern for the former President's health. He explains that he believes that years must pass before Nixon can get a fair trial and that it would be unjust to keep him suffering under this cloud.

The nation, he argues, would again be polarized and hurt by a revival of "ugly passions." Insisting, "I cannot rely upon public-opinion polls to tell me what is right," he adds, "If I am wrong ten angels swearing I was right would make no difference." He concludes, "I feel that Richard Nixon and his loved ones have suffered enough," and grants "a full, free and absolute" pardon to the former President for "all offenses against the United States" committed while in office.

Ford adds fuel to the fire by asking Congress for $800,000 in "transitional" expenses for Nixon and by arranging to turn over

President Ford signs the document that grants Richard Nixon a "full, free and absolute pardon" for all offenses he may have committed while in office.

the Nixon tapes and White House papers to the former President as his private property. The White House is instantly engulfed in another storm of protest against what most Americans see as a blatant violation of the code of equal justice under the law. Telegrams and phone calls run 6 to 1 against the pardon.

The media and most Americans are suspicious that a deal was made before Nixon's resignation—Nixon stepping down to make Ford President in exchange for the pledge of a pardon. Ford's credibility is suddenly badly damaged, especially after having answered, when he was asked at his confirmation hearing for Vice-President how he felt about a pardon for Nixon if he became President, that, "I don't think the public would stand for it."

Nixon issues a statement, accepting the pardon without admitting any criminal guilt. He again tries to make his offenses seem only political mistakes, professing, "I know that many fair-minded people believe that my motivations and actions in the Watergate affair were intentionally self-serving and illegal. I now understand how my own mistakes and misjudgments have contributed to that belief and seemed to support it. . . . That the way I tried to deal with Watergate was the wrong way is a burden I shall bear for every day of the life that is left to me." His offense, he implies, was only "in not acting more decisively and more forthrightly" in exposing Watergate.

The protests grow so furious that it is clear the pardon has wiped out almost all the goodwill, trust, confidence, and hope Ford had inspired since taking office. Ford's press secretary, Jerald F. terHorst, resigns in protest, rather than face reporters in an attempt to justify the President's action.

"This is the final chapter of the Watergate cover-up," declares Senator Floyd Haskell of Colorado. He points out it will "only confirm what too many Americans already believe: that there is one set of laws for the rich and powerful, another for everyone else."

Newsweek's letters run 25 to 1 against the pardon. The comments are devastating: "Jerald F. terHorst has helped many Americans to hold their heads high when the President's action has made most hold their noses"; "Do you suppose Dick had the presence of mind to shut off the recorders when he and Jerry cooked up the pardon deal?"; "President Ford has named himself still another participant in the Watergate cover-up"; "We are tired of Watergate, but we are not tired of justice and . . . equality under the law."

Judges and lawyers across the nation are dismayed that the President has apparently established a double standard of justice for the nation. One judge angrily refuses any longer to convict traffic offenders, and another orders the release of prisoners jailed for nonviolent crimes. Harvard Law professor Raoul Berger worries the pardon "will breed disrespect for the law."

President Ford expected criticism, but he is shaken by the magnitude of the protest. He realizes that the pardon cannot be explained away as an act of mercy while objectors to the Vietnam War, draft evaders, and military deserters are still in jail or exile, and while Nixon's former aides are in jail or under indictment. Is mercy a commodity to be dealt out only to ex-Presidents?

President Ford now makes his second mistake. He has a White House spokesman reveal that he is also studying the possibility of pardoning *everyone* involved in Watergate. The President is now accused of trying to pull off the supreme cover-up of Watergate, where Nixon had failed. If the trials of Nixon's chief aides do not take place, the nation will never hear all the legal evidence establishing the Nixon Administration's guilt or innocence once and for all.

The new uproar brings a hasty correction from the White House. The statement that the President would consider a blanket pardon for the Watergate defendants was "misunderstood," and Ford has no such intention. The trial of Haldeman, Ehrlichman, Mitchell, Mardian, and Parkinson for the Watergate cover-up will go forward.

Public outrage continues so high that President Ford is forced to make several speeches admitting that his pardon of Nixon is highly unpopular. "I'm still convinced," he insists, "despite the public reaction so far, that the decision I made was the right one." Answering criticism that he had permitted Nixon to escape trial without even confessing guilt, Ford declares, "The acceptance of a pardon, I think, can be construed by many, if not all, as an admission of guilt." Rockefeller also expresses this view. The former President has been punished by the "shame and disgrace" of his downfall.

Many Americans feel that Ford's earlier talk about amnesty for Vietnam draft resisters and deserters was principally an attempt to make the pardon of Nixon palatable. On September 16, Ford hastily introduces an amnesty plan to let them "earn their way back into American society" by two years of compulsory public-service work. Outraged liberals point out that no such requirement was imposed upon Richard Nixon.

Few American exiles in Canada or Sweden accept Ford's

conditional amnesty. "The government was wrong in waging an illegal, immoral war," declares their spokesman in Canada, "not us in resisting the draft out of conscience."

Many Americans worry that since Nixon has been able to escape trial without admitting his guilt, his defenders may try to make a martyr out of him, claiming he has been unjustly driven from office by a conspiracy of the press and the Democratic party. For this reason the House Judiciary Committee completes its report, despite Nixon's resignation, and submits it to the full House as a matter of official record.

In a unanimous final judgment, the House Judiciary Committee finds "that from shortly after the break-in on June 17, 1972, President Nixon personally directed his subordinates to take action designed to delay, impede, and obstruct the investigation of the Watergate break-in; to cover up, conceal and protect those responsible; and to conceal . . . other unlawful covert activities."

An addendum on behalf of the Republican members of the committee adds, "We hope . . . that it will not hereafter be said by many that Richard Nixon was 'toppled from office,' for that is not true. It was Richard Nixon, not his longtime critics, who impeded the FBI's investigation of the Watergate affair by wrongfully trying to implicate the CIA. It was Richard Nixon, not seasoned Nixon-baiters, who created and preserved the damning evidence of that transgression and who, knowing that it had been subpoenaed by both this committee and the special prosecutor, concealed its terrible import until he could do so no longer."

As the Watergate cover-up trial opens on October 1, 1974, Nixon is hospitalized in California with phlebitis, and physicians determine that he will be unable to travel for at least three months. A subsequent operation enables him to avoid subpoenas requiring him to appear as a witness.

Nevertheless, Ehrlichman, bitter at Nixon's refusal to pardon him while he had the chance, is now determined to prove that the former President was the real mastermind behind the cover-up, and that criminal acts carried out by his aides were at his specific direction.

"Richard Nixon deceived, misled, lied and used John

Ehrlichman to cover up his own knowledge and his own activities," Ehrlichman's lawyer, John Frates, asserts. But Dean testifies at the trial that Ehrlichman was active in the Watergate cover-up from the start. Dean is also unshaken in his testimony implicating Mitchell, Haldeman, Mardian, and Parkinson as participants in the conspiracy.

When public indignation over Nixon's pardon refuses to die down, President Ford feels compelled to appear before the House Subcommittee on Criminal Justice on October 17, 1974, to answer questions about circumstances surrounding the pardon. He is the only President other than Washington and Lincoln to appear before a Congressional committee while in office.

Giving his reasons once more for the pardon, and explaining the talks he had had about it beforehand, he declares, "I want to assure you, the members of this subcommittee, members of the Congress and the American people, there was no deal, period, under no circumstances."

Congress nevertheless remains angry about his agreement to turn Nixon's tapes and White House papers over to the former President. It passes special legislation nullifying this arrangement and keeping these records at the White House.

On November 6, 1974, the Democrats win a sweeping victory in congressional and state elections, as the American people register their anger at the Republicans for the Watergate disaster and the presidential pardon. The four House Judiciary Committee Republicans who defended Nixon to the end— Charles Sandman and Joseph Maraziti of New Jersey, Wiley Mayne of Iowa and David Dennis of Indiana—are all resoundingly defeated. "I didn't think Watergate would carry this far," Sandman admits, "but it has."

As the Watergate cover-up trial winds to its conclusion, Judge Sirica instructs the jury that Richard Nixon's pardon should make no difference to their judging the defendants. After over fifteen hours of deliberation, the jury brings in its verdict on January 1, 1975.

Mitchell and Haldeman are found guilty of conspiracy, obstruction of justice, and three counts each of perjury. Ehrlichman is convicted of conspiracy, obstruction of justice, and two counts of perjury. Mardian is found guilty of conspiracy. Only Parkinson is acquitted.

Millions of Americans protest that justice has not been done because President Ford's controversial pardon before trial has let the chief conspirator off scot-free while those who obeyed his criminal orders are being sent to prison. "San Clemente for Nixon," says one of the defendants' lawyers bitterly, "and San Quentin for everybody else."

But Special Prosecutor Leon Jaworski declares, "I'm not troubled by the fact that the former President is not going to jail. No President has ever suffered the infamy and disgrace that this one did. It was even more ignominious than sitting in the slammer. What sank him was his lying."

Nixon's immunity to punishment is too much for Judge Sirica, however. Early in January he orders the early release from jail of John Dean, Jeb Magruder, and Herbert Kalmbach. They, at least, had confessed their crimes and cooperated with the prosecution. Soon afterward, Judge Byrne similarly orders the early release of Colson, because of his cooperation as well as "serious family problems."

On January 1, 1975, President Ford signs into law the most sweeping political campaign reform bill in the nation's history, preventing repetition of the abuses that had been at the heart of the Watergate scandal.

So, at last, the final chapter has been written on the fantastic story that began with the arrest of five burglars in the Democratic National Headquarters on June 17, 1972.

22

What Did It All Mean?

Never before in American history had there been anything like it. A President who had won re-election by a huge electoral majority was forced to divest himself of his whole administrative staff. Facing certain impeachment, conviction, and removal from office, he was forced to resign.

How did it all happen?

Nixon's fantastically expensive and corrupt campaign for re-election obviously hoodwinked the vast majority of those Americans who took the trouble to vote. They were sold an image of Richard Nixon the President as a great exponent of law and order, morality, virtue, patriotism, and accomplishment in office. His opponent, George McGovern, was successfully characterized as an indecisive bungler and an unpatriotic, dangerous radical.

"When you look back on Mr. Nixon's career," Robert M. Hutchins, former chairman of the Center for the Study of Democratic Institutions, points out, "starting from the days when he ran against Jerry Voorhis and Helen Gahagan Douglas, there is something very familiar about Watergate. . . . I find that hard to ignore."

The flaws in Richard Nixon's own character drove him to ruthless lengths to hold the White House as his personal fiefdom for eight years and had then led to his downfall. A man with an insatiable desire for power and praise, he was opportunistic, vain, arrogant, insincere, and cunning. His insecurity made him suspect plots against him everywhere, and filled him with fear, spite, and hatred.

He behaved, columnist Stewart Alsop noted, as if he were waging war, not politics. He recklessly disregarded the legal limits of the democratic process to destroy those he marked as his enemies. Calling for "national unity," he actually divided the country, manipulating public opinion against his critics.

It was possibly Nixon's appetite for self-glorification that led him to install secret tape recorders to preserve every word he spoke in the White House. He then made the fatal error of failing to destroy those tapes with evidence of his misdeeds, never imagining that the tapes could be pried from his control. Without this proof that he persistently lied in his protestations of innocence, Richard Nixon might well have succeeded in his cover-up of Watergate, his abuses of power, his obstructions of justice, his defiance of Congress.

The Watergate scandal convinced Americans that money was, indeed, the root of all evil in the nation's politics, corrupting candidates who accepted in secret large illegal sums from powerful special interests. Under the prevailing rules, money was buying elections for politicians pledged to favor those interests at the expense of the public.

Watergate also revealed that Nixon had turned American democracy into a semiautocracy, under which great and secret power was wielded. "The power of government," said Senator Weicker, "was used not on behalf of change or on behalf of the weak, but on behalf of the status quo and on behalf of the strong—and to stifle dissent."

Senator Walter Mondale of Minnesota observed, "Ironically, at a time when Mr. Nixon said he was conducting his foreign policy to establish dialogue and to ease the tensions of the Cold War abroad, he was invoking the Cold War national security rationale to stifle dialogue and dissent at home. The techniques of foreign espionage have been used to distort the domestic political process."

Even while posing as a peacemaker, Nixon waged unconstitutional warfare in Cambodia and Laos, without the knowledge or consent of Congress. Only after Watergate did Americans grow aware of how weak and enfeebled Congress had become, abdicating its responsibility to keep the executive branch of the government from exercising dictatorial powers.

When a CBS newsman asked Ehrlichman if Nixon wasn't turning the government into one-man rule, the President's top adviser for domestic affairs replied, "Sure, that's what the President of the United States is for."

Nixon had not been the first President to misuse his powers. Senator J. William Fulbright, describing earlier holders of the office, once called such abuse of the Presidency "the arrogance of power." This arrogance was made possible by excessive glorification of the Chief Executive far beyond that accorded by any other democratic people to their elected leaders. The American tendency to venerate the occupant of the White House led Richard Nixon to behave more and more like a monarch. John Cogley, editor of *Center Magazine*, noted "the blare of trumpets before the First Family's appearance; the deliberate, majestic descent down the stairs, with all eyes on the Leader and his lady."

Former Secretary of Defense Clark Clifford observed that the pomp of the Presidency under Nixon and his rule of the nation from two splendid government-subsidized private homes in California and Florida were a far cry from the notion of the office held by the Founding Fathers.

"When the present incumbent moves to one of his other 'White Houses,'" Clifford observed during the Nixon era, "it is almost as though the czar were moving to his summer quarters and taking his court with him. . . . A President does not have to live that way. . . . The man who holds the office begins to accept the concept that he is a ruler whose powers do not come from the people. . . . This is where an exalted, distorted, and corrupted view of the presidency has led us today."

"Our problem," said Father Theodore M. Hesburgh, president of Notre Dame, "is that we keep looking for a single leader on a white horse." This exaltation of the national leader contributed to the Watergate syndrome. The men around Nixon gave their allegiance not to the Constitution, but to the President personally. Such blind loyalty led them to commit criminal acts to shield Nixon from the consequences of his credo that any means were justified to keep him for eight years in the White House.

Richard Kleindienst, Nixon's second Attorney General, insisted that three million government employees of the Federal civil service owed the President their allegiance. Yet the civil-service system had been set up originally for the very purpose of removing governmental jobs from political control.

Nixon and his men acted on the assumption that whatever served him best—personally, politically, and diplomatically— benefited the nation. Vanity soon led him to confuse himself with his high office. He was fond of referring to himself in the third person: "The President will not do this"; "The President intends to do that." In suppressing Watergate evidence, he sought to convince the nation that he was concerned only with protecting "the Presidency," not with his personal survival in office.

While posing as a great champion of government economy, Nixon continued a trend begun by his predecessors by expanding the presidential staff to a swollen bureaucracy of five thousand people. Before then, President Franklin D. Roosevelt had had only eight. Nixon used his huge staff of "faceless men" to exercise great authority in his name, free of scrutiny by Congress or the press, until Watergate set off a national alarm.

The AFL-CIO saw Watergate as a "large-scale subversion of the democratic political process . . . when one party, because of its access to vast and excessive sums of money, can exercise the advantages of wealth and power to pervert the Justice Department and the White House itself to undermine its opposition and cement its grip on the reins of government."

During the Nixon Presidency Americans lived under an arbitrary government by men, instead of a government by law. The laws of the land were often broken by the high officials sworn to administer them. When the process by which Americans choose their leaders was sabotaged, the democratic system itself was placed in jeopardy.

Former Senator Wayne Morse of Oregon warned in June 1973, "Most Americans have not faced the fact, or refuse to believe, that our country is being led toward a police state. Ten years before the Third Reich, the German people didn't think theirs was either." There was an unmistakable parallel between what the Nixon Administration tried to do, and the police state's use of a "ministry of justice" to throttle all dissent and political opposition.

No sooner had Nixon been elected in 1968 by a slim victory over Hubert Humphrey than he began scheming how to stay in power for two terms. To Nixon and his men, governing the country became a continuation of the election campaign.

The illegal wiretaps, political espionage, and other early misdeeds of the Nixon Administration represented, in large part, an attempt to weed out government officials who could not be relied upon to be absolutely loyal to the President. Nixon also sought to keep the press from finding out matters that he was keeping secret from Congress and the public, such as the bombings of Cambodia. It became routine for his top aides to resort to police-state tactics for these ends.

Jeb Magruder confessed that somewhere along the way he lost his "ethical compass"—his own home training which had taught him to know right from wrong. He and other Watergate defendants admitted that illegal behavior had simply become a "way of life" in the White House and at CRP. The Nixon Administration operated in behalf of its own welfare, not the good of the nation. As Dwight Chapin insisted, "The important thing is to protect the President."

Trapped in the successful attempt to steal a second term for Nixon and to conceal their tracks, his aides ultimately gave the excuse Hitler's aides gave at the Nuremberg Trials: "We were only following orders." These fiercely ambitious men, noted William V. Shannon in *The New York Times*, "served only their own careers. They had no abiding ethic except to do what their bosses wanted." One did not get ahead in the Nixon Administration by protesting to one's superior, "But what you are ordering me to do is against the law."

The only morality among those high up in the Nixon Administration was "deniability"—shielding oneself from being put on record as knowing of a criminal act, while nevertheless approving it. Thus, when Hugh Sloan tried to find out what the large cash payments to Liddy were for, Maurice Stans told him,

"I don't know . . . and I don't think you ought to try to know."
Ehrlichman did not want to know, either.

Donald Segretti explained to a recruit for his dirty-tricks
campaign: "Nixon knows that something is being done. It's a
typical deal: don't-tell-me-anything-and-I-won't-know." Gordon
Liddy told McCord he was confident his Gemstone budget would
be approved if John Mitchell could be assured of "deniability."
Charles Colson stopped taking phone calls for blackmail because
"I wanted to be able to say I don't know the first —— thing
about it." And the President, though he was told about the
cover-up within one week after the Watergate arrests, kept
denying to the American people that *he* had known. "There has
been an effort to conceal the facts . . . from me," he vowed.

Nixon also did not want to know the truth about opposition
to his policies. His executive staff served to isolate him from
reality. The elaborate precautions of his aides to keep anti-Nixon
demonstrators out of his sight exemplified their dedication to
letting him see and hear only what he wanted to, not what a
President must know in order to govern wisely.

To win re-election the President and his men sought to sell
their Administration as a public-relations package. Many of
Nixon's aides were, in fact, professional "PR men." His fury at
the press stemmed from the refusal of some reporters to feed the
public White House handouts, insisting instead upon searching
out and reporting the facts.

Nixon's paranoia led him to insist that Daniel Ellsberg was
a traitor for publishing the Pentagon Papers; that the Russians
were involved; that the McGovern campaign had ties to
politically violent radical movements; and that foreign enemies
were financing the political opposition to a second Nixon term.
He was infuriated with the FBI and CIA for failing to find any
evidence to support his dark suspicions.

He set up his own secret intelligence network to prove
himself right. Spying on the political opposition, and all the
crimes of Watergate, were inevitable consequences. When the
Plumbers, too, failed to confirm Nixon's suspicions, White House
aides did not hesitate to forge proof. Hunt forged the Kennedy
cables on Colson's orders. Colson spread malicious slanders to

discredit Ellsberg and smear anti-Vietnam Democrats. Colson admitted that almost every dirty trick he carried out for the Administration was on the orders of the President.

To some extent Nixon's actions reflected his fear of the nation's "counterculture" that so upset the Establishment during the 1960's—the antiwar demonstrators, the civil-rights marchers, the college students who rejected all the values Nixon and his neat, short-haired aides stood for. He saw them and political opponents who sympathized with them as a ring of subversive enemies who had to be paralyzed at all costs and by all means.

To destroy this "conspiracy" against him, Nixon persecuted dissenters with illegal arrests and political trials, and harassed through Federal agencies important opponents on his enemies list.

He persistently demanded television time to make "presidential" speeches that were thinly disguised polemics against his critics. Ironically, the more the nation heard him, the less convincing he became. Skepticism followed a growing awareness of Nixon's artificiality—his self-conscious gestures of emphasis; his prefacing of evasive statements with the phrase, "Let me make this perfectly clear"; his accusations followed by the disclaimer, "But I'm not blaming anyone," and a forced smile. Even at the end, in a typical exercise of duplicity he accepted the "responsibility" for Watergate, but not the "blame."

He and his aides accused the media, the Congress, the special prosecutor, the Senate Watergate Committee, Judge Sirica, and the House Judiciary Committee of trying to "get the President." As a growing flood of forced disclosures made their case more desperate, they sought to hold the support of Nixon's true believers by convincing them of a huge conspiracy against the Administration.

In retrospect it seems incredible that a politician whose career had made it plain that he was unscrupulous, a liar, an opportunist, and in some respects a fool, could have deceived so many millions of Americans for so long, hoodwinking them into respecting, believing, and voting for him.

Even had he himself not been at the center of the Watergate web, history is unlikely to be generous to a President whose judgment was so poor that he chose as his top aides men who did not hesitate to commit criminal acts. "The sordid clique which he brought into the White House," observed Britain's conservative *Daily Telegraph,* "and with which he talked in a sleazy and obscenely vulgar style . . . seems to have corroded part of his character."

Under the Nixon Administration the pretext of national security was used with almost ritual persistence to excuse and hide every immoral and illegal act it committed, even to the extent of tarnishing the reputations of the FBI, the Department of Justice, and the CIA. "Perhaps the best thing about Watergate," observed Yale political scientist Ronald Steel, "will be that it will make the American people realize how they have been manipulated and exploited by their leaders in the name of 'national security.' "

Watergate had a disastrous effect on both domestic and foreign policy. Nixon and his men were so preoccupied working up "scenarios" to fend off new disclosures erupting day after day, that the business of government was paralyzed for long periods of time. Foreign nations grew wary of committing themselves too fully to agreements with a President who had clearly lost his influence with Congress and was likely to be forced out of office.

The American people were understandably dismayed and disheartened by the unraveling of the whole Watergate scandal. They began to realize that Congress, by failing to exercise its Constitutional powers, had let first Lyndon Johnson and then Richard Nixon lead the nation into a decade of disaster. A new appreciation grew of the wisdom of the system of governmental checks and balances written into the Constitution by the founders of the nation.

President Franklin D. Roosevelt observed, "The Presidency . . . is preeminently a place of moral leadership." Watergate revealed the Nixon Administration to have been a quagmire of immoral leadership that put expediency above the law, ends above means, self-interest above public service.

"The Watergate," said John Gardner, former Secretary of Health, Education, and Welfare under Johnson and presently the head of Common Cause, "is a story of what men will do for power, and how the public process is corrupted by money and secrecy."

The final official judgment of the House Judiciary Committee on the impeachment that Richard Nixon evaded by resigning is set on the record in its 528-page report, backed by 200 pages of incriminating evidence. The Judiciary Committee unanimously held that he deserved impeachment, and the full House accepted this judgment by a vote of 412 to 3.

Washington columnist Joseph Kraft termed the Nixon Administration "the first criminal Presidency in our country." Senator Weicker called the conspirators "the men who almost stole America." Lyndon Johnson's former press secretary, William B. Moyers, observed, "It was close. It almost worked, but not quite. Something basic in our traditions held."

But during the televised House Judiciary Committee debate on impeachment, Representative James Mann of South Carolina warned the American people, "Next time there may be no watchmen in the night"—no Frank Wills to detect government burglars and trigger exposure of the whole Watergate conspiracy. As historian Arthur Schlesinger, Jr., noted, "If they had avoided a few dangerous corners, Nixon, Haldeman, Ehrlichman, and all the rest would still be riding high." Calling Nixon's "the most lawless Administration in American history," Schlesinger noted with irony that the President's farewell address had made him sound like the "innocent victim of a hit-and-run driver."

During the Judiciary Committee debate Representative Paul S. Sarbanes of Maryland drove home the importance of curbing the power of any President to violate the civil liberties of American citizens: "I ask every doctor and lawyer and every insurance agent and accountant in the country what kind of land you would be living in if a group of hired hands have the power to come into your office in the dead of the night."

"What destroyed Richard Nixon," said a penitent Donald Segretti, "was not the media, not the acts of his subordinates, but rather his handling of his own response to the scandal. We must now demand that our country be governed in the open, so that all citizens may observe what our leaders are doing and why."

The full truth about Watergate and the crisis it brought to the nation in its wake needs to be an important part of every American's education. One of Nixon's appointees to the Supreme Court, Justice Harry Blackmun, acknowledged, "The pall of

Watergate . . . is something that necessarily touches us all, irrespective of political inclination."

Yale psychohistorian Robert Jay Lifton believes that Watergate must not be forgotten but studied and discussed to prevent anything like it in the future. "If we gloss over Watergate and the resignation," he cautions, "we will learn nothing from it."

Long ago Machiavelli, the famous political cynic, warned, "If a citizen who has rendered some eminent service to the state should add, to the reputation and influence which he has thereby acquired, the confident audacity of being able to commit any wrong without fear of punishment, he will in a little while become so insolent and overbearing as to put an end to all power of the law." That prophecy was written over 450 years before Richard Nixon and Watergate.

New generations of Americans have reason to be grateful to a handful of heroic countrymen for the return of their nation to the principles of an open democracy—night watchman Frank Wills; the Washington police who responded to his call; Bernstein and Woodward, the intrepid reporters of the *Washington Post*; their secret government informants; John Sirica, the honest judge who broke the silence of the Watergate burglars; two incorruptible special prosecutors, Archibald Cox and Leon D. Jaworski; Nixon appointees Richardson and Ruckelshaus who defied the President's order to fire Cox; the Senate Watergate Committee headed by Constitutional defender Sam Ervin; the members of the House Judiciary Committee, whose fair and just hearings under Chairman Peter Rodino convinced the majority of Americans of Nixon's guilt; and John Doar, chief counsel for the House Judiciary Committee.

When Judge Sirica sentenced the first seven Watergate criminals, he declared, "I am convinced that the greatest benefit that can come from this prosecution will be its impact as a spur to corrective action so that the type of activities revealed by the evidence at trial will not be repeated in our nation." The Congress subsequently moved in that direction.

The deserved praise and fame won by the *Washington Post* for its tenacious Watergate exposé, despite the punitive campaign waged against it by the Nixon Administration, encouraged the media in a new vigilance as watchdogs of the public interest.

The successful persistence of Special Prosecutor Archibald Cox and of his successor, Leon Jaworski, in going after the evidence of crimes committed by officials of the Nixon Administration and bringing them to justice, demonstrated the importance of keeping politics entirely out of the Department of Justice and the FBI, a change that is likely to be written into law.

There was great educational value, demonstrating the functioning of our system of government under the Constitution at its best, when the deliberations of the House Judiciary Committee on impeachment were televised to the nation.

That the full House had ordered such deliberations, and the Senate had prepared for a trial, indicated a new independence by Congress, an awakening after too many years of inertia and intimidation by the power of the White House. The impeachment proceedings served notice on future Presidents that they are not above the law, and can expect to be turned out of office for "high crimes and misdemeanors."

Watergate cut the Presidency down to size, putting it once more in balance with Congress and the courts.

"Some say this is a sad day in America's history," observed Representative Charles B. Rangel of New York during the House Judiciary Committee debate. "I think it could perhaps be one of our brightest days . . . [because it shows] that when this or any other President violates his sacred oath of office, the people are not left helpless."

Although America's Constitutional system had taken a long time to work, it finally forced Nixon out of office and quietly installed a new President in his place. And this had happened without tanks surrounding the White House or mobs taking to the streets.

"This is a revolution," observed historian Henry Steele Commager. "In most countries of the globe it would be a violent revolution, but in the U.S. it is peaceful and legal. It is indeed a Constitutional revolution."

One of the great ironies of Watergate was the outcome of the sign "Bring Us Together," held up by a teen-ager during the 1968 campaign. "That will be the great objective of this Administration at the outset," Nixon declared, "to bring the American people together." James Reston of *The New York Times* observed that in his downfall Nixon had kept that promise, at least, "not for his leadership and tactics, but against them." Republicans and Democrats, liberals and conservatives alike, were united by the conviction that his removal from office was in the best interests of the nation.

There was little sympathy for the man who had betrayed every principle and every friend in a desperate, unsuccessful effort to save his own skin. There was widespread anger at his failure to admit guilt, either in resigning or in accepting a pardon. Because he had never acted as President of all the people, but only of those who supported him uncritically, millions who had felt unrepresented in the White House were understandably relieved at his downfall.

"In the end," noted Joseph Kraft, "Nixon was alone, divorced from friends and reality in a psychic bunker of his own making."

Some critics felt Watergate was not the fault of Richard Nixon alone, but of the American people who had elected him as a reflection of their own self-satisfaction, their self-righteous interventions in the affairs of other governments, their intolerance of dissent and change.

"In the future," suggested Senator Mondale, "we ought to ask our Presidents to symbolize a mature people who now realize—especially after Vietnam—that they are no better than any other people, that they are capable of a great deal of evil as well as a great deal of good, and that they are just as subject to the temptations of power as any other people in history. This kind of symbolizing might do us all a lot of good."

Others felt that Watergate indicated the moral bankruptcy of the American political system. In August 1973, Senator Edward Kennedy declared on the Senate floor, "The United States has the best political system that money can buy—and it is a disgrace to every principle on which our republic stands."

Former New York City mayor John Lindsay agreed: "Watergate sums up everything that is the absolute worst about politics, about governmental powers and about public morality. . . . The contributions of Vesco, ITT, milk producers, airlines and others financed this kind of thing, whether they knew it or not. And most of them did know that, in return, they were buying some kind of political protection—an air-route franchise, immunity from SEC or antitrust protection. . . . A politician can't help but feel indebted to donors."

The *Washington Star-News* suggested, "The change needed is the legal assumption that if a corporation makes a substantial political donation which is followed or preceded by favorable government action on a large scale, this coincidence in itself is prima facie evidence of an intent to corrupt. That, coupled with automatic and absolutely unavoidable good, stiff jail sentences for the chairman, the president, the treasurer and the bagman of the offending corporation, would wipe out that particular kind of political corruption in a month."

Some observers felt that Watergate represented only the moral bankruptcy of Nixon and his men and that the American system had worked beautifully in getting them out of office. "The Watergate disclosures need not bring only dismay to Americans," observed Shakil Ahmed from Calcutta, India. "They have revealed a true, sound and untainted democracy. Without this democracy news of Watergate would just never have reached us. When democracy by and large has become a great sham, it is blissful to realize there is still one place left where tampering with it—even by the head of state—does not go uncondoned."

Speaking perhaps for a broad cross-section of Americans, the *Poughkeepsie Journal* in upstate New York declared, "We must accept the error of Richard M. Nixon as a people, and profit by the experiences. We should make a solemn promise to ourselves that the likes of this will never happen again."

Congress was spurred by Watergate to pass new legislation to control campaign contributions, making it difficult in the future for candidates supported by wealthy special interests to buy a presidential election. Now such elections will be largely financed by public funds assembled from $1 contributions indicated on everyone's income tax returns, providing $20,000,000 for each major candidate.

New regulations put severe limits on private contributions, set ceilings on overall campaign spending, require comprehensive disclosure of contributions, and provide a strong enforcement apparatus to ensure that these regulations work. Senator Charles

Percy called the new Federal election law "a silver lining in the black cloud of Watergate."

State legislatures also felt the impact of Watergate. Massachusetts House Speaker David Bartley believed it would make voters more skeptical—"not necessarily a bad thing if it promotes more public interest in the political-government process." Oregon state senator Victor Atiydh declared, "Necessary campaign reform and open government has been easier to institute because of the influence of Watergate."

Since the scandal broke, many states have passed their own reform laws on campaign finances. Colorado state senator Roy Kogovsek declared, "It's going to make state officials aware that people are watching more closely." The need for just such a close watch was emphasized during the congressional hearing on Rockefeller's nomination as Vice-President, when it was indicated that he had given huge gifts to New York State politicians in his campaign to win the Republican nomination for governor.

In California, Common Cause sponsored a sweeping new Political Reform Act. In a public referendum, Californians voted for it by a huge majority. California lobbyists can now spend no more than $10 a month on any legislator and cannot make campaign contributions at all. Office-holders must file annual statements of income and holdings. Every contributor of more than $50 to a campaign must be listed by name, address, and employer. Campaign spending is limited to a few cents per voter, and those in office are allowed 10 percent less than challengers. A bipartisan enforcement commission now supervises all California elections and investigates all violations, with penalties for the guilty.

Other states have passed similar legislation. Alabama placed tight restrictions on what office-holders can do in their private businesses, requiring them to make full disclosure of these interests. Many states now compel office-holders and candidates to tell how much they own and where it came from. Colorado compels lobbyists to list the amounts of money or gifts given legislators, and to whom. In Texas it is now a crime to give a legislator money or gifts to influence legislation. Some states have passed such strict laws that many office-holders refused to run for re-election.

Americans might also consider borrowing a few of Great Britain's election laws. Active electioneering there is limited to only eight days, with polling on the ninth. A candidate's manager has to account for every cent received and spent, and this is limited to roughly four cents a voter. In local elections televised political broadcasts must include representatives of all parties. It is illegal to make a false statement in relation to the personal character or conduct of a candidate during an election, preventing last-minute defamatory attacks.

There is also food for thought in comparing Britain's political machinery for getting rid of a chief executive who clearly no longer has the confidence of the people. Whereas in the United States it took a long, cumbersome, and painful exercise of the impeachment machinery to bring this about, in England all it takes is a vote of "no confidence" in the House of Commons and the government falls, with a date set for new elections as early as practical.

Watergate has made it likely that we have seen an end to what John Gardner calls "unbridled Presidential power . . . accumulated over the last four decades." Future Congresses can be expected to guard the nation against such presidential blunders and excesses as the secret bombing in Cambodia, the creation of a secret White House police force, the use of government agencies to punish political opponents, and illegal espionage against citizens.

"In this society of ours," declared Senator Philip Hart, "we depend on diffusion of power as the best means of achieving political democracy." Senator Jacob Javits introduced a bill to limit the scope of executive secrecy and domestic intelligence gathering. Congress has made it clear to the White House that the CIA will no longer be able to conduct secret wars or have a free hand in overturning foreign governments.

Other changes are being considered. Some congressmen want a single six-year term for the President, so that he can concentrate on dealing with the nation's problems instead of on re-election. Some want an independent ombudsman operating within each Administration, to protect the rights of citizen-con-sumers. This system is presently being used with great success by the Scandinavian countries, where elected ombudsmen act on every complaint to secure justice for citizens who are unfairly pushed around by government bureaucrats.

Berkeley law professor Paul J. Mishkin proposed that such an office be created under the title of Counsel General of the United States, combining the functions of ombudsman and special prosecutor. He suggested that the Counsel General be appointed for a dozen years or so by the Supreme Court, with the advice and consent of Congress.

Yale law professor Thomas Emerson urged drastic restrictions on what information can be classified secret. "Secrecy in government accompanies evil in government . . . ," he pointed out. "Government wrongs are kept secret because they are evil; and evil is done because it can be kept secret."

Certainly it will no longer be acceptable for any press secretary of a President to give the media false information month after month, then suddenly inform reporters that all these White House statements are "inoperative." Jerald terHorst underscored that when he resigned after the White House had misled him about Nixon's pardon. Replacing him, NBC's Ron Nessen told reporters that he was "another Ron" but no Ziegler, and he, too, would refuse to lie to them.

The widespread publicity given to prison sentences for the Watergate defendants will give pause to future campaigners about the tactics they use to win elections. Stricter new laws will also make future elections cleaner.

Public disillusionment with Watergate has made voters more open to new faces—candidates who are young, female, and representative of ethnic groups. Sociologist Gunnar Myrdal, in a study of America, noted, "Generally speaking, the lower classes in America have been inarticulate and powerless." Black author James Baldwin underscored that bitterly, observing, "If he lived on my street in Harlem, Nixon would be in jail." Now one result of Watergate may be a greater willingness of voters to listen to candidates who are not professional politicians.

The University of Chicago now offers a course for students called "Constitutional Aspects of Watergate." The lessons of this period when the United States fell into deep crisis, its democratic institutions subverted and threatened, will undoubtedly be studied for decades to come as a crucial turning point in our history.

Watergate, then, may eventually prove to have produced many constructive new changes in the America of tomorrow, namely:

- Greater citizen watchfulness and participation in government at all levels.
- Greater care in selecting and voting for public officials, especially for high office.
- Restrictions on the ability of big business to influence political parties or officials by campaign contributions.
- Greater courage and vigilance by the media in keeping the public informed and the government honest.
- More independence by the Justice Department in prosecuting high crimes and misdemeanors.
- Stricter curbs on the use of bugging, wiretaps, and other invasions of privacy by Federal agencies.
- More open government and public information; less chance to hide official skulduggery behind "top secret" and "national security" classifications.
- A stronger role played by Congress in the checks and balances of governmental operations.
- Vigilance by new civic "watchdog" groups to protect the Constitution and Bill of Rights from officials in high places who seek to subvert them.
- New awareness by government officials of public skepticism about them, putting them under greater pressure to be truthful and honest if they want to stay in office.
- New election laws to clean up dirty politics.
- Increased use of TV to cover important national debates in Congress, so that the people can be directly informed.
- An end to White House treatment of citizens and their representatives in Congress as adversaries, with recognition by the President that he is their servant, not master.
- Closer public scrutiny of presidential expenditures, so that the President and his staff are not encouraged to live—and therefore to think—like royalty.
- Increased incentive for future Presidents to be candid with the American people, publicly acknowledging mistakes when they have been made, rather than covering them up.

- Closer ties between the President and his political party, which represents a broad cross-section of the people.
- New awareness by the American people of the importance of candidates for Vice-President on political tickets.

"[Watergate] has done a tremendous amount of good for better government," declares the Watergate special prosecutor, Leon Jaworski. "Those who seek office know there's a very high standard expected of them . . . . There aren't many who now think they can depart from the straight line. There'll be less use of influence. The attention given to this case will give its results a more lasting effect. It has made its impressions deep-rooted. The good that comes out of it won't be a passing fancy."

"Watergate, in short, may well prove a great benefit," observes historian Henry Steele Commager, who is vice-chairman of the National Committee for an Effective Congress, "a turning point in the political and moral history of this generation. It may provide just that catharsis necessary to cleanse our political system. Watergate may rally the Congress to a sense of its power and its responsibility, rally the public to the danger threatening to undermine the nation, and reinvigorate those principles which the Founding Fathers knew to be essential to the Republic."

If this happens, Watergate will turn out in the long run to have been not just a dreadful nightmare of "White House horrors" but a crisis that awakened all Americans from that nightmare to join together in restoring our country to its original ideals.

Cast of Characters

Agnew, Spiro T. Vice-President. Resigned, October 10, 1973, convicted, disbarred.

Anderson, Jack. Syndicated columnist.

Andreas, Dwayne. Millionaire contributor to CRP.

Baker, Howard H., Jr. Republican, Tennessee. Vice-Chairman, Senate Watergate Committee.

Baldwin, Alfred C., III. Watergate lookout and wire-tap monitor.

Barker, Bernard L. Leader of Cuban burglars in Dr. Fielding and Watergate break-ins. Jailed.

Barrett, John. Arresting policeman at Watergate.

Beard, Dita. ITT lobbyist.

Bernstein, Carl. Washington Post reporter.

Butterfield, Alexander P. Assistant to Haldeman.

Buzhardt, J. Fred. Counsel to Nixon.

Byrne, W. Matthew, Jr. Presiding judge in Ellsberg-Russo trial.

Caddy, Douglas. Original lawyer for Watergate burglars.

Casey, William J. Chairman, Securities and Exchange Commission.

Caulfield, John J. White House intelligence agent.

Chapin, Dwight L. Presidential appointments secretary. Jailed.

Clawson, Kenneth W. Communications director for CRP.

Colson, Charles W. Special counsel to Nixon. Jailed, disbarred.

Connally, John B. Secretary of the Treasury, adviser to Nixon. Indicted.*

---

* An indictment only charges a person with a crime, and must not be considered evidence of guilt. Many aspects of the Watergate case were still in jurisdiction when this book was completed in January of 1975.

Cook, G. Bradford. Successor to Casey as chairman of Securities and Exchange Commission.

Cox, Archibald. Special prosecutor for Watergate until October 20, 1973.

Cushman, Robert E., Jr. CIA Deputy Director.

Dahlberg, Kenneth H. Midwest finance chairman for CRP.

Dash, Samuel. Chief counsel, Senate Watergate Committee.

Dean, John W., III. White House counsel, chief coordinator of the Watergate cover-up. Jailed.

De Diego, Felipe. Cuban member of Plumbers. Indicted.

Ehrlichman, John D. Assistant to the President for Domestic Affairs. Convicted, sentenced.

Ellsberg, Daniel J. Former Pentagon analyst who released Pentagon Papers to *The New York Times.*

Ervin, Sam, Jr. Democrat, North Carolina. Chairman, Senate Watergate Committee.

Fielding, Fred. Assistant to John Dean.

Fielding, Dr. Lewis J. Daniel Ellsberg's psychiatrist.

Ford, Gerald R. Appointed Vice-President October 12, 1973. Became President August 9, 1974.

Geneen, Harold. President of ITT.

Gesell, Gerhard. Judge in Dr. Fielding break-in trial.

Gonzales, Virgilio R. Cuban Watergate burglar. Jailed.

Gray, L. Patrick, III. FBI acting director.

Gregory, Thomas J. Spy for CRP.

Gurney, Edward J. Republican, Florida. Member Senate Watergate Committee.

Haig, Alexander M., Jr. Nixon chief of staff after Haldeman.

Haldeman, H. R. White House chief of staff. Convicted.

Harmony, Sally H. Secretary to G. Gordon Liddy.

Helms, Richard. CIA Director.

Higby, Lawrence. Aide to Haldeman.

Hoover, J. Edgar. FBI Director.

Hughes, Howard. Billionaire contributor to Nixon campaign.

Hunt, Dorothy. Wife of E. Howard Hunt, payoff money courier.

Hunt, E. Howard, Jr. Former CIA agent, secret operative for Colson, co-head of Plumbers, participant in break-ins. Jailed.

Huston, Tom Charles. White House project officer, author of Huston plan for secret White House intelligence agency.

Inouye, Daniel K. Democrat, Hawaii. Member Senate Watergate Committee.

Jaworski, Leon. Successor to Cox as special prosecutor for Watergate.

Kalmbach, Herbert W. Personal attorney to President Nixon. Jailed.

Kissinger, Henry A. Presidential advisor on foreign affairs, later Secretary of State.

Kleindienst, Richard. Attorney General after Mitchell. Convicted, sentence suspended.

Krogh, Egil, Jr. White House aide, co-head of Plumbers. Jailed.

LaRue, Frederick C. Special assistant to Mitchell. Indicted.

Liddy, G. Gordon. Spymaster for CRP, leader of Dr. Fielding and Watergate break-ins. Jailed.

McCord, James W., Jr. Former CIA agent, security coordinator for CRP, leader of Watergate burglary team. Jailed.

McGregor, Clark. Successor to Mitchell as CRP head.

Magruder, Jeb Stuart. Deputy Director of CRP. Jailed.

Mardian, Robert C. Political coordinator of CRP. Convicted.

Martinez, Eugenio R. Cuban Watergate burglar. Jailed.

Merrian, William. ITT Vice President.

Mitchell, John N. Attorney General, later head of CRP. Acquitted in Vesco trial. Convicted for Watergate cover-up.

Mitchell, Martha. Wife of John Mitchell.

Montoya, Joseph M. Democrat, New Mexico. Member Senate Watergate Committee.

Moore, Richard. Special counsel to President Nixon.

Nixon, Richard M. President. Resigned August 9, 1974.

O'Brien, Lawrence F. Chairman, Democratic National Committee.

O'Brien, Paul. Attorney for CRP.

Odle, Robert C., Jr. Personnel director for CRP.

Parkinson, Kenneth W. Attorney for CRP. Indicted, acquitted.

Patman, Wright. Democrat, Texas. Chairman House Banking and Currency Committee.

Petersen, Henry E. Assistant Attorney General in charge of Justice Department's Watergate investigation.

Porter, Herbert L. Scheduling director of CRP. Jailed.

Rebozo, Charles G. (Bebe). Nixon's closest friend.

Reinecke, Edward. Lieutenant Governor, California. Resigned, convicted.

Rhodes, John. Republican, Arizona. Succeeded Ford as minority leader of the House.

Richardson, Elliot L. Attorney General after Kleindienst.

Rockefeller, Nelson A. Succeeded Ford as Vice-President.

Rodino, Peter W., Jr. Democrat, New Jersey. Chairman, House Judiciary Committee.

Rohatyn, Felix. ITT lobbyist.

Scott, Hugh. Republican, Pennsylvania. Minority leader of Senate.

Sears, Harry L. Attorney for Vesco. Indicted.

Segretti, Donald H. Head of dirty-tricks campaign. Jailed.

Silbert, Earl J. Assistant U.S. Attorney, original chief prosecutor at Watergate break-in trial.

Sirica, John J. U.S. District Court, Washington, D.C. Judge in all Watergate trials.

Sloan, Hugh W., Jr. CRP treasurer under Stans.

St. Clair, James. Nixon's Watergate defense attorney.

Stans, Maurice H. Chairman, CRP Finance Committee. Indicted in Vesco case, acquitted.

Strachan, Gordon C. Assistant to Haldeman. Indicted.

Sturgis, Frank (Frank Fiorini). Cuban Watergate burglar. Jailed.

Talmadge, Herman E. Democrat, Georgia. Member Senate Watergate Committee.

terHorst, Jerald. Press secretary to President Ford.

Thompson, Fred D. Chief minority counsel, Senate Watergate Committee.

Ulasewicz, Anthony T. Caulfield aide, made payoffs for Kalmbach.

Vesco, Robert L. Financier, contributor to Nixon re-election campaign. Indicted, fled to Central America.

Walters, Vernon A. CIA Deputy Director.

Weicker, Lowell P., Jr. Republican, Connecticut. Member Senate Watergate Committee.

Wiggins, Charles. Republican, California. Member House Judiciary Committee.

Wills, Frank. Watergate security guard.

Woods, Rose Mary. Personal secretary to President Nixon.

Woodward, Bob. Washington Post reporter.

Young, David R., Jr. Co-head with Krogh of Plumbers.

Ziegler, Ronald L. Press secretary to Nixon.

House Judiciary Committee

Brooks, Jack (D., Texas)
Butler, M. Caldwell (R., Virginia)
Cohen, William S. (R., Maine)
Conyers, John, Jr. (D., Michigan)
Danielson, George E. (D., California)
Dennis, David W. (R., Indiana)
Donohue, Harold D.
  (D., Massachusetts)
Drinan, Robert F.
  (D., Massachusetts)
Edwards, Don (D., California)
Eilberg, Joshua (D., Pennsylvania)
Fish, Hamilton, Jr. (R., New York)
Flowers, Walter (D., Alabama)
Froehlich, Harold V. (R., Wisconsin)
Hogan, Lawrence J. (R., Maryland)
Holtzman, Elizabeth (D., New York)
Hungate, William L. (D., Missouri)
Hutchinson, Edward (R., Michigan)
Jordan, Barbara (D., Texas)
Kastenmeier, Robert W.
  (D., Wisconsin)

Latta, Delbert (R., Ohio)
Lott, Trent (R., Mississippi)
McClory, Robert (R., Illinois)
Mann, James R. (D., South Carolina)
Maraziti, Joseph J. (R., New Jersey)
Mayne, Wiley (R., Iowa)
Mezvinsky, Edward (D., Iowa)
Moorhead, Carlos J. (R., California)
Owens, Wayne (D., Utah)
Railsback, Tom (R., Illinois)
Rangel, Charles B. (D., New York)
Rodino, Peter W., Jr. (D., New
  Jersey), chairman
Sandman, Charles W., Jr. (R., New
  Jersey)
Sarbanes, Paul S. (D., Maryland)
Seiberling, John T. (D., Ohio)
Smith, Henry P., III (R., New York)
Thornton, Ray (D., Arkansas)
Waldie, Jerome R. (D., California)
Wiggins, Charles E. (R., California)

Bibliography

AFL-CIO Executive Council Report. *Watergate: An Unfinished Story of Money and Politics.* 1973.

Bernstein, Carl, and Bob Woodward. *All the President's Men.* New York: Simon and Schuster, 1974.

Hunt, E. Howard. *Undercover: Memoirs of an American Secret Agent.* New York: Putnam, 1974.

Lurie, Leonard. *The Impeachment of Richard Nixon.* New York: Berkley Publishing Corporation, 1973.

McCarthy, Mary. *The Mask of State: Watergate Portraits.* New York and London: Harcourt Brace Jovanovich, 1973.

McCord, James W., Jr. *A Piece of Tape: The Watergate Story Fact and Fiction.* Rockville, Md.: privately printed, 1974.

McGinniss, Joe. *The Selling of the President.* New York: Trident Press, 1969.

Magruder, Jeb Stuart. *An American Life: One Man's Road to Watergate.* New York: Atheneum, 1974.

Mazlish, Bruce. *In Search of Nixon.* Baltimore: Penguin Books, 1973.

Mazo, Earl. *Richard Nixon.* New York: Avon Books, 1960.

Mosher, Frederick C., ed. *Watergate: Implications for Responsible Government.* New York: Basic Books, 1974.

Nordland, Rod, ed. *The Watergate File.* New York, London: Flash Books, 1973.

Osborne, John. *The Nixon Watch.* New York: Liveright, 1970.

———. *The Second Year of the Nixon Watch.* New York: Liveright, 1971.

Sampson, Anthony. *The Sovereign State of ITT.* Greenwich, Conn.: Fawcett Publications, 1974.

Sussman, Barry. *The Great Coverup: Nixon and the Scandal of Watergate.* New York: Thomas Y. Crowell Company, 1974.

The New York Times. *The End of a Presidency.* New York: Bantam Books, 1974.

United Press International and The World Almanac, comp. *The Impeachment Report.* New York: New American Library, 1974.

Vidal, Gore. *An Evening with Richard Nixon.* New York: Random House, 1972.

Voorhis, Jerry. *The Strange Case of Richard Milhous Nixon.* New York: Popular Library, 1973.

Washington Post. *The Presidential Transcripts.* New York: Dell Publishing Company, 1974.

Wills, Garry. *Nixon Agonistes.* Boston: Houghton Mifflin Company, 1970.

Also consulted were issues of *The Atlantic Monthly, The Center Magazine, The Center Report, Civil Liberties, Congressional Record, Lithopinion, The Nation, Newsweek, New York, The New York Times, The New York Times Magazine, The New York Post, Playboy, Time, TV Guide,* and *Variety.*

Index

About the Author

Jules Archer first became interested in writing for young people when his three sons were in high school, and in the years since then he has written more than forty books of history and biography. Among the topics he has considered are the role of dissent in American society, the Philippines' fight for independence, and the rise of new leaders and new nations in Africa. His biographies include men as diverse as Metternich and Mao Tse-tung. In all his books, Mr. Archer's basic premise has been that if young readers are to make the intelligent judgments essential to a functioning democracy they must be given the whole truth about our society—our failures as well as our successes.

Born in New York City and educated at the College of the City of New York, Mr. Archer has been a copywriter for film companies and a war correspondent. With his wife, Eleanor, who assists him in his research, he lives in Pine Plains, New York.